Frontier Law and Order

Frontier Law and Order

TEN ESSAYS

BY

PHILIP D. JORDAN

UNIVERSITY OF NEBRASKA PRESS   LINCOLN

Manufactured in the United States of America

To Nibs

my beloved first grandson

Contents

Preface

This volume collects ten essays pertaining to frontier law and order. Unlike the traditional treatment of this subject matter, which is largely devoted to infamous brawls, feuds, and the exploits of famous peace officers, the emphasis here is upon the nature of the law—statutes and ordinances—which the bad man and the evil woman transgressed. Preoccupation with the cattle rustlers and gunslingers and renegade cowboys of the plains and the Far West has prevented us from realizing that they were no different, except in dress and equipment, from lawbreakers on earlier frontiers—no different from the pirates who preyed on the traffic on the Lower Mississippi River during the Spanish and American periods, or from the counterfeiters, horse thieves, and bluelegs who terrorized the Old Northwest in its formative period, or from the practitioners of mayhem and murder along the Atlantic seaboard during the early nineteenth century, or from the Brown gang of Iowa or the Murrell gang of the Tennessee country.

After both the Mexican and Civil wars, lawlessness reached epidemic proportions in village and city, township and county, sedate communities and raw hinterland. Middle western and far western towns relied for protection on the town marshal, who, in addition to providing lamps for city councils, collected taxes, chased hogs from the street, tended the local lock-up, and supervised elections. When a police force was organized, the marshal usually became its chief. The county sheriff was the marshal's counterpart: elected by the people, he constantly sought to conduct himself so that he might enjoy the fruits of reelection. The pathetic point underlying these essays is that the American people never wanted law and order badly enough to support any pay for effective enforcement.

Three of the essays—"Bayonet, Bowie Knife, and Bloody Jack," " 'Gimme a Hoss I Kin Ride!,' " and "The Law—Western Style"—are published here for the first time. Seven originally appeared in historical journals; they are reprinted as they first appeared except for alterations in the footnoting to make it consistent, and are used with the permission and through the courtesy of the original publishers: "The Wearing of Weapons in the Western Country," which was published in the *Filson Club History Quarterly*, vol. 42 (July 1968), pp. 205–21; "The Mississippi—Spillway of Sin," which appeared in *Arizona and the West*, vol. 9 (Winter 1967), pp. 317–32; "Lincoln's Views on Mob Action," published in the *Lincoln Herald*, vol. 70 (Summer 1968), pp. 73–76; "Lady Luck and Her Knights of the Royal Flush," published in the *Southwestern Historical Quarterly*, vol. 62 (January 1969), pp. 295–312; "The Derringer and the Ace of Spades: Reflections on Middle Border Law and Order," which appeared in *Louisiana Studies*, vol. 6 (Winter 1967), pp. 313–31; "Come Back Soon, Honey," published in the Chicago Corral's *Westerners Brand Book*, vol. 26 (March, April, May 1969), pp. 1–8, 12–14, 23–24; and "The Close and Stinking Jail," which appeared in the *Pacific Northwest Quarterly*, vol. 60 (January 1969), pp. 1–9.

The author acknowledges with gratitude grants from the Graduate School, University of Minnesota, which permitted him to research the general field of law and order in the United States during the nineteenth century. He appreciates also the co-operation of Professor Robert S. Hoyt, chairman of the History Department; of Professor Bruno Greene, of the university law library; and of graduate students who not only contributed snips and pieces but also, upon occasion, whole bolts of historical cloth ready for the cutting and the patterning. Two students, Mr. Patrick Nolan and Mr. John Schneider, deserve special recognition. To list the innumerable persons in historical societies and private and public libraries, and owners of special collections would result in two lengthy a catalogue, yet I am indebted to each and every one. Sheriffs, police officials, city clerks, and county officials went out of their way to be helpful. To these and others, I say thank you!

PHILIP D. JORDAN

Frontier Law and Order

CHAPTER ONE

The Wearing of Weapons
in the Western Country

The tools of assault are many—the poniard that severs soul from body, the whip that lacerates bare back, the pistol that points the path to eternity, the sharp-honed thumbnail that gouges the eye from its socket. The heavy bowie knife hefts well, and the lyncher's knot tightens .well. The six-gun upon occasion was a greater equalizer than was the ballot box. Deadly weapons, grasped by men of vengeance and men of passion and held hard in the clutch of gentlemen at stand on the early morning duelling field, were common to the western country. Powder and ball and blade scarred an advancing frontier, seared low country and high country, and scorched and blistered a land of promise with unbelievable violence, so that murder and mayhem were thought by many to symbolize an age.

An old saw says that guns don't kill—that the man behind the gun does the slaying. It is equally true that, lacking a weapon, a man can neither threaten nor wound nor kill with it. Yet over-simplification deceives, and there are times when deadly devices are a necessity and, when properly used, support and strengthen society. Wise and prudent individuals know quite well what the fool and the bully never compre-hend—the possession of weapons does not put the whole world in their hands.

Both purveyors and wearers of weapons throughout the western coun-try justified the carrying of knives and hand-guns on grounds of self-defense. Scores of frontier lawyers, brought up on Blackstone, quoted his commentaries with enthusiasm. These backwoods legalists learned from the English jurist that self-defense is "The *defense* of one's self, or the mutual and reciprocal defense of such as stand in the relations of husband and wife, parent and child, master and servant." In such cases,

1

continued Blackstone, if the party himself or *any* of his relations be forcibly attacked in person or property, "it is lawful for him to repel force by force; and the breach of the peace which happens is chargeable upon him only who began the affray." The commentaries, appearing in the first American reprint in 1771 and selling some twenty-five hundred copies in America before the Declaration of Independence, also carried a warning: "Care must be taken that the resistance does not exceed the bounds of mere defence and prevention; for then the defender would himself become an aggressor."[1]

Blackstone's definition of self-defense, generally speaking, was accepted and written into state statutes and eventually found its way into manuals published for the guidance of justices of the peace, sheriffs, constables, and marshals. The law usually sought to prevent the need for an individual to defend himself, his kin, and his property by stipulating either that weapons not be carried openly or not be worn concealed. Tennessee, for example, in 1801 passed an act making it illegal for persons to "publicly ride or go armed to the terror of the people, or privately carry any dirk, large knife, pistol, or any other dangerous, weapon, to the fear or terror of any person."[2]

A little more than a decade later, Louisiana statutes made it unlawful for persons to carry weapons concealed in their bosoms, coats or any other place, and permitted peace officers to stop and search those whom they suspected of doing so.[3] Free colored persons in Louisiana were permitted to carry weapons only if they secured a permit from a justice of the peace, and slaves were forbidden, either by day or night, to carry visible or hidden arms.[4] An Alabama act of 1841 was most specific, saying that when a killing in any sudden encounter or affray was caused by an assailant, "by the use of a deadly weapon, concealed before the commencement of the fight, his adversary having no deadly weapon drawn," such a slaying would be deemed murder in the second degree, but stipulated that a jury would not be precluded from finding the assail-

[1] William Blackstone, *Commentaries on the Laws of England*, ed. with an introduction and notes by George Sharwood, 3 vols. (Philadelphia: J. B. Lippincott & Co., 1872, 1873), vol. 2, bk. 3, pp. 2–4; see also John H. Wigmore, *A Panorama of the World's Legal Systems*, 3 vols. (St. Paul: West Publishing Co., 1928), 3:1094–95.

[2] Edward Scott, comp., *Laws of the State of Tennessee ... 1715–1820*, 2 vols. (Knoxville: Heiskell & Brown, 1821), 1:710.

[3] Meinrad Greiner, comp., *Louisiana Digest, 1804–1841* (New Orleans: Benjamin Levy, 1841), p. 13.

[4] Ibid., pp. 219, 500.

ant guilty in the first degree.[5] Shopkeepers and vendors of Georgia were forbidden in 1837 to sell, keep in stock, or have about their persons bowie or other knives or pistols, dirks, sword canes, and spears.[6]

How deadly dangerous weapons were is made dramatically clear by the language of indictments for murder drawn up in courts throughout the Kentucky country: "That whereas AB late of the county of . . . merchant, and CD . . . laborer, not having the fear of God before their eyes, but seduced by the instigation of the devil" assaulted and killed EF and that AB with a pistol "then and there charged with gun powder, and a leaden bullet, which gun the said AB in his right hand held upon EF and feloniously, voluntarily and of his malice aforethought, did shoot off and discharge" resulting in a fatal wound in the breast half an inch wide and five inches deep.[7]

As the frontier worked its illegal will upon the land, territories and states sought by statute to discourage the wearing of weapons openly or concealed. From the laurel-crowned Alleghenies to the towering Rocky Mountains, toward Colorado mining camps and on to sites where diggers in California courted Lady Luck, the struggle was waged. It continued throughout the Mississippi River basin and on into the southwest. An Illinois act, rather ambiguous, stipulated a fine of not more than a hundred dollars or imprisonment for anyone having "upon him any pistol, gun, knife, dirk, bludgeon, or other offensive weapon."[8] The words "upon him" could prove tricky in a court presided over by a justice of the peace, for too many were notoriously ignorant of the law, eager to collect their fees, and not anxious, unless imperative, to flaunt popular custom.

It is equally difficult to learn precisely whether a Minnesota statute prohibited the carrying of concealed weapons, although the presumption is, if the law be read literally, that the act proscribed the wearing

[5] *Alabama Acts, 1839–1841* (Tuscaloosa: Hale & Eaton, 1840), p. 123.

[6] *Digest of Statute Laws of Georgia, 1851* (Athens: Christy, Kelsea & Burke, 1851), p. 848; this entire statute was considered and declared *unconstitutional*, so far as it *prohibited* the carrying of weapons; and *constitutional*, as it *prescribed the mode of carrying them* (1 Kelly, p. 243).

[7] John Bradford, *The General Instructor; or, The Office, Duty, and Authority of Justices of the Peace, Sheriffs, Coroners and Constables of the State of Kentucky . . .* (Lexington: John Bradford, 1800), pp. 75–76. See also Abraham E. Gwynne, *A Practical Treatise on the Law of Sheriff and Coroner, with Forms and References to the Statutes of Ohio, Indiana and Kentucky* (Cincinnati: Derby, 1849); William Littell, *The Statute Law of Kentucky* (Frankfort: Robert Johnson, 1814).

[8] *Illinois Revised Laws, 1832–1833* (Vandalia: Greiner & Sherman, 1833), p. 202.

of weapons openly or concealed. On the other hand, it most likely did neither, for it seemed to imply that a person might bear arms, either concealed or not, if he had "reasonable cause to fear an assault or other injury or violence to his person, or to his family or property."[9] On the other hand, a Nebraska act hinged upon the "intent" factor, and mere intent, upon occasion, is difficult to prove. This act, crisply put, held that a person might carry hidden or open weapons if he had no intent to make an assault.[10]

The code of North Dakota forbade the carrying of concealed arms, but said nothing about carrying them openly.[11] The Territory of Arizona forbade the concealment on the person of dirks, bowie knives, slung shots, brass knuckles, and pistols only within towns, villages, and cities. In addition, it stipulated that every person who, not in necessary self-defense, in the presence of two or more persons, drew or exhibited any deadly weapon in a "rude, angry, or threatening manner" was guilty of a misdemeanor.[12] A Texas act, making no mention of how a weapon was worn, offered somewhat of an innovation by stating that any person killed with a bowie knife or dagger, under circumstances which would otherwise render the homicide a case of manslaughter, "the killing shall nevertheless be deemed murder, and punished accordingly." The law, in this instance, defined a bowie knife and a dagger as any knife intended to be worn upon the person, which was capable of inflicting death, and "not commonly known as a pocket knife."[13] Such examples could be multiplied many times, but these are sufficiently typical to demonstrate the law's confusion, or, at least, its inconsistency.

Not until the frontier—that so-called "rough and wooly" period—was drawing its last gasp on the hangman's tree of public opinion which persisted in viewing the frontier only as lawless, did statutes become satisfactorily specific. Both the laws of New Mexico and of Oklahoma, extensive in their provisions and precise enough in their language, made

[9] Moses Sherburne and William Hollinshead, comps., *Public Statutes of the State of Minnesota, 1849–1858* (St. Paul: Pioneer Printing Co., 1859), p. 742.

[10] E. Estabrooke, comp., *Statutes of Nebraska* (Chicago: Page & Hoyne, 1867), p. 624.

[11] *Revised Codes of North Dakota* (Bismarck: Tribune Co., 1896), p. 1293.

[12] Cameron H. King, comp., *Revised Statutes of Arizona* (Prescott: Prescott Courier Print, 1887), p. 726.

[13] *Penal Code of State of Texas* (Galveston: News Office, 1857), p. 96. See also S. Garfielde and E. A. Snyder, comps., *Laws of the State of California, 1850–1853* (Benicia: S. Garfielde, 1853), pp. 642, 645.

clear how weapons were to be borne, defined deadly weapons, and indicated where they might or might not be carried.

The New Mexico statute of 1880 stated categorically that it was unlawful for persons to carry deadly weapons, concealed or otherwise, within any settlement except in the lawful defense of themselves, their families, or their property, which, then and there, were threatened with danger. It defined deadly weapons, by whatever name they might be called, as those with which a dangerous wound could be inflicted. Conviction carried a fine of not less than ten dollars nor more than fifty dollars, or imprisonment of not less than ten days nor more than fifty days at the discretion of the jury trying the case. It provided penalties for persons who drew or used a deadly weapon at any ball, dance, election poll, or any other public place. It permitted travelers to carry arms within territorial settlements or towns for one hour after arriving and while traveling out of towns and away from settlements. It directed that operators of hotels, boarding-houses, and drinking saloons post in conspicuous places a "plain notice in both Spanish and English, to travelers to divest themselves of their weapons." Finally, the act stipulated that every person taking out a license for a ball, dance, or fandango must swear to preserve good order and enforce the law.[14]

The Oklahoma statute of 1890, although kin to the New Mexico act, offered significant variations. This act made it illegal to carry *concealed* on a person, on a saddle, or in saddlebags, any pistol, revolver, bowie knife, dirk, dagger, slung shot, sword cane, spear, metal knuckles, or any type of knife or instrument manufactured or sold for the purpose of defense. It also proscribed the carrying *openly* of the weapons just enumerated. The only arms persons were permitted to carry were shotguns and rifles for hunting or for repair, for killing animals, for use at public musters or militia drills, or while traveling from one place to another. It was made unlawful to sell or give deadly weapons to minors. It was unlawful for anyone, except a peace officer, to carry weapons to church, schools, places of amusement, shows, circuses, or into ballrooms, social parties or gatherings, or to any resort where intoxicating liquors were sold. The act permitted public officers to wear arms only while on duty or while going to and from their homes from their place of duty.[15]

---

[14] L. Bradford Price, comp., *General Laws of New Mexico* (Albany, N.Y.: W. C. Little & Co., 1880), pp. 312–15.
[15] Will T. Little et al., comps., *Statutes of Oklahoma, 1890* (Guthrie: State Capital Printing Co., 1891), pp. 495–96.

Territorial and state statutes concerning the wearing of weapons were, in a manner, reflected in village, town, and city ordinances. A few examples must suffice. All were passed by western frontier municipalities. On May 6, 1837, the trustees of the recently incorporated town of Burlington, Iowa, then the Territory of Wisconsin, passed the following ordinance: "Any person who shall, except in defence of his person or property, shoot, discharge, or cause to be discharged any firearms of any description" upon conviction was subject to a fine of not less than five dollars, nor more than ten dollars.[16] Three years later Quincy, Illinois, forbade the firing of any musket, fowling-piece or other firearms, except in case of necessity, or in the performance of some public or lawful duty.[17] About the same time St. Louis passed similar ordinances.[18] Memphis, Tennessee, and other southern cities proscribed the firing of guns and pistols within city limits.[19] Not one of these examples, it will be seen, deals directly with the wearing of weapons, openly or concealed. City officials felt that their ordinances forbidding the discharge of guns covered, in a sense, the carrying of them. Furthermore, prosecution could always be initiated under state statutes.

The law then, on both state and local levels, seemed plain enough concerning both the carrying and the firing of weapons. Moreover, acts were equally clear when they spoke of the wearing and use of arms used for thrusting, cutting, and stabbing. Yet, as most persons should know, there is a chasm of difference between the passing of an act and its successful execution. A back-country lawyer once put it to me succinctly: "There's a helluva lot of difference between them legislators writin' an

[16] Journal of the Proceeding of the Board of Trustees of the Town of Burlington, in the Territory of Wisconsin, Elected Agreeably to the Provisions of an Act of the Legislative Assembly of the Said Territory, Entitled "An Act to Incorporate the Inhabitants of Such Towns as Wish to be Incorporated," December 6, 1836, MS, City Clerk's Office, Burlington, Iowa.

[17] Quincy, Illinois, Ordinance Book, 1840–1856, p. 13, MS, City Clerk's Office, Quincy, Illinois.

[18] St. Louis, *Revised Ordinances . . . 1835–1836* (St. Louis: Missouri Argus, 1846), p. 197; also St. Louis, *Revised Ordinances . . . Revised and Digested by the Fifth City Council . . .* (St. Louis: Chambers & Knapp, 1843), p. 300.

[19] *Digest of the Ordinances of the City Council of Memphis, 1826–1857* (Memphis: Memphis Bulletin Co., 1857), p. 161; see *Vicksburg Register*, September 18, 1834: "Be it ordained by the President and Selectmen of the town of Vicksburg, That if any person shall discharge a gun, pistol or other firearms within the limits of the town of Vicksburg, he or she shall incur a penalty of ten dollars for such offense . . . and it shall be the duty of the Town Constable to report to the president all violations of this ordinance."

act and passin' hit and gettin' enybody from the sheriff on down to enforcin' er obeying hit."

"The law," said the *New Orleans Bee*, "is tolerably strong relative to carrying dirks, pistols or other weapons of assault. Why is it not enforced?"[20] Three dynamic, viable factors thwarted the law. First, men liked weapons, wanted weapons, enjoyed the power that weapons lent them, and insisted on having and using and carrying and handling them as they pleased. Second, a good many gentlemen of one kind or another—some jurists and some vagrants—were disciples of a religion known as the "higher law." Third, personal weapons, upon occasion, were urgently needed for self-defense.

Arms of every description were easy to come by, and there was scarcely a town in the western country which did not boast of a gunsmith who, in addition to repairing weapons, also peddled them. In cities, several specialty shops and a variety of general stores catered to the gun trade. Newspapers advertised bowie knives, tomahawks, pistols, and daggers for sale not only to gamblers but also to sportsmen.[21] The *Philadelphia Public Ledger* complained in 1837 of the alarming extent to which its citizens were carrying concealed weapons.[22] "No excuse whatever can be used for this practice," said the editor. "As a measure of defence, knives, dirks, and sword canes are entirely useless. They are fit only for attack, and all such attacks are of murderous character. Whoever carries such a weapon has prepared himself for homicide."[23]

Alexander Marjoribanks, an English traveler, found the use of the bowie knife and revolving pistol most prevalent in Cincinnati, and thought that, in this respect, the Queen City was outstripping New Orleans.[24] Another Englishman, surveying the United States, said that throughout New Orleans stalls selling pocket pistols and knives were "scattered in all directions,"[25] T. H. Gladstone observed that "every white stripling in the South may carry a dirk-knife in his pocket, and play with a revolver before he has learned to swim."[26] Foreigners,

---

[20] *New Orleans Bee*, August 10, 1835.

[21] *Philadelphia Mirror*, October 10, 1836.

[22] *Philadelphia Public Ledger*, March 20, 1837.

[23] Ibid., January 25, 1837.

[24] Alexander Marjoribanks, *Travels in South and North America* (London: Simpkin, Marshall, & Co., 1853), p. 277.

[25] James Logan, *Notes of a Journey Through Canada, the United States of America, and the West Indies* (Edinburgh: Fraser & Co., 1838), p. 178.

[26] T. H. Gladstone, *The Englishman in Kansas* (New York: Miller & Co., 1857), p. xxviii.

however, were not alone in describing both the prevalence and the use of weapons. Many a Yankee, such as a native of Maine and a clergyman from Minnesota, spoke as did visitors from abroad. The man from Maine taught languages at Jefferson College, Mississippi, and his elaborate literary style reflected his profession. He wrote of moonbeams touching bright hilts of Spanish knives stuck in the open bosoms of nearly every New Orleans gentleman. The minister, later to become the first Episcopal bishop of Minnesota, jotted in his diary that, although it was a penitentiary offense for Alabamians to carry concealed weapons in the streets, the law was broken daily.[27]

Wayfarers and travelers, no matter what their calling, were apt to see through a distorted lens and to write contrived observations. If a corrective is needed for those mistaken, out-of-focus, itinerant snoopers of American society, the native newspaper editor provided balance. But both visitors and journalists, however they might bicker over some aspects of frontier life, agreed that the wearing of weapons was both threat and hazard. The national press constantly reported assaults and murders with arms. "Every day," an editor said, "exhibits some portion of the *sovereign* people in arms against the laws of God and the country, and against their own rights and the rights of others." The *Boston Evening Transcript* in 1841 could never recollect a time when there was such an "extensive system of frauds, villainies, and robberies, and all kinds of rascalities." A Minnesota editor, a few years later, spoke of daily lists of sickening, bloody murders.[28] Nor must it be believed, although many travelers did think so and some scholars still do, that the South was more lawless during its frontier period than were other areas during their formative years.[29]

[27] Joseph H. Ingraham, *The South-West; by a Yankee*, 2 vols. (New York: Harper & Bros., 1835), 1:90; Lester B. Shippee, ed., *Bishop Whipple's Southern Diary, 1843–1844* (Minneapolis: University of Minnesota Press, 1937), pp. 86–87.

[28] *Philadelphia Public Ledger*, October 29, 1840; *Boston Daily Evening Transcript*, May 22, 1841; *Winona* (Minnesota) *Argus*, May 14, 1857. For additional editorial comment, see "The Mississippi—Spillway of Sin" and "The Derringer and the Ace of Spades: Reflections on Middle Border Law and Order," pp. 23 and 99, respectively, of this volume.

[29] At least some Southerners held this view. See A. B. Carlson, *The Law of Homicide, Together with the Trial for Murder of Judge Wilkinson, Dr. Wilkinson, and Mr. Murdaugh . . .* (Cincinnati: Robert Clarke & Co., 1882), p. 194, for the argument of Benjamin Hardin: "If you go into the Northern States, it is a rare thing if you can find a man in ten thousand with a deadly weapon on his person. Go into other States that shall be nameless, and you will hear of them as often as of corn-shuckings in an Indian summer. Go further South—to Arkansas or Mississippi, for instance, and

Everywhere, north, east, south, and west of the Bluegrass Country, rogues in buckskin and aristocrats in broadcloth snuffed out lives, and afterwards pleaded self-defense or invoked the higher law. The arguments made by both the prosecution and the defense in the famous Galt House murder are perfect examples of nineteenth-century attitudes. This unsavory affair occurred in Louisville, Kentucky, on December 15, 1838. In a barroom brawl, three Mississippians killed a local tailor and bartender in an argument over the fit of a suit of clothes. Feeling ran so high that a change of venue was taken from Louisville, Jefferson County, to Harrodsburg, Mercer County, and trial began on March 11, 1839. Prosecuting was the State, and both plaintiff and defendants were represented by legal talent, among whom were Benjamin Hardin, for the State, and Sergeant S. Prentiss, of Mississippi, for the defense.[30] Among the murder weapons was a bowie knife, "probably," so a witness described, "from eight to ten inches long in the blade, two inches wide, heavy, and shaped at the point like other knives of the same name."[31]

Prentiss, through the trial, harped upon the self-defense theme. "Why," he asked, "is the step of the Kentuckian free as that of the bounding deer; firm, manly and confident as that of the McGregor when his foot was on the heather of his native hills, and eye on the peak of Ben Lomond? It is because he feels independent in the knowledge of his rights, and proud in the generous consciousness of ability and courage to defend them, not only in his own person, but in the persons of those who are dear to him." Warming to his subject, the defense attorney continued: "When the rattlesnake gives warning of his fatal purpose, the wary traveler waits not for the poisonous blow, but plants upon the head his armed heel, and crushes out, at once, his 'venom and his strength.'" There was more to come. "When the hunter hears the rustling in the jungle, and beholds the large green eyes of the spotted tiger glaring upon him, he waits not for the deadly spring, but sends at

---

though you would be a peaceable man, shuddering at the name of a 'tooth-pick' in the North, in these States you would arm yourself to the teeth, and track your steps in blood with impunity. Why is this, but from the relaxation of the laws that are elsewhere enforced and obeyed?"

[30] Ibid., T. Egerton Browne, *Trial of Judge Wilkinson, Dr. Wilkinson and Mr. Murdaugh, on Indictments for the Murder of John Rothwell and Alexander H. Meeks . . .* (Louisville: T. E. Browne & Co., 1839).

[31] Carlson, *Law of Homicide*, p. 15. For accounts and descriptions of the bowie knife, see J. Frank Dobie, "Bowie and the Bowie Knife," *Southwest Review* 16 (April 1931): 351–68; *Niles' Register*, September 29, 1838. Innumerable foreign travellers and American newspapers commented upon both the knife and its use.

once through the brain of his crouching enemy the swift and leaden death." [32]

The defense's purple prose grew deeper and richer when it justified the substitution of the higher law for man-made statutes. Nowhere in legal pleading appears a better exposition:

> Sirs, there are sins against individuals, as well as sins against heaven, which can only be expiated by blood—and the law of Kentucky is, that the man who is attempted to be *cowhided*, not only *may*, but *must*, if by any possibility he can, *at the time*, kill the man who attempts thus to degrade him. I do not refer to a law of Kentucky, enacted by the Legislature of this State; I mean a law paramount to any enacted by the Kentucky Legislature, a law that emanates from the *hearts* of the people of Kentucky, and is sanctioned by their *heads*—a law that is promulgated in the *os ad coelum* of every Kentuckian, and proclaimed in the sparkling of every eye of *both* sexes and *all* ages—a law, the force of which every one feels, the import of which every one perceives by intuition. It is the law of the *Kentucky instinct* —none are so ignorant as not to know this law; few are so dastardly as to deny its injunction. [33]

Hardin, for the prosecution, generally deplored the wider latitude given to the restraints of law in southern states as against stricter enforcement in northern communities. He told the court that climate affected character, arguing that "he who on the iron-bound coast of the frozen North or on the arid rocks of New Plymouth, would illustrate every noble virtue of his nature, not less distinguished for his piety than his patriotism, for his endurance than his courage, and for his generosity than his bravery, when transplanted to the enervating regions of the South may become different and degenerated, trusting more to his interests than his patriotism, and to concealed weapons than to bravery."

Hardin attacked also Louisville's taverns and saloons, maintaining that their existence was due to political favoritism. "Even the municipal government," he charged, "is either influenced by paltry mercenary motives in its avidity for the revenue of licenses, or it has not the nerve or public interest to grapple with the monster." As no New Englanders turned wayward Southerners were involved in the case and as the only bar involved in the murder was the taproom of the Galt House, Hardin's arguments scarcely seem germane. He was on better, but still

[32] These and subsequent quotations are all taken from Carlson, *Law of Homicide*, pp. 150–51.

[33] J. S. Buckingham published this passage in his *The Eastern and Western States of America*, 3 vols. (London: Fisher, Son, & Co., 1842), 3:33.

shaky, grounds when he attacked the wearing of weapons; "Are we to tolerate this bowie-knife system under the false pretense of self-defense? I say, let your verdict act like the ax laid to the root of the tree, and many a prayer will bless you for your timely check of its growth. Many a woman is made a mourning widow, many a child made a pitiable orphan, and many a father childless by the use of this accursed weapon. Whenever you see men wearing bowie-knives and daggers—hunt them down as you would bears and their cubs, from whom you can expect nothing but injury."

Hardin's pleas proved most unpopular. In the first place, the defendants were being tried for murder, not for carrying weapons. Kentuckians and citizens of other states long had been accustomed to saunter about bearing what pistols and knives they pleased. Indeed, no Kentucky statute prevented them from so doing. It is true that, on February 3, 1813, the legislature had prohibited persons from wearing concealed weapons, but this act was declared unconstitutional by the Court of Appeals in 1822.[34] A similar prohibition was not passed until March 22, 1871.[35] In short, for almost fifty years, the carrying of weapons

[34] C. S. Morehead and Mason Brown, comps., *Digest of Statute Laws of Kentucky*, 2 vols. (Frankfort: Albert H. Hodges, 1835), 2:1289–90. Act to prevent persons in this Commonwealth from wearing concealed Arms, except in certain cases, February 3, 1813: "That any person in this commonwealth who shall hereafter wear a pocket pistol, dirk, large knife, or sword in a cane, concealed as a weapon, unless travelling on a journey, shall be fined in any sum not less than one hundred dollars; which may be recovered in any court having jurisdiction of like sums, by action of debt, or on the presentment of a grand jury; and a prosecutor in such presentment shall not be necessary. One half of such fine shall be to the use of the informer, and the other to the use of this commonwealth." This act declared unconstitutional, *Bliss* v. *Commonwealth*, 2 Litt. 90.

[35] *Kentucky Acts, Adjourned Session, 1871* (Frankfort: Kentucky Yeoman Office, 1871), pp. 89–90. Act to prohibit the carrying of Concealed Deadly Weapons, March 22, 1871: "That if any person shall hereafter carry concealed any deadly weapon upon their persons other than an ordinary pocket-knife, except as provided for in the next session, he shall be fined, on the first conviction, not less than twenty-five dollars, nor more than one hundred dollars, or imprisoned not less than thirty days nor more than sixty days, or both so fined and imprisoned; and on any subsequent conviction not less than one hundred nor more than four hundred dollars, or imprisoned not less than two months nor more than six months, or both. That the carrying of concealed deadly weapons shall be legal in the following cases: 1st. Where the person has reasonable grounds to believe his person, or the person of some of his family, or his property, is in danger from violence or crime. 2d. Where sheriffs, constables, marshals, and policemen carry such concealed weapons as are necessary to their protection in the efficient discharge of their duty. 3d. Where persons are required by their business or occupation to travel during the night, and carrying

openly or concealed was both permissible and allowable. Moreover,
public sentiment favored it. One is not unduly surprised, then, to learn
that the defendants in the Galt House murder trial were acquitted.

Many a man throughout the western country, as the frontier moved
steadily toward the setting sun, believed firmly that his right to bear
arms was guaranteed by the constitution of the United States, which
recites that "a well-regulated militia being necessary to the security of
a free state, the right of the people to keep and bear arms shall not be
infringed." State constitutions carried similar provisions. Indeed, a
curious act was passed by the governor and judges of the Northwest
Territory under the Ordinance of 1787. This act not only sought to
suppress gambling for money, but also attempted to restrain the "disorderly" practice of discharging firearms. Guns were not to be fired
near houses nor between sunrise and sunset. Every person shooting
at wild game was prohibited from aiming in the direction of settled
communities. But the law was careful, in its list of exceptions, to permit
the use of weapons in self-defense.[36] There seems little doubt but that
the territorial act influenced comparable laws in Ohio and other states
carved from the territory.[37]

----

concealed deadly weapons during such travel." The act defined "concealed" as
follows: "That it shall be deemed concealed to carry deadly weapons in a scabbard
or belt, if the belt is under the coat, fastened around the person."

[36] Salmon P. Chase, ed., *Statutes of Ohio and of the Northwest Territory, 1788–
1833*, 3 vols. (Cincinnati: Corey & Fairbank, 1833), 1:106. Act for suppressing and
prohibiting every species of gaming for money or other property, and for making
void all contracts and payments made in consequence thereof, and also for restraining
the disorderly practice of discharging firearms at certain hours and places, July 26,
1790: "That nothing herein contained shall be deemed or construed to extend to any
person lawfully using fire-arms as offensive or defensive weapons, in annoying, or
opposing a common enemy, or defending his or her person or property, or the
person or property of any other, against the invasion or depredations of any enemy,
or in support of the laws of government; or against the attacks of rebels, highwaymen, robbers, thieves, or others unlawfully assailing him or her, or in any other
manner where such opposition, defence, or resistance is allowed by the law of the
land." The passage relative to wild game is interesting: "Every person shooting at
any of such game [buffalo, bears, deer, turkeys, geese, rabbits, etc.] is hereby required
to discharge the ball or balls, shot, or missile weapon so employed in a direction
from such city, town, or village, or station towards the country so as such ball or
balls, missile weapon, or shot, shall pass by or from, and go clear of the buildings
pertaining to the same."

[37] *Ohio Acts, Fifty-Third General Assembly, 2nd. Sess., January, 1859* (Columbus:
Richard Nevins, 1859), pp. 56–67. Act to prohibit the carrying of concealed weapons,
March 18, 1859: "That whoever shall carry a weapon or weapons, concealed on or

The "constitutional" right of the people to keep and bear arms, no matter what the popular mind believed either in the nineteenth century or today, does not appear to be a common-law right, like that of trial by jury. The Statute of Northampton of 1328 forbade Englishmen to "go nor ride armed by night or by day in fairs, markets, nor in the presence of the justices or other ministers, nor in no part elsewhere . . ." Upon the basis of this and other English statutes, it seems clear that the right to keep and bear arms was not regarded as a "fundamental" right of every Englishman. It must be remembered also that the phrase "to bear arms" is a military one, for an individual carrying weapons is not correctly spoken of as "bearing arms." [38]

The middle decades of the nineteenth century witnessed a series of legal wrangles which pivoted on this knotty question of the right of Americans to keep and bear arms. The earliest of these disputes in the western country involved the Kentucky act of 1813, which was ruled unconstitutional nine years later. The Kentucky constitution provided that "the right of the citizens to bear arms in defence of themselves and the state *shall not be questioned.*" Therefore, the court of appeals, one of three judges dissenting, held the 1813 act to be in conflict with the constitutional guaranty, and hence void.

The court said: "That the provisions of the act in question do not import an entire destruction of the right of citizens to bear arms in defence of themselves and the state, will not be controverted by the court; for though the citizens are forbid wearing weapons *concealed* in the manner described in the act, they may nevertheless, bear arms in any other admissible form. But to be in conflict with the constitution it is not essential that the act should contain a prohibition against

---

about his person, such as a pistol, bowie knife, dirk, or any other dangerous weapon, shall be deemed guilty of a misdemeanor, and on conviction of the first offense shall be fined not exceeding two hundred dollars, or imprisoned in the county jail not more than thirty days; and for the second offense, not exceeding five hundred dollars, or imprisoned in the county jail not more than two months, or both, at the discretion of the court. If it shall be proved to the jury, from the testimony on the trial of any case presented under the first section of this act, that the accused was, at the time of carrying any of the weapon or weapons aforesaid, engaged in the pursuit of any lawful business, calling, or employment, and that the circumstances in which he was placed at the time aforesaid were such as to justify a prudent man in carrying the weapon or weapons aforesaid for the defense of his person, property or family, the jury shall acquit the accused."

[38] Lucilius A. Emery, "The Constitutional Right to Bear Arms," *Harvard Law Review* 28 (March 1914): 473–77. See also J. P. Chamberlain, "Legislatures and the Pistol Problem," *American Bar Association Journal* 11 (September 1925): 596–98.

bearing arms in every possible form. It is the *right* to bear arms in defence of the citizens, and the state that is secured by the constitution,
and whatever restrains the full and complete exercise of that right,
though not an entire destruction of it, is forbidden by the explicit
language of the constitution. If, therefore, the act in question imposes
any restraint upon the right, immaterial what appellation may be given
to the act, whether it be an act *regulating* the manner of bearing arms
of any other, the consequence, in reference to the constitution, is precisely the same, and its collision with that instrument equally obvious."
And the court further on declared that "in principle there is no difference between a law prohibiting the wearing of *concealed* arms and a
law forbidding the wearing of such as are exposed." And, therefore,
the defendant having been convicted and fined for carrying a sword
concealed in a cane, the judgment was reversed.[39]

Such, at times, is the caprice of the legal mind that in 1833 the
Supreme Court of Indiana handed down a diametrically opposed ruling
to that in the Kentucky case. And this ruling was followed in 1840 by
the Supreme Court of Alabama and again a few years later.[40] The
Alabama law forbade the wearing of concealed weapons, and the court
held that the statute was not in conflict with the state constitution, which
provided that citizens enjoyed the right to bear arms in defense of
themselves and the state.

In the Alabama case of 1840, the court wrote that the state constitution in declaring that every citizen has the right to bear arms in defense of himself and the state, "has neither expressly nor by implication
denied the legislature the right to enact laws in regard to the *manner*
in which arms shall be borne. The right guaranteed to the citizen is not
to bear arms upon all occasions and in all places, but merely 'in defence
of himself and the state.' The terms in which this provision is phrased
seemed to us necessarily to leave with the legislature the authority to
adopt such regulations of police as may be dictated by the safety of the
people and the advancement of public morals."[41]

[39] "The Right to Keep and Bear Arms for Private and Public Defence," *Central
Law Journal* (St. Louis), nos. 22–23 (May 28 and June 4, 11, and 18, 1874), pp. 259–
61, 273–75, 285–87, 295. No more succinct synopsis of *Bliss* v. *Commonwealth*, 2
Littell 90, is in print, and my account of the case is taken verbatim from p. 260
without quotation marks, except those originally used. To the unsigned author, I
acknowledge appreciation.
[40] Alabama, *The State* v. *Reid*, I Ala. 612; *Owen* v. *The State*, 31 Ala. 387.
[41] Quoted from *Central Law Review*, p. 260, referring to *The State* v. *Reid*.

In the second Alabama case, the court, after viewing with approbation the findings in the 1840 case, commented further: "We do not desire to be understood as maintaining that in regulating the manner of bearing arms, the authority of the legislature has no other limit than its own discretion. A statute, which, under pretence of *regulating* the manner of bearing arms, amounts to a destruction of the right, or which requires arms to be so borne as to render them wholly useless for the purpose of defence, would be clearly unconstitutional. But a law which is intended merely to promote personal security, and to put down lawless aggression and violence, and to that end inhibits the wearing of certain weapons in such a manner as is calculated to exert an unhappy influence upon the moral feelings of the wearer, by making him less regardful of the personal security of others, does not come in collision with the constitution." The court continued: "Under the provision of our constitution, we incline to the opinion that the legislature cannot inhibit the citizen from bearing arms *openly*, because it authorizes him to bear them for the purpose of defending himself and the state, and it is only when carried openly that they can be effectively used for defence." [42]

Another question remains: did a state possess authority, under its constitution to forbid the concealed wearing of *certain* kinds of weapons? Tennessee's constitution, for example, stipulated that free white men held the right to keep and bear arms "for their common defence." The legislature enacted a statute providing proper punishment for persons who carried concealed under their clothes any "bowie-knife, or Arkansas tooth-pick, or other knife or weapon that shall in form, shape or size resemble a bowie-knife, or Arkansas tooth-pick."

The act was challenged and moved up the legal ladder to the high court, which upheld its constitutionality. The court held, in what has been called the most instructive case on this particular point, that: "As the object for which the right to keep and bear arms is secured, is of a *general* and *public* nature, to be exercised by the people in a body for their *common* defence, so the *arms*, the right to keep which is secured, are those which are usually employed in civilized warfare, and that constitute the ordinary military equipment. If the citizens have these arms in their hands, they are prepared in the best possible manner to repel any encroachments upon their rights by those in authority. They need not, for such a purpose, the use of those weapons which are

[42] Ibid., referring to *Owen* v. *The State.*

usually employed in private broils, and which are efficient only in the hands of the robber and the assassin."[43]

Neither must it be believed that a person might carry a concealed weapon and justify both the carrying and concealment on the grounds that he, in the past, had been attacked and now, as a result, was wearing a weapon in self-defense. A Kentuckian, arrested and convicted of carrying a concealed weapon, justified his action by proving that he had been shot at by strangers more than two years previously and that, since that attempted assault, he habitually had worn concealed arms. The court declared these facts wholly irrelevant, because there was "neither proof nor cause for apprehension of any such impending danger." The conviction was upheld.[44]

When the frontier was closed formally in 1890, the time-honored, traditional, and established hobby of carrying and drawing deadly weapons had been curtailed in most states throughout the Union.[45] No longer was it legal to comport one's self as did many a disconsolate lover in a multitude of bathetic folk songs:

> She then drew out the silver dagger,
> And sank it in her snow-white breast,
> At first she reeled and then she staggered,
> Saying fare you well, I'm going to rest.

> He then drew out the silver dagger
> And sank it in his manly heart,
> Saying this should be an awful warning
> That all true lovers should never part.[46]

The law would not have approved such antics, for involved were the wearing of a concealed weapon, the carrying of a forbidden type of weapon, a suicide, and, in another version of the song, a homicide.

---

[43] Ibid., p. 273, referring to Tennessee, *Aymette* v. *State*, 2 Humph. 154. See also Tennessee, *Andrews* v. *The State*, 3 Heiskell, 165.

[44] Ibid., p. 286, referring to Kentucky, *Hopkins* v. *Commonwealth*, 3 Bush, Ky. 480.

[45] See the attached schedule of the statutes of the several states relative to the carrying or drawing of weapons. The schedule was compiled from Frederick H. Wines, "Report on Crime, Pauperism, and Benevolence in the United States," *Eleventh Census, 1890* (Washington: G.P.O., 1896), vol. 3, pt. 1, pp. 383, 398–411. John Edgar Hoover, *Uniform Crime Reports for the United States* (Washington: G.P.O., 1967), p. 113, reports a total arrest, all ages, of 51,474 for carrying and possessing weapons in 1966.

[46] Vance Randolph, ed., *Ozark Folksongs*, 4 vols. (Columbia: State Historical Society of Missouri, 1946–1950), 2:58.

Yet, to perpetuate a bromide, truth is stranger than folk song, and crimes of love and lust, passion and politics, avarice and arson plus a variety of crafty and cunning improvisations continued to haunt society.

Appendix

CARRYING OR DRAWING WEAPON, STATUTES OF THE SEVERAL STATES IN 1890

North Atlantic Division

		Min.	Max	
1	Maine	—	—	Persons who go armed may be bound over for one year to keep the peace.
2	New Hampshire	None	2 yrs.	Or fine not exceeding $20, or both fine and imprisonment.
3	Vermont	None	2 yrs.	Or fine not exceeding $200, or fine and imprisonment; for slung shot no more than five years.
4	Mass.	None	1 yr.	Or fine not exceeding $50.
5	Rhode Island	—	—	—
6	Conn.	—	—	—
7	New York	—	—	—
8	New Jersey	None	3 mos.	—
9	Penn.	None	1 yr.	Or fine not exceeding $50, or both fine and imprisonment.

South Atlantic Division

		Min.	Max	
10	Delaware	10 days	30 days	Or fine not less than $25 nor more than $100, or both fine and imprisonment.
11	Maryland	None	6 mos.	Or fine not exceeding $500.
12	Dist. of Columbia	None	6 mos.	Or fine not less than $50 nor more than $500, or both fine and imprisonment.

13	Virginia	Fine	Fine	Fine not less than $20 nor more than $100.
14	West Virginia	1 mo.	1 yr.	And fine not less than $25 nor more than $200.
15	North Carolina	—	—	Punishable by fine and imprisonment at discretion of court.
16	South Carolina	None	1 yr.	Or fine not exceeding $200, or both fine and imprisonment.
17	Georgia	None	18 mos.	Punishable under sec. 4310 of Georgia Code: "Accessories after the fact shall be punished by fine not to exceed $1,000, imprisonment not to exceed 6 months, to work in the chain gang on the public works or such other works as the county authorities may employ the chain gang, not to exceed 12 months, and any one or more of these punishments may be ordered, in the discretion of the judge: Provided, That nothing herein contained shall authorize the giving the control of convicts to private persons, or their employment by the county authorities in such mechanical pursuits as will bring the products of their labor into competition with the products of free labor."
18	Florida	None	6 mos.	Or fine not exceeding $100.

North Central Division

| 19 | Ohio | — | 30 days | Or fine not exceeding $200. |

20	Indiana	Fine	Fine	Fine not exceeding $500.
21	Illinois	Fine	Fine	Fine not less than $20 nor more than $100.
22	Michigan	None	3 mos.	Or fine, not exceeding $100, or both fine and imprisonment.
23	Wisconsin	None	6 mos.	Or fine not exceeding $100.
24	Minnesota	None	3 mos.	Or fine not exceeding $100; persons who go armed may be bound over for one year to keep the peace.
25	Iowa	—	30 days	Or fine not exceeding $100.
26	Missouri	5 days	6 mos.	Or fine not less than $50 nor more than $200, or both fine and imprisonment.
27	North Dakota	None	1 yr.	Or fine not exceeding $500, or both fine and imprisonment.
28	South Dakota	None	1 yr.	Or fine not exceeding $500, or both fine and imprisonment.
29	Nebraska	None	30 days	Or fine not exceeding $100.
30	Kansas	None	3 mos.	Or fine not exceeding $100, or both fine and imprisonment.

South Central Division

31	Kentucky	10 days	30 days	And fine not less than $25 nor more than $100.
32	Tennessee	3 mos.	5 years	The penalty for carrying concealed weapons is imprisonment not less than 3 nor more than 6 months, and fine not less than $200 nor more than $500; for drawing a concealed weapon for purpose of assault or intimidation, imprisonment not less than 3 nor more than 5 years.

33	Alabama	None	6 mos.	Fine not less than $50 nor more than $500, and the offender may also be imprisoned in the county jail or sentenced to hard labor for the county for not more than 6 months. The penalty prescribed is for carrying concealed about the person a bowie knife, or knife or instrument of like kind, or a firearm of any kind or description, or an air gun, or weapon of like description. The penalty in Alabama for carrying a rifle or shotgun cane is imprisonment in the penitentiary not less than 2 years and fine not less than $500 nor more than $1,000, or both such fine and imprisonment.
34	Mississippi	1 mo.	3 mos.	Or fine not less than $25 nor more than $100, or both fine and imprisonment.
35	Louisiana	None	3 mos.	And fine not less than $25 nor more than $1,000.
36	Texas	10 days	30 days	And fine not less than $25 nor more than $200.
37	Arkansas	Fine	Fine	Fine not less than $50 nor more than $200.

Western Division

| 38 | Montana | Fine | 3 mos. | The penalty for carrying concealed weapons is fine not less than $10 nor more than $100; for drawing deadly weapons, imprison- |

				ment not less than 1 nor more than 3 months, or fine not less than $10 nor more than $100, or both fine and imprisonment.
39	Wyoming	5 days	20 days	And fine not less than $5 nor more than $50. The penalty in the table is for carrying deadly weapons whether concealed or not. Any one who has in his possession or upon his person any offensive weapon with intent to commit an assult is punishable by imprisonment not more than 6 months or fine not exceeding $500.
40	Colorado	None	30 days	Or fine not exceeding $100, or both fine and imprisonment.
41	New Mexico	10 days	50 days	Or fine not less than $10 nor more than $300.
42	Arizona	Fine	Fine	Fine not less than $50 nor more than $300.
43	Utah	None	6 mos.	Or fine not less than $300, or both fine and imprisonment.
44	Nevada	None	6 mos.	Or fine not exceeding $500. This penalty is for drawing a deadly weapon. The penalty for carrying concealed weapons by minors is imprisonment not less than 30 days nor more than 6 months, or fine not less than $20 nor more than $200.
45	Idaho	20 days	50 days	Or fine not less than $50 nor more than $100, or

				both fine and imprison-ment.
46	Washington	None	30 days	Or fine not less than $20 nor more than $100, or both fine and imprison-ment.
47	Oregon	5 days	100 days	Or fine not less than $10 nor more than $200, or both fine and imprison-ment.
48	California	None	6 mos.	Or fine not exceeding $500, or both fine and imprison-ment.

CHAPTER TWO

The Mississippi—
Spillway of Sin

The Mississippi flows a long course, twisting and turning as if it were a fugitive escaping from its own misdeeds. Many have depicted the stream's beauty—its verdant islands, secluded swamps, pictured rocks. Lovers of the Great River sing of it as an explorer's highway, as a personality which helped tie a nation together, as the pulsing heart of the Valley of Democracy. Few have conceived of the river as a highway for highwaymen and as a waterway down which coursed a flood of crime and sin. Concealed beneath the river queen's royal robes of romance were the filthy rags of the vagrant, and, although she beckoned with a swamp lily, she wore a dirk at her belt. To some who knew her and lived with her, she was a lovely Cinderella, symbol of the happy ending; to others she was the beguiling prostitute of mid-America, companion of thieves, gamblers, and murderers.

The Mississippi was both the Green Thumb and the Black Thumb, and these are interesting expressions whose origins are shrouded in uncertainty but whose meaning is unmistakable. The Green Thumbs, so an old river rat told me when I was a boy foolish enough to pole a leaky skiff through the sloughs of Big Island, were those honest settlers up and down the river who took up land, plowed it, and forced it to bring forth corn and rye and wheat. They tended to their own business and bothered no man.

The Black Thumbs were the bearded ones with their slatternly women who never settled down, but who followed the gospel of force and rape and pillage. They were the horse thieves, the makers of bogus green, the river pirates. When I asked my grandfather about the Green Thumbs and the Black Thumbs, he recognized the terms and said his father, who had come into the Iowa country in the 1840s, spoke of honest folk as Green Thumbs and of dishonest folk as Black Thumbs.

Samuel Clemens caught the spirit of the black-thumbed villain. In his first river yarn, published at age sixteen in the *Carpet-Bag* of May 1, 1852, the youthful author portrays a bully with Bowie knife thrust in his belt and a large horse pistol in each hand who seeks to humiliate a brawny woodsman.[1] This, however, took no particular perspicacity on the part of Hannibal's young Mark Twain, for river brutality and lawlessness not only had been shameful outrages for decades, but also had been the subject of persistent personal conversation, newspaper stories, and editorial comment.

The crimes and sins, both of commission and omission, along the river equalled those of the Commandments, and the American, with Yankee ingenuity, managed without apparent difficulty to improvise additional transgressions which might have startled even Moses. From jerry-built St. Anthony in the Minnesota country to rowdy St. Louis and on to wicked New Orleans, the Mississippi carried the lawless, coddled organized outlaw gangs, and gave haven to banditti.

On steamboats, stern-wheelers and side-wheelers, traveled not only the pious but also the rascals. Many a man, sedate enough at home on land, succumbed to river pleasures once he heard the beckoning call of the calliope and was safe aboard.[2] Practically every boat offered alcohol and games of chance. Whiskey was not regarded as a luxury, but as a necessity. There was a saying on the river that "if a man owned a bar on a popular packet, it was better than possessing a gold mine." Those who held bar concessions—as, for example, Billy Henderson of St. Louis, who bought the bars on all boats of the Northern Line—became wealthy. Bartenders were skilled in mixing whiskey cocktails for Easterners, mint juleps for Southerners, and in concocting a superior French brandy by mixing burnt peach stones, nitric acid, and cod-liver oil with Kentucky whiskey three weeks from the still.[3]

[1] Franklin J. Meine, *Mark Twain's First Story* (Iowa City: Prairie Press, 1966).

[2] The date of the introduction of the calliope varies, although it probably was during the middle 1850s. Philip Graham, *Showboats: The History of an American Institution* (Austin: University of Texas Press, 1951), p. 30, says that the first calliope installed on a showboat was placed on the *Palace* after 1858. On page 78 he writes that the calliope made its debut on July 4, 1856, and that it had been invented by Joshua C. Stoddard, of Worcester, Massachusetts, who organized the Steam Music Company. Miteford M. Mathews, *A Dictionary of Americanisms on Historical Principles*, 2 vols. (Chicago: University of Chicago Press, 1951), 1:248, gives 1858. The steam whistle was in use as early as 1843.

[3] George B. Merrick, *Old Times on the Mississippi* (Cleveland: Arthur H. Clark Co., 1909), pp. 132, 135.

Foreigners, coming to see the strange new America for themselves, frequently commented not only upon the variety of alcoholic beverages —sherry cobblers, brandy smash, milk punch, sangarees, egg nog and plain whiskey, brandy, gin, and rum—but also upon the astonishing appetite of Americans for strong drink. An English visitor spoke of passenger behavior aboard the *Monson*, bound from Cairo to St. Louis: "Drinking went on freely . . . among the coloured as well as the white people, some presents of rum in bottles having been sent from the cabin passengers to some of the negroes on the lower deck, and these getting drunk, became vociferously pious in their potations, and sang, with great fervour, and in full chorus, the Methodist hymn—'We are bound for the land of canaan.'"[4]

Not until after the Civil War, when steamboat traffic had fallen off, was an attempt made to abolish bars and dry out the boats. Captain William F. Davidson, shrewd owner of the Keokuk Northern Line of the upper river, moved from St. Paul to St. Louis. There, at a revival meeting on the levee, he got religion, an event which caused an editor to comment: "What Christ ever wanted of Commodore William F. Davidson is more than we can tell."[5] By 1877 bars were abolished on Davidson's boats. His rewards were great. Elected president of the St. Louis Bethel Association, he was besieged by requests for free passes not only from temperance advocates but also from clergymen of many denominations. In short, Davidson's reformation cost him not only profits from the sale of liquor but also income from the sale of tickets.

Ardent spirits, cardsharks knew and many passengers regretfully learned, went well with aces. Filling an inside straight when filled with brandy smash is no easy task. So prevalent was gambling throughout the entire nation and so firmly entrenched was it as a national pastime, that gaming on river boats should not receive undue emphasis. No one found fault with or complained about an honest game either ashore or afloat. Many river steamers displayed signs warning that gentlemen who played cards did so at their own risk.

[4] Alexander Marjoribanks, *Travels in South and North America* (London: Simpkin, Marshall, & Co., 1853), p. 398; J. S. Buckingham, *The Eastern and Western States of America*, 3 vols. (London: Fisher, Son, & Co., 1842), 3:84.

[5] Undated, unidentified clipping in the William F. Davidson papers, Box 2, Minnesota Historical Society, St. Paul. See also Robert C. Toole, "The Early Career of William F. Davidson," *Minnesota History* 36 (September 1959):250–58; and his "Steamboats at the Bar: The Keokuk Northern Line, 1873–1888," *Missouri Historical Review* 59 (April 1965):300–321.

Contrary to general belief, the play was not inordinately high on the upper river, although it might run to a tidy sum on the lower river. It was a stupid individual, indeed, who had not heard that gambling was hazardous and that professional crooks were an ever-present menace on the river. In reality, only a sucker could be suckered. George Devol, whose memoirs must be taken at somewhat less than face value, said he once had fleeced a passenger of $10,000, only to discover that the money was counterfeit. On another occasion, $8,000 changed hands, with Devol the big winner.[6]

With no limits to bets, a game, beginning as low as twenty-five cents and taking only from two to five minutes to play, might run into thousands of dollars. Craps, poker, and vingt-et-un were so manipulated with loaded dice, stripper decks, and marked cards that neither luck nor knowledge of the game could result in anything but loss for the unprofessional player. "Every man," said a gambler, "who is not a professed gambler, is inevitably bound to get up loser." Yet, despite odds, there were those who believed in gambling, and, said one, "that's about all I do believe in."[7]

E. M. Grandine, 41 Liberty Street, New York City, was a major supplier of advantage and marked-back playing cards. With these, river gamblers could easily read both the size and suit of cards by looking at either their faces or backs. Such marked cards retailed at $1.25 a pack, $10.00 a dozen, and $85.00 a gross. Loaded dice of the best ivory retailed for $5.00 for nine dice—three high, three low, and three square. A sleeve machine, which secreted extra cards and weighed only four ounces, cost $35.00. A vest hold-out was both complicated and rather expensive. Designed to conceal cards in a gambler's waistcoat, it was worked by the foot with spiral coils and catgut and sold for $25.00. Stamped cards apparently were first printed in the United States about 1834. Three years later New Orleans became a center for the manufacture of stamped cards.[8]

Passengers frequently carried arms, and nimble-fingered, professional cardmen usually wore weapons. On October 10, 1836, the *Philadelphia Mirror* printed the following: "NOTICE TO GAMBLERS AND

[6] Merrick, *Old Times*, p. 138; George H. Devol, *Forty Years a Gambler on the Mississippi* (New York: Henry Holt, 1926), pp. 22, 40.

[7] J. H. Green, *An Exposure of the Arts and Miseries of Gambling* (Cincinnati: U. P. James, 1843), p. 29; P.C.S., "A Steam-boat Scene," *American Home Missionary and Pastor's Journal* 6 (March 1834): 207–208.

[8] [John O'Connor], *Wanderings of a Vagabond: An Autobiography* (New York: The Author, 1873), pp. 235–40, 428.

OTHER SPORTSMEN—Bowie knives and tomahawks sold here."
Some years later, an English traveler tarried in the City of Brotherly
Love and described the knives on display. One was "a large clasp
knife, the blade of which when opened is caught by a spring which
prevents its shutting again until you touch the spring." The other knife
resembled "a small straight poniard or dagger" which could be carried
"in a sheath under the waistcoat on the left side," and could be drawn
"in an instant." [9] A Philadelphia editor wrote in 1837 that "one-third
of the male bipeds in this city, between youth and middle age, the
Friends always excepted," carried dirks or Bowie knives.[10] About the
same time, both Mississippi and Alabama passed acts forbidding the
carrying of such weapons.[11]

No state statute or municipal ordinance succeeded in removing
weapons from the American's pocket. Laws were not enforced, and
assaults with knives and pistols continued not only in unsettled, frontier
areas, but also in settled urban communities of the East.[12]

Passengers on river steamers were no different than men elsewhere.

[9] Marjoribanks, *Travels in South and North America*, pp. 437–38. See also Buckingham, *Eastern and Western States*, 3:31–32; T. H. Gladstone, *The Englishman in
Kansas* (New York: Miller & Co., 1857), pp. 128, 281; James Logan, *Notes of a
Journey Through Canada, the United States of America, and the West Indies* (Edinburgh: Fraser & Co., 1838), p. 172; *Missouri Argus* (St. Louis), April 19, 1836.
Foreigners and natives frequently referred to almost any type of knife used as a
weapon as a Bowie knife.

[10] *Philadelphia Public Ledger*, March 18, 1837. For discussion on the inventor of
the Bowie knife, see *Niles' Register*, September 29, 1838.

[11] *Niles' Register*, September 16, 1837, printed a partial text of the Alabama act
approved on June 30, 1837: "That if any person carrying any knife or weapon,
known as Bowie knives or Arkansas tooth picks ... shall cut or stab another with
such a knife, by reason of which he dies, it shall be adjudged murder, as if the killing
had been by malice and aforethought." A tax of one hundred dollars was put on
every Bowie knife sold, given, or otherwise disposed of. See also Lester B. Shippee,
ed., *Bishop Whipple's Southern Diary, 1843–1844* (Minneapolis: University of Minnesota Press, 1937); "What Harm Is There in a Bowie-Knife?" *New Orleans Picayune*,
July 30, 1840; and J. Cutler Andrews, "The Confederate Press and the Public Morale,"
Journal of Southern History 32 (November 1966):461.

[12] *New Orleans Bee*, August 10, 1835; *Minnesota Republican* (St. Anthony),
December 4, 1857. For instances of assault with weapons during the decades prior
to the Civil War, see the following: *Washington National Intelligencer*, June 10,
1830; *Boston Courier*, October 11, 1831; *Philadelphia Public Ledger*, September 8,
1836; *Boston Evening Transcript*, April 24, 1841; *St. Louis Reveille*, June 4, 1844;
Chicago Tribune, June 22, 1849; *London Times*, September 9, 1851; and issues of St.
Paul *Minnesota Pioneer* for 1853. Newspapers of New Orleans, Louisville, St. Louis,
and other river communities printed many episodes.

They passed bogus money, drank too much, gambled against tremendous odds, and delighted in the wearing of weapons. These were the practices which gave both the Mississippi River and its elaborate, floating palaces an unsavory reputation. The steamboat, however, in furnishing liquor and games of chance, was only following contemporary social customs common throughout the growing nation. Passengers passing counterfeit notes and carrying weapons were acting no differently than were men elsewhere. It is a grave mistake to believe that life on the river was somehow an exception to life on shore. The pattern of lawlessness was the same everywhere. The steamboat only mirrored the sins of all America.

The major illegal acts found on the boats—drinking, gambling, carrying weapons, counterfeiting—have crept quietly into this narrative. Yet they are the factors which gave boats a bad reputation. Again, it must be emphasized that not one of these practices originated on the boats, and although the boats offered opportunity for misdeeds, they most certainly proferred them in smaller numbers than did towns and cities not only along the river but also in non-river communities.

Generally speaking, drinking, cardplaying, and the use of personal weapons injured individuals more than they hurt society. But counterfeiting was a different matter. It threatened and harmed and did violence to the entire social structure. This is not to say, as any reasonable individual knows, that society benefits from intemperance, gambling, and the injudicious use of knives and guns. It is to say that the making and passing of fraudulent coins and bills struck at the very roots of the economic system.

Nations recognized this from earliest times. In England, during the reigns of Edward III and of Queen Mary, acts were passed to curtail counterfeiting. Ireland was such a prolific market for fake coins that it was said that there is "scarce an Irish laborer who does not exchange his week's wage for base money, taking a mixture of shillings, sixpence, and copper." Emigrants during the colonial period introduced counterfeiting to British America.[13]

By the 1830s long green was prevalent on the frontier and along western rivers. Indeed, as early as 1818, *Niles' Register* was complaining:

[13] Patrick Colquhoun, *A Treatise on the Police of the Metropolis* (London: Bye & Law, 1806), pp. 189, 192; Arthur C. Hall, *Crime and Its Relations to Social Progress* (New York: Columbia University Press, 1902), p. 211; Kenneth Scott, *Counterfeiting in Colonial America* (New York: American Numismatic Society, 1953).

"We can hardly open a newspaper without seemingly hearing a bellow-
ing aloud of *'counterfeiters'*—*'more counterfeiters'*—*'beware of counterfeiters'*—*'forgery'*—*'more forgery,'* and the like." [14] The country drained
by the Mississippi was during the 1840s fairly saturated with wildcat
money which was called by a variety of names—shinplasters, redbacks,
bluebacks, greenbacks, red horse, blue pup, rag tag, brindle pup, and
stump tail. Steamboat captains not infrequently arrested passengers
who attempted to pay for passage with counterfeit notes. In Minnesota,
during the 1850s, wildcatting caused consternation, and worthless notes
from practically every state in the Union went downriver.[15]

St. Louis, to offer one example, was flooded with long green. Time
and again, merchants and citizens were warned of counterfeit bills.
George Reader, a Mormon, was apprehended on a steamboat passing
fake American half-dollars and spurious Spanish quarter-dollars. A
William Anderson, alias Reynolds, was arrested while circulating counterfeit coin on board the *Comet*. Such examples could be multiplied
many times over. Counterfeit notes were passed on banks of Kentucky,
Ohio, Indiana, Tennessee, Illinois, Virginia, Pennsylvania, North Carolina, and Louisiana to mention only a few. For years New Orleans had
been a favorite city in which to circulate worthless currency. Such
money flowed into the city not only from upriver communities but also
from such centers as Detroit.[16]

Bankers, businessmen, and pursers on river boats protected themselves as best they could by subscribing to and using periodicals called
bank note reporters and counterfeit detectors. These contained detailed
descriptions of fake bills. The first such periodical probably was

14 *Niles' Register*, September 19, November 21, December 12, 1818; January 9,
1819; August 26, 1820; September 2, November 18, December 9, 1820; January 13,
1821; March 30, April 6, July 6, 1822; June 14, 1823; May 21, July 30, 1825;
September 8, November 17, 1832; August 24, 1833; November 25, 1837; December
15, 22, 1838.

15 William H. Dillistin, *Bank Note Reporters and Counterfeit Detectors, 1826–
1866* (New York: American Numismatic Society, 1949), pp. 65–70. See also Niel
Carothers, *Fractional Money: A History of Small Coins and Fractional Paper Currency
of the United States* (New York: John Wiley & Sons, 1930). Anti-counterfeiting
measures are discussed on page 128. *Boston Evening Transcript*, May 20, 1841; Sydney
A. Patchin, "The Development of Banking in Minnesota," *Minnesota History Bulletin* 2 (August 1917):126.

16 *St. Louis Reveille*, May 25, June 1, July 2, October 14, 1844; July 8, 26, November 7, 1845; July 12, 17, 1846; June 15, August 2, 1850. See, for example, *New Orleans
Bee*, February 2, 1832; February 7, 1833; May 24, 1834; June 10, 1835.

issued in Boston in 1805. Those most generally relied upon by merchants doing business in river towns were the *Western Manifest and Counterfeit Detector* and *Clark's Counterfeit Detector*, each printed in St. Louis.[17]

Senator Thomas H. Benton once saw a list of ninety-nine varieties of counterfeits on the Bank of the United States and its branches. An editor of an English financial journal maintained that issues of every good bank in the United States had been counterfeited, and said that in America "counterfeiting has long been practiced on a scale which to many will appear incredible." A British visitor to America suggested that "unless the traveler is provided with a 'Bank-Note Reporter,' published monthly, and continually consults it, he is sure to be imposed upon."[18]

Sometimes narrators, in their haste with river history, forget that it was the Mississippi that brought the towns along its banks into existence, and that river and town were bound together as firmly as Siamese twins. The sins of the one were shared with the other. A "river town" possessed a unique personality not shared by inland settlements. The white-winged stern-wheeler, laden with cargo and with band playing, would have gone to early rot had it not been for flood-scarred Winona in Minnesota, old Fort Madison in Iowa, sleepy Alexandria in Missouri, and, below St. Louis, the towns of Memphis, Vicksburg, Natchez, and New Orleans. And these centers, large or small, would have withered had not the steamboat infused them with the invigorating life of new people and increasing commerce. Such interaction and interdependence were responsible also for the variety and extent of illegal activities.

The man who set himself against the law took both the river and the urban community as his frontier. The latter offered more oppor-

---

[17] Dilliston, *Bank Note Reporters*, pp. 25–26; *St. Louis Reveille*, February 13, April 8, May 1–2, June 1, 12, July 1, August 7, September 3, November 15, 1845; June 10, 1848; June 15, 1850. A widely used and popular reporter after the Civil War was [Laban Heath], *Heath's Greatly Improved and Enlarged, Infallible Government Counterfeit Detector* (Boston: Laban Heath, 1866).

[18] Thomas H. Benton, ed., *Abridgement of the Debates of Congress*, 16 vols. (New York: D. Appleton & Co., 1857–1863), 11:375; "Progress of American Counterfeiting," *Bankers' Magazine and Journal of the Money Market* (London) 22 (October 1862):621–24. See Arthur A. Smith, "Bank Note Detecting in the Era of State Banks," *Mississippi Valley Historical Review* 29 (December 1942):371–86; Charles R. Weld, *A Vacation Tour in The United States and Canada* (London: Longman, Brown, Green, & Longmans, 1855), p. 217.

tunities for antisocial behavior than the former. Rural areas were ideal
for hit-and-run raids, for secluded caves in which to manufacture counterfeit coins and paper, and for concealment in timber hideaways. The
city, as it always had been, was the primary breeding ground, and the
focal point for those with black thumbs. Thieves, confidence men, and
murderers considered the Mississippi as a handy escape route and a
convenient way to move swiftly from one town to another.

Indeed, those of the underworld regularly migrated with the seasons,
not only before but also after the Civil War. Unsavory characters,
during the hot, disease-ridden summer months, left the South to ply
their trade in cooler communities of the upper river. In winter, when
frost's touch nipped the North Country, vagrants, burglars, and ladies
of the evening emigrated to resume business in a more salubrious
southern clime. "This is the period," said the *New Orleans Bee* on
July 15, 1835, "when New Orleans is annually doomed to depredations
and burglaries of every kind in almost every ward." On September
12, 1846, the *St. Louis Reveille* commented: "In our valley of the Mississippi there at present exists, and is daily increasing, a desperate band
of robbers who are continually passing from city to city." The *Minneapolis Tribune* on April 25, 1868, warned of a gang of thieves and
burglars on their way up the river. Four years later, on August 15, 1872,
the *Tribune* spoke of the arrival of a large number of thieves, burglars,
and pickpockets, saying: "They are most of them from New Orleans
and other large Southern cities."

By the 1830s the pattern of lawlessness in the area drained by the
Great River was not only all too apparent but also was reaching alarming proportions. Yet this upsurge was not restricted to the Valley of the
Mississippi. The Mississippi country only reflected what was occurring
throughout the nation. Editors, foreign travelers, and just plain citizens
cried out against lynchings, warned of floods of bogus money, protested
thefts, riots, rapes, and assaults, and charged that police were ineffective,
inefficient, and dishonest—as indeed, they were.

"Society," wrote Hezekiah Niles in his *Register*, "seems everywhere
unhinged, and the demon of 'blood and slaughter' has been let loose
upon us." He exclaimed that "we have executions, and murders, and
riots to the utmost limits of the union!" The *New York Advertiser* was
quoted in the *Boston Courier* of March 12, 1833, as saying: "We think
there has seldom or never been a period known in this country when
crimes were so numerous." A Philadelphia editor on September 7,
1836, feared that before long the City of Brotherly Love would "outstrip

in the infamy of a reputation, for depravity, any city in the civilized West." [19]

The *Boston Evening Transcript* of May 22, 1841, could not recollect "a period when there has been such an extensive system of frauds, villainies, and robberies. . . ." And the *Chicago Tribune* noted a bit pathetically on November 23, 1853, that crime and civilization go together, and "our city gives daily proof of its rapid advancement by the increasing number of criminal cases we are daily called on to record." Lincoln's first address before the Young Men's Lyceum in Springfield, Illinois, in 1837, painted a picture of the nation's growing disregard for the law. [20]

Niles was not wrong when he wrote that society was everywhere un-hinged, but neither he nor other contemporary commentators, although they tried, were able to dissect out fundamental causes. What was there in a new land of abundance, of political equality, and of individualism which resulted in excessive pillaging, in more murders per annum than any European nation, in endemic riots, in such widespread counter-feiting that daily business transactions were jeopardized? Why did citizens of St. Louis wrest from peace officers a Negro and crisp him, while still alive, at a burning stake? [21]

Why were steamboat passengers constantly fearful that their pockets would be picked, their trunks looted, and the bottoms of their carpet-bags slit? What caused the gangs of juvenile delinquents up and down the river who were as mean, vicious, and destructive of peace and order as are their counterparts today? What was there in the American scene or character that prompted editors from St. Paul to New Orleans to say repeatedly that law enforcement agencies were unable and unwilling to protect citizens and maintain the peace?

Why, after the mass lynching of gamblers in Vicksburg on the Fourth of July, 1835, and the eviction of the Knights of the Royal Flush in other Midwestern communities—Natchez, Mobile, Louisville, Cincinnati—why, after all this, did gambling not only continue but increase? [22] Why, after repeated raids and riots by citizens from the

[19] *Niles' Register*, September 5, November 28, 1835; *Philadelphia Public Ledger*, September 7, 1836.

[20] John G. Nicolay and John Hay, eds., *Complete Works of Abraham Lincoln*, 12 vols. (New York: Francis D. Tandy Co., 1905), 1:37–44.

[21] J. Thomas Scharf, *History of St. Louis City and County*, 2 vols. (Philadelphia: Louis H. Evarts & Co., 1883), 2:1091–93.

[22] *Vicksburg Register*, July 9, 30, August 13, 27, September 10, 24, 1835.

pineries of Minnesota to the swamps of Louisiana, did prostitution
continue to flourish? One thing seems certain: the crib that rocked the
child was not the crib that welcomed the man.

The roots of the lawlessness which pocked both river and town were
identical with the factors which nourished crime elsewhere. Misbehavior is all of a yardage, and the pattern runs the length of the cloth.
Yet, as Jean Baptiste Racine pointed out in the seventeenth century:
"Crime like virtue has its degrees." In short, the law since Roman times
has recognized gradations between and among offenses. First degree
murder, for example, is a greater threat to society than is simple
assault. And, upon occasion, many feel that ordinances and statutes
prohibiting certain actions are not only unreasonable but also are in
error. Always it must be remembered that each addition to the criminal
code creates new criminals. The more laws, the greater the number of
lawbreakers.

Intemperance, gambling, duelling, and prostitution, major types of
antisocial behavior, generally were thought of as peccadilloes not to be
regarded as in the same category with pickpocketing, arson, rape, or
forgery and counterfeiting. Reformers might rail against the cardsharp,
the duellist, and the soiled dove, but their efforts accomplished little.
Cold-water advocates got nowhere singing: "King Alcohol has many
forms by which he catches men / He is a beast of many forms and ever
thus has been." [23]

Minor offenses were tolerated—and in some instances approved—not
only because they satisfied a need but also because they swelled municipal and state coffers. Two examples must suffice. For the decade beginning in 1824, the receipts realized from the sale of licenses for gambling
houses in Louisiana totaled $563,500. This sum was used for the support
of the male and female orphan asylums, the primary schools of New
Orleans, the College of Louisiana, the Charity Hospital, and for "ordinary" purposes. The practice ended April 17, 1835, when the legislature passed a bill to prevent gambling. [24]

Although practically every river municipality early in its history
passed ordinances relative to disorderly houses, houses of ill fame, and
common prostitutes, enforcement was at best perfunctory. Arrests were
made and fines levied. But soon the fines became more important than
the eradication of prostitution. "The social evil was again remunerative

[23] Philip D. Jordan and Lillian Kessler, comps., *Songs of Yesterday* (New York:
Doubleday, Doran, & Co., 1941), p. 326.
[24] *New Orleans Bee*, March 5, April 25, 1835.

to the city," said the *Minneapolis Tribune* on October 10, 1879, "by the arraignment and fining of Nettie Connelly and three of her helpers."

River residents, although generally tolerating picayunish impieties, reacted violently to threats against property, purse, and person. It was one thing for a gentleman to be found sprawling in a brothel with his waistcoat open, and another to be found sprawling in his countinghouse with a Bowie knife in his chest. There was a difference between losing a fortune at the hands of a faro dealer and losing a treasure at the hands of a burglar. During its January 1831 term, the New Orleans criminal court heard some nine cases of larceny, six of assault and battery, three of murder, and one each of forgery and swindling. Captain Frederick Marryat, the British traveler, wrote in 1839: "At one time the murders in the city of New Orleans were just as frequent as in all the States contiguous to the Mississippi."[25]

Yet the slayer boldly faced or stealthily stalked his victim in cities other than New Orleans and in the cabin backcountry. In the Galt House of Louisville in 1838, three Mississippians killed a local hatter and a bartender in an argument over the fit of a suit of clothes. In this instance, the identity of the assailants was known.[26] In contrast to this was the brutal slaying of the Spencer family—a father and four children—near Luray, Missouri, in 1877, a crime which shocked the nation and threw such fear among citizens of river towns that some dared not venture from home after dark. Although a suspect was tried and acquitted for the Spencer murders, he was seized and hanged by the Anti-Horse Thief Association and went to his death protesting his innocence.[27] To this day no one is sure of the real murderer's identity. To murder and not be apprehended is clever; but even more talented is he whose murders appear to be accidents or natural deaths and never are discovered.

One cannot easily shrug off increasing homicides with the casual expression, "Life was cheap." Cheap it might have been along the

[25] Frederick Marryat, *A Diary in America*, 3 vols. (*London*: Longman, Orme, Brown, Green, & Longmans, 1839), 2:262–63.

[26] T. Egerton Browne, *Trial of Judge Wilkinson, and Mr. Murdaugh, on Indictments for the Murder of John Rothwell and Alexander H. Meeks* . . . (Louisville: T. E. Browne & Co., 1839).

[27] John W. Murphy, *Outlaws of the Fox River Country* . . . (Hannibal, Mo.: Hannibal Printing Co., 1882); Paul Rowe, ed., *The Trail of Bill Young* (Kahoka, Mo.: Kahoka Gazette-Herald, 1965); Patrick B. Nolan, "*Outlaws of the Fox River Country*: A Study in the Validation of Source Materials" (Master's thesis, University of Minnesota, 1967).

river's borders, but it was not so expendable that slayings went un-
noticed. A new country, bleeding from the cutting edge of the frontier,
was a grim place and a hard one for the symbolic lady who held aloft
the scales of justice. Her servants, particularly city police and hayseed
sheriffs, themselves were frequently ignorant of the law, unskilled in
gathering evidence, and politically ridden. The legal profession received
scant respect, and courts too often were a mockery. Those extralegal
handmaidens, vigilante committees, anti-horse thief associations, and
spur-of-the-moment mobs, upon summation accomplished more evil
than good.

Both native and foreigner, coming to break the prairie and to fell
the timberlands, seem to have been equally contemptuous of the law.
The Irish, like Abou ben Adhem, led all the rest in the per capita con-
sumption of spirits. At least this is what police court records indicate.
Immigrants robbed because they were needy, natives because they were
greedy. Who knows what various motives lie in the hearts of men when
they snuff out lives with the strangler's noose, the robber's pistol and
Bowie knife, the poisoner's vial, the rustic's pitchfork?

The underlying, fundamental reasons why wrongdoing and lawlessness flourished through the Mississippi Valley and the expanding
nation were first, there was no disposition on the part of a sufficient
number of citizens for order; and, second, there were no adequate law-
enforcement agencies which received proper support from the citizenry.
Any community, urban or rural, can enforce the law if it has the will and
the money; but no police force, without the backing of the community
and without adequate funds, ever can maintain the peace.

Police protection was first based upon the "watch" system imported
from England. Through the lanes, streets, and alleys of New York,
Boston, Philadelphia, and Baltimore the un-uniformed night watch,
sounding its rattles, went its appointed rounds. As men moved westward they carried the watch system with them, establishing watches in
Minneapolis, Chicago, St. Louis, Cincinnati, New Orleans and elsewhere throughout the Middle Border.

Yet the system was dated and dead. Anyone scanning police reports
or reading newspapers should have known it. Cities like St. Louis,
which still maintained a night watch in 1850, had they been enterprising
might have again looked across the Atlantic. Had they done so, they
would have discovered that the Liverpool police force was created in
1824, and that five years later Sir Robert Peel was responsible for the
metropolitan police act which set up a commissioner and assistant

commissioner of police with headquarters at Scotland Yard. Had their vision stopped this side of the Atlantic, they would have seen that New York City had abandoned the watch system in 1844.[28]

With the passing of the steamboat and the arrival of the iron railroad horse, the Mississippi lost much of its former traffic, but little of its original sin. Indeed, the decades following the Civil War witnessed an upsurge in criminal activities of every variety. Armies of tramps, among them Federal and Confederate veterans, terrorized entire communities, so that it was not uncommon for governors each spring to issue proclamations of warning against this breed of jungle cat.[29] Lynchings were more numerous than before the war. Clark County, Missouri, which bordered the river, during the 1870s was an unbelievable area of violence.

River pirates of the lower river still looted and sacked. An editor wrote in March of 1870: "It has become evident from cases that have occurred of late, that a steamer had almost as well be wrecked on the coast of Africa or amongst the piratical islands of the Chinese seas, as on the Lower Mississippi."[30] The New Orleans riots of 1866, in which city police played the role of killers, surpassed in ferocity almost any such outbreak of the pre-war period.

Gambling did not decline, and prostitution increased. In 1874 a fire broke out in one of Chicago's "worst and vilest" districts. About twenty blocks were destroyed and more than five hundred prostitutes lost "costly fittings and robes." Many of the girls emigrated to river communities, including St. Louis and St. Paul. When an enterprising madam was picked up by police, she exclaimed bitterly: "Burned out in Chicago and jailed the first night in St. Paul!" In 1880 the federal census reported 365 houses of ill fame in New Orleans, seven in St. Paul, four in Minneapolis, and three in Winona, Minnesota. In Iowa, Muscatine acknowledged five and Keokuk four. Rock Island, Illinois, listed two. St. Louis, with becoming modesty, made no return; but in 1871 there were in the city 136 bawdy houses, six assignation houses, and six keepers of single rooms.[31]

[28] Asa Briggs, *The Age of Improvement* (London: Longmans, Green, & Co., 1959), pp. 213, 218.

[29] *Keokuk Daily Constitution*, April 2, 1879; *New Orleans Bee*, July 17, 1835; *Burlington Hawk-Eye*, April 4, 1867.

[30] *Minneapolis Tribune*, August 12, 1876.

[31] *St. Paul Daily Press*, April 20, 1869; July 16, 19, 22, August 27, 1874; Frederick H. Wines, "Report on Crime, Pauperism, and Benevolence in the United States," *Eleventh Census, 1890* (Washington: G.P.O., 1896), vol. 3, pt. 1, p. 126; See *St. Louis Reveille* for 1871 for many references to prostitution.

Black Thumbs, although centering their nefarious activities in river cities, did not confine their lawlessness to heavily populated centers. They spread from the river, ranging far and wide, to ally themselves with the Bald Knobbers of the Ozarks, to engage in gun battles with Iowa Marshals, and to puzzle the already addled talents of sheriffs in a score of counties.

Perhaps a fair knowledge of the sheriff's concept of law enforcement was expressed by a hillbilly who in the 1880s rode into a rural village which boasted of two stores. "I stopped at one of them," he said, "and the first thing I knew a man spoke ter me and used a string of cuss words. I whaled loose and hit him with two knucks. Tore his neck open and knocked him down so hard it busted the board he fell on. . . . The sheriff came and took me ter a little shop and sot me down on a workbench. Then he went ter look 'bout the dead man. I figured I'd better take out. So I got my horse and rid five miles to my grandpap's. The man didn't die, and nobody ever bothered me 'bout it." [32]

[32] Lucile Morris, *Bald Knobbers* (Caldwell, Ida.: Caxton Printers, 1939), p. 16.

CHAPTER THREE

Lincoln and Mob Rule

When Lincoln delivered his address on the perpetuation of free institutions before the Young Men's Lyceum in Springfield, Illinois, on January 27, 1838, he spoke of the "increasing disregard for law which pervades the country." To support this statement he specifically cited the lynching of gamblers by outraged citizens of Vicksburg, Mississippi, and the burning alive of a Negro by a mob in St. Louis.[1]

Curiously enough, little is known today of the details of these two offenses against law and order. Indeed, it is not generally understood that American society during the 1830s was torn and disrupted by the bloody activities of vigilante discipline. Yet, during this decade, editors throughout the nation were, as did Lincoln, deploring not only a soaring crime rate but also a rising tide of mob action, an epidemic of taking the law into one's own hands.

"We have executions, and murders, and riots to the utmost limits of the union!" said *Niles' Weekly Register* in 1835. Later that year the *Register* warned the people of the United States that "unless they look well to themselves, the day of their destruction is at hand. . . . We disclaim every man who advises the people to take the law into their own hands, no matter for what cause, no matter for what good reason, no matter to answer what end of justice, no matter how much good may for once be done thereby." In 1836, the *Register* stated bluntly that blood was the order of the day in the nation.[2] Lincoln was only echoing such sentiments when he admonished the Young Men's Lyceum, "let every man remember that to violate the law, is to trample on the blood

[1] Roy P. Basler, Marion D. Pratt, and Lloyd A. Dunlap, eds., *The Collected Works of Abraham Lincoln*, 9 vols. (New Brunswick, N.J.: Rutgers University Press, 1953), 1:109; Joseph F. Newton, *Lincoln and Herndon* (Cedar Rapids, Ia.: Torch Press, 1910), pp. 9–10; James E. Cutler, *Lynch Law* (New York: Longmans, Green, & Co., 1905), p. 110.

[2] *Niles' Register*, September 5, November 28, 1835; January 30, 1836.

of his father, and to tear the character [charter] of his own and his children's liberty."[3]

Lincoln, like many another American, was particularly incensed by two outstanding and particularly horrible episodes: the extra-legal punishment of professional gamblers at Vicksburg in 1835 and the burning of a St. Louis Negro in 1836. He described these outrages as dangerous examples and as revolting to humanity.[4] No doubt the young attorney gained knowledge of each event from newspapers, for press accounts were detailed and editorial condemnation was general.[5] Both foreign and domestic travelers commented upon the hanging and the burning.[6] The Vicksburg lynching was referred to obliquely, but clearly, in the famous trial of the Galt House murderers in Louisville, Kentucky, in December, 1838. The eloquent Benjamin Hardin, attorney for the prosecution, said that the "revolutionary and disorganized proceedings of mobs in New York, in Mississippi, and at other points in a few years past, have tarnished the fair character of our country."[7]

Judge John Rowan, representing the defense, repudiated Hardin's argument, declaring that the Vicksburg proceeding was not a deliberate,

[3] Basler, *Collected Works of Lincoln*, 1:112.

[4] Ibid., 1:109–110.

[5] See, for example, *Niles' Register*, July 25, August 1, 8, 22, November 21, 1835; *Daily National Intelligencer* (Washington), July 25, 29, August 3, 5, 6, November 21, 1835; *New Orleans Bee*, July 13, 14, 16, 1835; *Louisville Journal*, quoted in *Daily National Intelligencer*, July 6, 1835, and *Cincinnati Gazette*, quoted in ibid, November 21, 1835.

[6] Captain Frederick Marryat, *A Diary in America* (London: Longmans, Orme, Brown, Green, & Longmans, 1839), 3:240–52; Michael Chevalier, *Society, Manners and Politics in the United States: Letters on North America*, ed. with an introduction by John W. Ward (New York: Doubleday & Co., 1961), p. 374; Lester B. Shippee, ed., *Bishop Whipple's Southern Diary*, 1843–1844 (Minneapolis: University of Minnesota Press, 1937), pp. 217–18; J. S. Buckingham, *The Eastern and Western States of America* (London: Fisher, Son & Co., 1842), 2:79–80. For the St. Louis atrocity, see *Niles' Register*, June 4, 1836; J. Thomas Scharf, *History of St. Louis City and County* (Philadelphia: Louis H. Everts & Co., 1883), 2:1824–25; Marryat, *Diary*, 3:238–40; Buckingham, *Society, Manners, and Politics*, 3:196–97; *Du Buque* (Wis. Terr.) *Visitor*, May 11, 1836.

[7] A. B. Carlson, *The Law of Homicide, Together with the Trial for Murder of Judge Wilkinson, Dr. Wilkinson, and Mr. Murdaugh* . . . (Cincinnati: Robert Clarke & Co., 1882), p. 170; T. Egerton Browne, *Trial of Judge Wilkinson, Dr. Wilkinson, and Mr. Murdaugh on Indictments for the Murder of John Rothwell and Alexander H. Meeks* . . . (Louisville: T. E. Browne & Co., 1837), passim. The trial, on change of venue from Louisville, Jefferson County, Kentucky, to Harrodsburg, Mercer County, began on March 4, 1839.

cold-blooded conspiracy of the bad against the good citizens of the place. "Judging, therefore, of the Vicksburg mob from its object and its cause," continued Rowan, "I find in it many mitigating circumstances; but am far, very far from approving it." Furthermore, Judge Rowan maintained that the happening was not unmingled with some of the elements of virtue and goodness.[8]

Lincoln, in his lyceum speech, was fairly vague concerning the lynching. He said only that Vicksburg citizens first commenced by hanging the "regular gamblers: a set of men, certainly not following for a livelihood, a very useful, or very honest occupation; but one which, so far from being forbidden by the laws, was actually licensed by an act of the Legislature, passed but a single year before."[9] This statement most certainly conveys the impression that the gamblers were punished merely because they were gamblers, and such is not the case. Two gamblers were tarred and feathered and ordered to vacate Vicksburg within forty-eight hours and five were hanged not because they were card sharks or were charged with dishonest dealing but because they made Vicksburg a place of rendezvous where "every species of transgression followed in their train."[10] They supported tippling houses, roamed the streets in armed groups, disturbed public meetings, insulted citizens, and defied civil authority.

On July 4, 1835, a gambler by the name of Cabler or Cakler attempted to break up a barbecue given by the Vicksburg Volunteers, insulted an officer, and struck a citizen. When two volunteers arrested Cabler, they found on his person a loaded pistol, a large knife, and a dagger. He was tied to a tree, whipped, and tarred and feathered. That evening citizens posted a public notice warning all gamblers to leave town within twenty-four hours. Some Knights of the Royal Flush heeded the instructions and left. But on July 6, five gamblers barricaded themselves in a house and refused to surrender themselves to the militia company and several hundred citizens. The house was surrounded, the back door kicked open, and shots fired from the interior. One bullet killed Dr. Hugh S. Bodley, a physician who had followed the crowd. It was the slaying of Bodley that caused militiamen and citizens to hang the five known only as North, Hullums, Dutch Bill, Smith, and McCall.

---

[8] Carlson, *Law of Homicide*, p. 243. For a brief sketch of John Rowan, see J. Winston Coleman, *Famous Kentucky Duels: The Story of the Code of Honor in the Bluegrass State* (Frankfort: Roberts Printing Co., 1953), pp. 12–13.

[9] Basler, *Collected Works of Lincoln*, 1:109.

[10] *Vicksburg Register*, July 9, 1835.

The residents of Vicksburg knew full well that their application of law to the lawless would bring criticism and censure of the type that Lincoln set down in his address. "It is not expected," they said, "that this act will pass without censure from those who had not an opportunity of knowing and feeling the dire necessity out of which it originated." They continued, "The laws, however severe in their provision, have never been sufficient to correct a vice which must be established by positive proof, and cannot, like others, be shown from circumstantial testimony." Citizens had borne with the lawbreaking of the gamblers until "to have suffered them any longer would not only have proved us to be destitute of every manly sentiment, but would also have implicated us in guilt of accessories to their origin." It was pointed out that the "revolution" against the gambling fraternity was conducted by the most respectable citizens of the community.[11]

The entire tone of Lincoln's remarks reflects adversely upon Vicksburg's citizenry because, unfortunately, he did not possess full and complete facts. He was entirely correct, of course, when he deplored mob rule, but in this instance he failed to understand that local law enforcement was inadequate and inefficient. And one may properly question the propriety of the death punishment administered to the five gamblers. Yet again it must be emphasized that the men were not hanged because they were gamblers. Their profession was legalized by the state legislature. They were punished because they disrupted the normal, orderly, social pattern. In addition, the gambling fraternity had for years infested the Mississippi Valley, and, in a score of communities, from St. Louis to New Orleans, had proved its members to be ruffians and disturbers of the peace.[12] Lincoln might well have mentioned that the Vicksburg lynchings stimulated other towns—Louisville, Natchez, Cincinnati, St. Louis—to take steps to rid themselves of professional gamblers.

Most unfortunately of all, Lincoln did not perceive that the Vicksburg vigilantes were by necessity combining the forces of obedience and revolution, that because of the lack of a sturdy social structure and of an effective police agency, it was necessary to utilize violent and illegal methods in order to achieve peace and social stability. The lynching of the gamblers was a means to an end. It was a temporary expedient. It was, as Professor Richard M. Brown says, "a measure of

[11] Ibid.

[12] For a discussion of gambling and other illegal activities in the area drained by the Mississippi River, see "The Mississippi—Spillway of Sin," p. 23 of this volume.

the intense devotion which respectable men of property give to the principles of law and order." [13]

Lincoln's judgment of the burning of the Negro in St. Louis on April 28, 1836, was sounder than was his interpretation of the Vicksburg incident.[14] The situation was this: Deputy Sheriff George Hammond and Deputy Constable William Mull arrested a powerful mulatto named McIntosh, charging him with interfering with officers while discharging their duty. In the ensuing struggle, McIntosh knifed Mull. When Hammond went to Mull's assistance, McIntosh cut Hammond's throat and killed him. Mull and local citizens recaptured McIntosh and jailed him. A crowd estimated at a thousand, broke the Negro out of jail, dragged him to a square at what is now Tenth and Market streets, tied him to a tree, piled dry resinous wood about him, and burned him alive.[15]

In short, citizens, without due cause, impeded the orderly process of the law, thwarted established authority which was in command of the situation, and illegally served as judge and jury. They refused to let the organized law take its course. In the Vicksburg situation, no functioning, organized law existed, and citizens, therefore, supplied that law on a temporary basis. Lincoln, however, was right in one particular—"the example in either case, was fearful."

[13] Richard M. Brown, *The South Carolina Regulators* (Cambridge: Belknap Press of Harvard University Press, 1963), p. 142.

[14] W. H. Herndon and Jesse W. Weik in their *Abraham Lincoln* (2d. ed., 1892), as quoted in Newton's *Lincoln and Herndon* (pp. 9–10), err when they state that the burning of McIntosh took place "a few weeks" before Lincoln delivered his lyceum address.

[15] Scharf, *History of St. Louis*, 1824–25; Cutler, *Lynch Law*, 108–10; Marryat, *Diary*, 3:238–40; *Niles' Register*, June 4, 1836. This was not the first nor was it to be the last burning alive of Negroes. A Negro was burned alive in the Choctaw Nation in 1832 and another near Natchez in 1842. See *Tennessee Statesman*, quoted in *Boston Courier*, April 17, 1832, and *Southern Statesmen*, quoted in *New Orleans Bee*, May 7, 1832; also *Boston Evening Transcript*, June 21, 1842. See also John L. Harr, "*Law and Lawlessness* in the Lower Mississippi Valley, 1815–1860," *Northwest Missouri State College Studies* 19 (June 1, 1955):50–70.

CHAPTER FOUR

Lady Luck and Her Knights
of the Royal Flush

Of all the enticing females who beguiled men the length and breadth of the rambunctious frontier, none was courted more assiduously than fickle Lady Luck. The patron saint of card sharps, dice tossers, and gamblers, amateur and professional, she also symbolized the chancy chore of putting together a new nation. Lady Luck represented the odds of the pioneer experience, the wager a man made with himself that he could succeed, the double-or-nothing bet that Manifest Destiny was as winning hand. She provided an escape—a catharsis—from the burden of the plow, the rigors of the trail, the loneliness of mountain men, cowboys, miners, and prairie travelers. The slap of cards on the table was solace even though the church damned gambling as sinful and the law thought of it as a misdemeanor. Yet neither moral persuasion nor statute nor ordinance, throughout the nineteenth century, succeeded in destroying Lady Luck's empire where her henchmen cut and dealt a deck or rolled the dice in taverns along the National Road, on steamboats plying western waters, or in saloons, or gambling parlors of scores of communities all the long way from the Missouri River, through the Southwest in New Mexico and Texas, and on to the Pacific slope.[1]

Opposition to gaming had been carried from England to the colonies in America. A series of acts in the mother country and the comments of

[1] In addition to references cited below, the following titles are useful: Donald R. Taft, *Criminology: A Cultural Interpretation*, rev. ed. (New York: Macmillan Co., 1950); Edwin H. Sutherland and Donald R. Cressey, *Principles of Criminology* (Philadelphia: J. B. Lippincott Co., 1966); M. P. Golding, ed., *The Nature of Law* (New York: Random House, 1966); Alexander Gardiner, *Canfield: The True Story of the Greatest Gambler* (Garden City, N.Y.: Doubleday & Co., 1930); David D. Allen, *The Nature of Gambling* (New York: Coward-McCann, 1953).

Blackstone, upon whom so many colonial lawyers leaned, provided plenty of precedent for legislation in America. Blackstone wrote that gaming "is an offense of the most alarming nature, tending by necessary consequence to promote public idleness, theft, and debauchery among those of the lower class." Among persons of a superior rank, he continued, "gambling hath frequently been attended with the sudden ruin and desolation of ancient and opulent families." Finally, said Blackstone, "gaming prostitutes every principle of honor and virtue."[2]

But, true or false, this did little to deter wagering on games of chance either in the Old World or the New World. Massachusetts, for example, in 1646, 1651, and 1670, passed laws prohibiting gambling in houses of public entertainment, and this included not only cards and dice but also shuffleboard and bowling.[3] In 1742 a general law stipulated that all security for money won at gaming or betting would be void, and that a loser, after payment of game losses, might recover those losses. If a loser did not wish to recover, any other person might sue and recover treble the amount lost to the winner. The act provided also that a winner must, under oath, disclose the amount he won. Repayment by the winner to the loser would, of course, excuse the winner from any penalty.[4] Among the earliest directives sent by James I to Governor Sir Francis Wyatt of Virginia, was one dated July 24, 1621, urging that drunkenness and gaming be suppressed.[5] Persons, both in England and her colonies in America, who played at unlawful games could be prosecuted under the vagrancy acts, which lumped together divers characters such as minstrels, jugglers, tinkers, peddlers, and curiously enough, all scholars of Oxford or Cambridge who begged without a license from the university.[6]

[2] William Blackstone, *Commentaries on the Laws of England*, ed. George Sharwood, 2 vols. (Philadelphia: J. B. Lippincott & Co., 1872, 1873), vol. 2, bk. 4, pp. 171–72. See Stat. 33 Hen. VIII, c. 9, 33 Geo. II, c. 24, 16 Car. II, c. 7, 9 Ann, c. 14.

[3] General Court, *Charter and General Laws of the Colony and Province of Massachusetts Bay* (Boston: T. B. Wait & Co., 1814), pp. 118–19.

[4] Ibid., pp. 541–43.

[5] William Waller Hening, ed., *The Statutes at Large: Being a Collection of All the Laws of Virginia From the First Session of the Legislature in the Year 1619*, 13 vols. (New York: R. & W. & G. Bartow, 1823), 1:114.

[6] Austin Van der Slice, "Elizabethan Houses of Correction," *Journal of the American Institute of Criminal Law and Criminology* 27 (May–June 1936):54; General Court, *Laws of the Commonwealth of Massachusetts, 1780–1807*, 3 vols. (Boston: F. T. Buckingham, 1807), 1:411–13. Other states included gamblers in vagrancy laws. See, for example, *Laws of the State of New Jersey* (Trenton: Joseph Justice, 1821), p. 49, where, in a definition of vagrancy, was included "all straggling persons,

Gambling with cards and dice increased between the American Revolution and the War of 1812 despite the fact that legislatures made strenuous effort to curtail the placing of bets and wagers. Both English and French packs of cards were easy enough to come by, and gaming tables were in parlor use as early as 1750. Imported dice were plentiful, and some were carved from whalebone within the country.[7] The popularity of billiards made it almost impossible to prevent an innkeeper from installing tables for the amusement of guests. So unpopular, indeed, was Rhode Island's act designed to prevent gambling at billiard tables in taverns and public houses that the statute was repealed in February, 1783.[8]

Tennessee sought to discourage gaming in October, 1799, in an act stipulating that all contracts, promises, and securities in consideration of gambling were void. Furthermore, a penalty of a fine of five dollars was set for persons who encouraged or took part in any gambling and a fine of ten dollars for each offense of any tavernkeeper who encouraged gambling. Any person losing in a game of chance might bring action to recover money or property lost.[9] North Carolina's tax on "A. B. C." and "E. O." tables not only is interesting from the legal viewpoint but also

---

who shall practise any unlawful gaming, to trick and deceive the people." Also L. Bradford Prince, comp., *General Laws of New Mexico* . . . (Albany, N.Y.: W. C. Little & Co., 1880), pp. 300–303, where "common gamblers and persons who go from plaza to plaza without any other means of visible support" are deemed vagrants.

[7] Two of the best histories of cards and gambling are Catherine Perry Hargrave, *History of Playing Cards and a Bibliography of Cards and Gaming* (Boston: Houghton Mifflin Co., 1930) and Henry Chafetz, *Play the Devil: A History of Gambling in the United States from 1492 to 1955* (New York: Clarkson N. Potter, 1960). See Ruth B. Davidson, "American Gaming Tables, 1750–1816," *Antiques* 54 (October 1953): 294–96. For a brief history of dice, see Alan Wykes, *The Complete Illustrated Guide to Gambling* (New York: Doubleday & Co., 1968), pp. 128–47. Cheap dice were made from the knucklebone of sheep, better quality from ivory.

[8] John Russell Bartlett, ed., *Records of the Colony of Rhode Island and Providence Plantations in New England, 1636–1792*, 10 vols. (Providence: Alfred Anthony, 1856–1865), 9:662.

[9] Edward Scott, comp., *Laws of the State of Tennessee . . . from the Year 1715 to the Year 1820 Inclusive*, 2 vols. (Knoxville: Heiskell & Brown, 1821), 1:722. An act of November 14, 1801, states: "That from and after the passing of this act, no money or any kind of property whatever, won by any species or mode of gaming shall be recoverable by law. . . ." An act of November 3, 1803, provided that fines from gaming convictions were to be divided in half, one half to go to the person who shall sue for the same, and the other half to go to the use of the county in which the offense was committed, "to be recovered by action of debt before any tribunal having cognizance thereof." (Ibid., 1:776–77).

because it plainly proves that such tables—games that later were to be most popular in the Middle West and the Far West—had been introduced into North Carolina by 1785. After this "evil species of gaming" proved popular "greatly to the prejudice of the good people," the legislature slapped a levy of 250 pounds on each and every "A. B. C." and "E. O." table.[10]

Most games of chance, except poker and its variations, were an established part of American life by 1800. New Jersey, for example, in 1797 forbade as gambling, all playing at cards, dice, or other games, with one or more dice, having one or more figures on them. "A. B. C." and "E. O." tables, faro, cockfights, tennis, bowls, and shuffleboard were forbidden. A New York statute of 1801 sought to prevent excessive and deceitful gambling. In the Deep South, an Alabama act of 1807 outlawed "A. B. C." and "E. O." tables, billiard tables, "rowley-powley" tables, rouge-et-noir, faro, or any other table or game in which money or property could be won or lost.[11]

Perhaps no southern state formulated and passed a more comprehensive anti-gambling law than did Georgia in its act of February 29, 1764. It, of course, was based upon English statutes. The act forbade lotteries in which chance played a part, that is, the use of dice, lots, cards, numbers, figures, or tickets, whether they be drawn from a box or a wheel. It proscribed wagering at cards, dice, and tables. It stipulated that vendors of liquor must not, under penalty of law, permit any gaming with cards, dice, draughts, shuffleboards, billiard tables, ninepins, or with any other games or implements of gambling. It instructed constables and justices of the peace to enforce the act. By 1819 revisions modernized the earlier statute. Among these was one which provided fine or imprisonment for keepers of disorderly houses in which were encouraged idleness, drinking, and gaming.[12] Maryland's criminal code

[10] Ibid., 1:335–36.

[11] *Laws of the State of New Jersey* (Trenton: Joseph Justice, 1821), pp. 267–69; William P. Van Ness and John Woodworth, eds., *Laws of the State of New-York, Revised, 1784–1813*, 2 vols. (Albany: H. C. Douthwick & Co., 1813), 1:152–54; Harry Toulmin, comp., *Digest of Laws of Alabama* (Cahawba: Ginn & Curtis, 1823), p. 378.

[12] Horatio Marbury and William H. Crawford, eds., *Digest of the Laws of the State of Georgia* ... (Savannah: Seymour, Woolhopter, & Stebbins, 1802), pp. 248–53; Augustus S. Clayton, *The Office and Duty of a Justice of the Peace, and a Guide to Clerks, Constables, Coroners, Executors, Administrators, Guardians, Sheriffs, Tax-Collectors, and Receivers, and other Civil Officers, According to the Laws of the State of Georgia* ... (Milledgeville: S. Grantland, 1819), p. 190.

forbade "E. O." tables and any other tables at which the games of "Pharo, Equality," or any game of chance was played for money.[13]

With the close of the War of 1812 and the growth of migration westward, gambling followed new frontiers, so that it became necessary, if only for appearance's sake, for new states to draft and enact legislation against the evils of gaming. The third session of the Illinois legislature prohibited the bringing of playing cards, dice, billiard balls, or any other gambling device into the state. Indiana's governor, speaking of gambling in 1829, fumed that "there is no offense in our penal code, which is more frequently committed; and no violation of law which escapes with such general license and impunity." A judge found the "besetting sin of early members of the bar to be intemperance and gambling," and said that "about nine-tenths of the members of the bar were slaves and victims of these vices." [14]

Although many members of the bar, justices of the peace, and judges were not averse to nipping from a bottle and most certainly enjoyed wagering at cards, one individual distinguished himself at these recreations. He was Judge Benjamin Johnson of the superior court of the Territory of Arkansas. One election day in Little Rock in 1829, the judge, wandering through a crowd which was listening to a political speech, told a citizen, in a rude and imperative manner, to be silent. The man refused. Several witnesses later testified, "The Judge being intoxicated, drew his knife and in violent terms abused and menaced him and ordered him to be silent and threatened him if he did not, he would kill him—and drew his arm back with his knife in his hand in a sabbing [*sic*] attitude." The judge's friends came and took him away. All this, of course, is not particularly startling to anyone knowing the antics of the frontier bar and bench, but the story is not quite ended, for one

[13] Virgil Maxcy, *Laws of Maryland . . .* , 3 vols. (Baltimore: Philip H. Nicklin & Co., 1811), 3:465.

[14] B. Carlyle Buley, *The Old Northwest Pioneer Period, 1815–1840*, 2 vols. (Indianapolis: Indiana Historical Society, 1950), 1:368, 370–71. Other governors spoke against gambling. See, for example, the *Washington Daily National Intelligencer*, November 4, 1835, which quotes Governor William S. Fulton of Arkansas: "The practice of gaming is decidedly condemned, and the insufficiency of laws in restraint of it being taken for granted, 'anti-gaming societies' are recommended. . . ." See also John C. Parish, *Robert Lucas* (Iowa City: State Historical Society of Iowa, 1907), pp. 180–81, 215. Lucas, governor of the Territory of Iowa in 1838, addressed the legislature and denounced the two vices of gambling and intemperance in severe terms. "These two vices," he said, "may be considered the fountains from which almost every other crime proceeds . . ." (ibid., p. 180).

normally does not expect a judge to fleece another judge. One evening, so the sworn testimony goes, Judge Johnson called on James Lemon, who, with two other gentlemen, operated a faro bank in Little Rock. The judge proposed to bring his colleague, Judge Joseph Seldon, to the faro establishment, induce him to bet, and to attempt to take his money from him. Johnson, in exchange for his friendly guide service, was to collect one-fourth of all Seldon lost. Lemon agreed, Johnson steered Seldon to the game, Seldon lost three hundred dollars, and Johnson received his one-fourth.[15]

The law, no matter how strict, frequently came out a poor second when pitted against practice, for Americans were addicted to wagering, were antagonistic to restrictions on their personal behavior and were convinced that it was their inalienable right to go to hell in any way they pleased. The states might draw tight legislation, but it was of little avail if enforcement were loose.[16]

Louisiana, in 1835, prohibited all gaming houses and banking games, but exempted licensed establishments until such time as those licenses expired.[17] Two years earlier Kentucky had amended its penal code as follows:

> That all persons hereafter guilty of playing with a free negro, mulatto or slave, any game at cards, or with dice, or any other game whatever, whereby money or property is won or lost, shall be guilty of a misdemeanor, and shall be fined therefor, at the discretion of a jury, a sum not exceeding fifty dollars, upon the presentment of a grand jury.[18]

[15] Clarence Edwin Carter, ed., *The Territorial Papers of the United States*, 24 vols. (Washington: G.P.O., 1934–1962), 21:623–26. See Mary Wheelhouse Berthel, *Horns of Thunder: The Life and Times of James M. Goodhue Including Selections from His Writings* (St. Paul: Minnesota Historical Society, 1948), p. 64, where the outspoken Goodhue, editor of the St. Paul *Minnesota Pioneer*, castigates a United States marshal and a territorial judge: "We never knew an instance of a debt being paid by either of them unless it be a gambling debt."

[16] Discussions of law enforcement may be found in Roger Lane, *Policing the City: Boston, 1822–1885* (Cambridge: Harvard University Press, 1967) and in Richard C. Wade, *The Urban Frontier: The Rise of Western Cities, 1790–1830* (Cambridge: Harvard University Press, 1959). For the role of the sheriff in law enforcement, see Bruce Smith, *Rural Crime Control* (New York: Columbia University Press, 1933) and his *Police Systems in the United States* (New York: Harper & Brothers, 1949). See also the President's Commission on Law Enforcement and Administration of Justice, *The Challenge of Crime in a Free Society* (Washington: G.P.O., 1967), p. 17.

[17] Meinrad Greiner, comp., *Louisiana Digest, 1804–1841* (New Orleans: Benjamin Levy, 1841), pp. 137–38.

[18] *Acts of the General Assembly of the Commonwealth of Kentucky, December Session, 1836* (Frankfort: A. G. Hodges, 1837), 305–6. The *New Orleans Bee*, March

As the nation, interrupted by both the Mexican and Civil wars, swept westward, the gambler kept pace with the soldier and sod-breaker. Legislators, territorial and state, put together criminal codes, which, of course, included crimes against what might be laughingly termed "public morality," but the gambler was as ubiquitous as sin itself. He invaded the mining camps of California, rode with Texas cattle herds, infested the saloons of New Mexico, and made himself available in the remoteness of the Dakotas, Nebraska, Montana, and Oklahoma, to mention only some places. Knights of the Royal Flush stopped en route at major cities—St. Louis, Minneapolis, Denver, Helena, Omaha, causing marshals and police chiefs no end of trouble.[19]

"Omaha," its chief of police said pathetically, "because of her geographical position, appears to be visited by and harbor more criminals than any of the Western cities which have a population greater than ours." In 1888 Omaha police confiscated gambling apparatus valued at thousands of dollars. The haul included a wheel of fortune, a faro outfit and checks, five faro and poker tables, two roulette tables, and "wheels complete, chuck-luck, faro boxes and complete outfit, check boxes, counters, drawers, etc. and about two bushels of chips."[20]

California licensed all gambling houses in an act of March 14, 1851. Briefly, the law provided that county treasurers should issue licenses. The fee for houses having any number of tables over three was fifteen hundred dollars quarterly; for houses with three tables or less, one thousand dollars quarterly, except in San Francisco, Sacramento, and Marysville, where the fee was thirty-five dollars a month for each table. Licenses, however, did not permit the playing of "French monte, three-card game, or the game known as Loop or String game, or the

---

27, 1838, carried a graphic account of Negroes gambling with dice in company with gamblers.

[19] The literature describing gambling and social evils in western communities is so abundant that the following titles are only suggestive: Forbes Parkhill, *The Wildest of the West* (New York: Henry Holt, 1951); John W. Horner, *Silver Town* (Caldwell, Ida.: Caxton Printers, 1950); Ronald D. Miller, *Shady Ladies of the West* (Los Angeles: Westernlore Press, 1964); Herbert Asbury, *The Barbary Coast: An Informal History of the San Francisco Underworld* (Garden City: Garden City Publishing Co., 1933); Nyle H. Miller and Joseph W. Snell, *Great Gunfighters of the Kansas Cowtowns* (Lincoln: University of Nebraska Press, 1963).

[20] *Omaha Municipal Reports, 1888* (Omaha: Dispatch Publishing Co., 1889), pp. 246, 256. For migration of lawbreakers in an earlier period, see "The Mississippi —Spillway of Sin" and "The Derringer and the Ace of Spades: Reflections on Middle Border Law and Order," pp. 23 and 99, respectively, in this volume.

game known as Thimbles, or the game known as Lottery." Poker and dice games were allowed.[21]

Texas, like California, forbade the gambling games of faro, monte, "viente-un," rouge-et-noir, roulette, "A. B. C.," chuck-luck, keno, pool, and rondo. The act attempted, in rather bumbling manner, to enumerate places where those courting Lady Luck might not gamble— houses that sold spiritous liquors, storehouses, taverns, inns, or any other public house, or in any street, highway, or other public place, or in any outhouse where people resort. Conviction carried a fine of not less than ten nor more than twenty-five dollars.[22]

Antigambling legislation in other western states was similar to that enacted by California and Texas. Montana forbade the playing for money of three-card monte and other games of chance as did Texas and California, but with one significant difference. The act specifically mentioned types of mechanical cheating: "If the keeper of any house, shop, tent, saloon, booth or other place shall knowingly permit . . . any other game or games, where fraud or cheating is practiced, or where loaded dice, marked cards, or waxed cards are used," the offender was subject, upon conviction, to a fine not exceeding one thousand dollars and the loss of his license.[23] Arizona licensed gambling establishments and prescribed stiff penalties for those who operated without licenses. The license fee of thirty dollars a month, collectable in advance, was placed on each and every gaming table or piece of gambling apparatus, including not only the usual games of faro, roulette, and keno but also stud-horse poker and all other banking or percentage games.[24]

Oklahoma and North Dakota proscribed the usual games, provided penalties for those who operated unlawfully, and extended the sites where addicts could not play from taverns, highways, and other public places to include vessels and floats. Both states made owners, agents, and superintendents of such places liable to a misdemeanor charge. The Oklahoma statute, however, was far more specific than that of North Dakota, for it stated that if any commander, owner, or lessee of any

[21] S. Garfielde and F. A. Snyder, comps., *Compiled Laws of the State of California, 1850–1853* (Benicia: S. Garfielde, 1853), pp. 826–27.

[22] *The Penal Code of the State of Texas* (Galveston: News Office, 1857), pp. 77–79. A tale, probably a literary fabrication, relates a gambling incident in Arkansas, after which the gambler "slopes" for Texas. See "Slopes for Texas," *Harper's New Monthly Magazine* 2 (January 1851):187–88.

[23] *Montana Revised Statutes . . . 1879* (Helena: Geo. E. Boos, 1881), p. 388.

[24] Cameron H. King et al., eds., *Revised Statutes of Arizona* (Prescott: Prescott Courier Print, 1887), pp. 397–98.

vessel or float knowingly permitted any gambling for money and did not immediately report the same, he was subject to a fine not exceeding five hundred dollars. In addition, he was liable to any party who lost money or property in a sum equal to the money or property lost. Such losses were to be recovered in a civil action.[25]

Normally state legislatures, when drawing up statutes, did not discriminate among races or men of color. A few southern states, such as Kentucky, did do so. With this in mind, an act of Washington comes as somewhat of a surprise. This law began, as had others, with a listing of games prohibited. Then it continued: "And every white man, Negro, half-breed, Indian, Kanaka or Chinaman" who shall gamble with "any Indian for fun, pleasure, luck, money, or anything of value whatever" shall, upon conviction, be fined not less than fifty and not more than five hundred dollars, or be subjected to both fine and imprisonment not exceeding six months.[26]

State statutes, of course, were reflected in village, town, and city ordinances, for these political units were authorized by state legislation to make such local laws as were necessary to manage communities and to keep the peace. Thus, to offer only a few typical examples, Columbus, Ohio, in 1826 passed an antigambling ordinance carrying a fine of from five to twenty dollars for each twenty-four hours of gaming of any kind. At St. Louis, Missouri, city fathers in 1835 passed an ordinance outlawing "A. B. C.," faro, and other games for money under penalty of a fine of five hundred dollars for each offense. All fines collected were to be turned over for use by the St. Louis Hospital. In 1837 trustees of the town of Burlington, Iowa, set a fine of five dollars for persons convicted of playing at any game or games for money in any tavern. Quincy, Illinois, enacted a similar ordinance in 1840.[27]

Ordinances designed to prevent vice and immorality and to preserve the public peace and good order became fairly standardized after the Civil War. There is only a slight difference, for example, between the 1871 gaming ordinance of Marquette, Michigan, a lumbering and

25 Will T. Little, L. G. Pitman, and R. J. Barker, comps., *Statutes of Oklahoma, 1890* (Guthrie: State Capital Printing Co., 1891), pp. 467–69; *Revised Codes of North Dakota 1895* (Bismarck: Tribune Co., 1895), pp. 1280–81.
26 *Code of Washington . . . 1881* (Olympia: C. B. Baglev, 1881), p. 179; also pp. 225–26 for an Act to Prevent and Punish Gambling, November 13, 1879.
27 Buley, *The Old Northwest*, 1:368; St. Louis, *Revised Ordinances . . . 1835–1836* (St. Louis: Office of Missouri Argus, 1836), p. 123; St. Louis *Missouri Argus*, June 5, 1835; Ordinance Book, 1837–1855, City Clerk's Office, Burlington, Iowa, p. 8; Ordinance Book, 1840–1856, City Clerk's Office, Quincy, Illinois, p. 13.

mining community situated on Lake Superior in the upper peninsula, and the 1883 ordinance of Dallas, Texas, a more cosmopolitan agricultural and wholesale center. Each forbade the keeping of gambling devices, each forbade betting and wagering, each made it illegal for persons to keep gambling rooms, and each prescribed penalties. There was, however, one difference: Marquette made it unlawful for students in any public or private educational institution to play at cards, dice, billiards, or any game of chance in any building where intoxicating liquors were sold.[28]

State statutes and municipal ordinances were often designed to protect the unsophisticated player from being fleeced by professional blacklegs and, by the license system, to raise funds for general city use or for some specific purpose, such as hospitals in St. Louis and New Orleans.[29] Not even the license system, however, guaranteed honest games. Relatively few persons complained about games run by respectable houses in a law-abiding manner, but practically everyone objected strenuously not only to the tricks of the trade but also to the high-handed contempt for law and the offensive, bellicose attitude assumed by those individual gamblers and groups of blacklegs who harassed steamboats and who threatened the peace and security of towns. Americans, during the middle of the nineteenth century, were tolerant enough of loose morals, but resented being mulcted and plucked. Constables, marshals, sheriffs, and peace officers generally were either unwilling or unable to enforce the law. A result was that gamblers grew bolder, building up a public hostility that expressed itself in journals and newspapers and eventually resulted in direct action against them by citizens who would no longer tolerate their arrogance.

By the mid-1830s, the gambling fraternity had become the target of editors and of native and foreign travelers. Shameful and corrupt activities on Ohio and Mississippi river steamboats coupled with wide-open towns—Cincinnati, St. Louis, New Orleans—brought a deluge of

[28] George B. Brown, comp., *Charter and Ordinances of the City of Marquette* (Marquette: Mining Journal Plant, 1898), pp. 128, 215–16, 218; Dallas City Council, *Charter and Ordinances of the City of Dallas* (Dallas: Herald Steam Printing House, 1884), pp. 109–11.

[29] *New Orleans Bee*, March 4, April 25, 1835. For the decade beginning in 1824, the receipts from the sale of licenses for gambling houses in Louisiana totaled $563,500. This sum was used for the support of male and female orphan asylums, the primary schools of New Orleans, the College of Louisiana, the Charity Hospital, and for "ordinary" purposes. The practice ended April 17, 1835, when the legislature passed a bill to prevent gambling. See "The Mississippi—Spillway of Sin," p. 23.

criticism. Gambling was said to destroy all the affections of man; to participate with a blackleg was unnatural; a gambler would not hesitate to play upon his brother's coffin or his father's grave; gambling was a sin of the deepest dye—one that strikes at the root of every good and virtuous feeling known to man's nature; and "the petty thief is zealously hunted and severely punished, but the *black legs*, the wholesale plunderers, the tempters and destroyers of our youth, are permitted to roam at large." [30]

Hezekiah Niles, published in his *Register* an account of a knife fight between a steamboat captain and a gambler; and editors of papers in New York, Philadelphia, New Orleans, and St. Louis gave space to raids on billiard parlors, on fashionable hotels where large amounts of money changed hands, and on dens of iniquity.[31] An Englishman, tarrying in Louisville, Kentucky, wrote that gamblers were readily recognizable "by the greater style of fashion and expensiveness in which they dress, and the air of dissipation by which they are marked from other men. Pistols and bowie-knives are carried by them all. . . ." A Yankee, visiting New Orleans, ventured into a temple of the goddess of fortune to see billiard tables surrounded by their "mace and cue" devotees.[32]

Impressions and opinions such as these stemmed in large part from shady practices, which long had been the gambler's stock in trade, and from the mass lynching of gamblers by outraged citizens of Vicksburg, Mississippi, in 1835. The professional gambler held supreme contempt for his fellow men, believing them to be suckers; he lived only to win, announcing to all who would listen that losers deserved to go to hell and that winners earned passage through the pearly gates. The professional was, indeed, a neurotic, who lived by chance, but refused to take any more chance than necessary. He frequently rationalized his

[30] *Western Messenger* 1 (August 1835):95; *Du Buque Visitor*, June 1, 1836; December 2, 1837; J. H. Green, *An Exposure of the Arts and Miseries of Gambling; Designed Especially as a Warning to the Youthful and Inexperienced, Against the Evils of that Odious and Destructive Vice* (Cincinnati: U. P. James, 1843), p. 8; Lester B. Shippee, ed., *Bishop Whipple's Southern Diary, 1843–1844* (Minneapolis: University of Minnesota Press, 1937), p. 87.

[31] See, for example, *Niles' Weekly Register*, October 24, 1835; *Philadelphia Mirror*, May 1, 1837; *New York Evening Post*, November 10, 1830; *New Orleans Bee*, June 14, 1833. The *St. Louis Reveille* carried innumerable articles relating to all forms of illegal behavior.

[32] J. S. Buckingham, *The Eastern and Western States of America*, 3 vols. (London: Fisher, Son, & Co., 1842), 3:10; Joseph H. Ingraham, *The South-West:Bye a Yankee*, 2 vols. (New York: Harper & Brothers, 1835), 1:126.

calling by maintaining that life itself is a gamble. He held immense respect for his own cleverness, and to demonstrate his superior cunning, he frequently resorted to marked cards, loaded dice, and mechanical devices.[33] He carried the same deceivers with him when he opened shop in South Dakota, Oklahoma, or Texas. It is a truism that when news of the discovery of gold in California arrived, the gambler exchanged his derringer for a six-shooter, his swordcane for brass knuckles, and his beaver hat for a sombrero.[34]

But no matter when or on what frontier he operated, the gambler did not forsake his Pandora's box stuffed with sleight-of-hand deceptions and gadgets designed to fleece the yokel, hoodwink the smart aleck, and empty the purse of the bumpkin and traveler. Nearly every sharper had his own method of marking the backs of cards. Some creased them with a thumb nail, others bent corners slightly, and still more curled half a deck, making what was called a *bridge*, for bending gave each card a slight curve. Even before the manufacturer of marked cards, gamblers had devised a cutter with which the edges and ends of selected cards might be stripped, thus making it possible to identify cards so marked in the pack.

Cards with marked backs apparently were first introduced in this country about 1834, at a time when poker was replacing three-card monte and vingt-et-un in gentlemanly preference. At first, like counterfeit money, they were manufactured in secret, but soon concerns in New York and elsewhere sold them openly. Between 1837 and 1854, a Doctor Cross of New Orleans did a thriving business. At first only three back designs were available—the star, the three-dots-and-chain, and the continual vine—but with these any gambler could identify every card in a deck. By 1843, at least seven "advantage" decks were available, some with calico, large clubs, or marble backs. Now and again, enterprising gamblers purchased blank backs and illicitly printed them with plates made expressly for that purpose. A gambler once remarked that every card with a colored or printed back "either has a secret mark upon it, or may, with the utmost facility, have one placed upon it, by which it may be instantly and certainly known."[35] E. M.

[33] For a brief but stimulating discussion of the psychology of gambling, see Robert D. Herman, ed., *Gambling* (New York: Harper & Row, 1967), pt. 3, "Gambling as a Pathology."

[34] R. E. Banta, "Gambling on the River," *American Heritage* 4 (Summer 1953):20–23.

[35] Green, *An Exposure of the Arts and Miseries of Gambling*, p. 308.

Grandine, 41 Liberty Street, New York, sold "advantage" and marked-back playing cards at $1.25 a pack, $10 a dozen, and $85 a gross. He also retailed loaded dice, of the best ivory, at $5.00 for a set of nine—three high, three low, and three square.[36]

Crooked dice and crooked cards, however, were only a portion of the gambler's tricks. Those professionals, some in black pantaloons, swallow-tailed coats, ruffled shirts with diamond studs, and fancy waistcoats and others in less picturesque dress, were also addicted to the "bag" and the "hold-out." A bag consisted of a thin bit of slightly bent metal—flat rod. A sharp point at one end of the rod was driven into the under side of a table. A flat bar ran parallel to and just touched the wood of the under side of the table. In this fashion, a crude "clip" was formed into which cards might be inserted and withdrawn at will. Holdouts were of several types, the most common and the simplest to use being a rubber affair, with hooks, which was placed up a sleeve. The hooked clips caught and held cards until they were released by pressing a small spring. Another holdout was concealed in the vest, and the "hand is held close to the body with the cards outspread while a string is pulled, and in that manner a card is shot into the hands under cover of the remaining cards."[37]

An even simpler device, and one much used, was merely a small pocket cut into the coat sleeve at the seam. Into this "pocket" an ace or other high card was inserted. A gambler with clever fingers could easily remove such a card without creating suspicion. Grandine sold sleeve holdouts at $35; retailed vest holdouts, which worked with spiral coils and catgut; and peddled "bugs," a contrivance for playing an extra card and "utterly defying detection" at $1.00. A ring holdout, worn on a finger, contained a flesh-colored small wire clip or spring which held a card concealed within the palm of the hand.[38]

It was not uncommon for those in the business professionally to use false wall mirrors, so designed as to reflect opponents' hands, to set convex mirrors in a poker chip, a pipe, or a snuffbox, or to use a signet ring. The signet swung on a pivot to reveal a mirror. Ceiling holes were bored above tables on steamboats and in gaming houses, so that a confederate might observe several hands and signal their contents to a

---

[36] John Morris [pseud.], *Wanderings of a Vagabond: An Autobiography* (New York: The Author, 1873), pp. 237, 239.

[37] Hereward Carrington, *Gamblers' Crooked Tricks* (Girard, Kans.: Haldeman–Julius, 1928), pp. 5–6.

[38] Ibid., pp. 6–7.

gambler at a table.[39] A house on Camp Street in New Orleans was rigged in an elaborate manner:

> In the backroom in the second story was a round table fixed in iron shoes so as to be immovable. Two of the legs of this table were hollow. Down the hollow legs wires were run to the floor, and along the floor in grooves, made for the purpose to the wall, then up the wall to the third story, thence to a point immediately above the center of the table. The wires were communicated from the table to the point above in the manner used in bell hanging. The grooves through which they run were inlaid with the softest buckskin, so as to prevent a noise in pulling them; the grooves were then covered over with thin copper and a carpet screened all from view—the grooves in the wall were papered over. . . . Immediately above the card table the ceiling was ornamented with a circular painting. . . . In the center of the painting was a hook as if to suspend a lamp. The ceiling was cut into small holes which could not be detected from below, because they represented certain portions of the figures of the painting. When a party was engaged at play, a person above could look down upon the hands and by pulling wires give his partner at the table any intimation as to the strength of the opposing hand which an agreed signal might indicate.[40]

It is little wonder that traits and tricks like these infuriated scores of persons whose money seemed to disappear magically during what victims believed to be only a social and relaxing game. George H. Devol, a longtime gambler, was right when he said that "Every man who is not a professional gambler, is inevitably bound to get up a loser."[41] And it is not surprising that public opinion finally boiled to a point where, in city after city, gamblers were run out.

Resentment and antagonism reached their peak and set in motion a chain reaction in Vicksburg, Mississippi, on the Fourth of July, 1835. No one could reasonably argue that Vicksburg was a city of saints, but generally, gamblers and their friends voluntarily segregated themselves from those who considered themselves to be law-abiding gentry. The community a year earlier had looked down its collective nose at Richmond, Virginia, when a mob marched upon and destroyed ten gambling houses.[42] "We could have wished," said the Vicksburg *Regis-*

[39] Green, *An Exposure of the Arts and Miseries of Gambling*, pp. 307–9; Morris, *Wanderings of a Vagabond*, pp. 240–47; Carrington, *Gamblers' Crooked Tricks*, pp. 5–9; George H. Devol, *Forty Years a Gambler on the Mississippi* (New York: Henry Holt, 1926), pp. 22–23, 45.

[40] *New Orleans Bee*, July 2, 1839.

[41] Devol, *Forty Years a Gambler on the Mississippi*, p. 7.

[42] Richmond had been plagued with gamblers for some time. On November 13, 1833, the *New Orleans Bee* reported that endeavors were under way in Richmond

ter, October 16, 1834, "that this most desirable result had been accomplished by other means. Mobs are dangerous weapons in a land of laws, their agency is greatly to be deprecated, however respectable the materials of which they may be composed." Indeed, the gamblers were tolerated when they first settled down in Vicksburg, for they were heavy spenders.

Yet it was not long before the brotherhood became a thorn in the corporate flesh, and citizens discovered that Lady Luck was no lady at all, but only a slut. The sharpers, a local editor wrote bitterly,

> supported a large number of tippling houses, to which they would decoy the youthful and unsuspecting and after stripping them of their possessions, send them forth into the world the ready and desperate instruments of vice. Our streets were ever resounding with the echoes of their drunken and obscene mirth, and no citizen was secure from their villainy. Frequently, in armed bodies, they have disturbed the good order of public assemblages, insulted our citizens, and defied our civil authorities.[43]

During the autumn of 1834, an infantry company had been formed in Vicksburg. This group of volunteers, together with citizens, celebrated the Fourth of July the next year with a splendid barbecue. After the feast and during the delivery of toasts honoring the Union, the state, and the town, a gambler named Cabler reportedly insulted an officer of the volunteers and struck a citizen. Cabler was seized by the volunteers and expelled from the scene. The company then marched to the public square to drill. During the exercises, word got about that Cabler was on his way to kill the volunteer who had been most active in hustling him from the barbecue. When Cabler, armed with a loaded pistol, a large knife, and a dagger, arrived at the square, he was seized and arrested by militiamen. They, together with a throng of citizens, took him into the woods, tied him to a tree, and not only whipped him but also tarred and feathered him.[44]

That evening citizens gathered at the court house, and there passed a resolution ordering all professional gamblers to leave town within twenty-four hours. Persons who permitted faro-dealing in their houses were notified they would be prosecuted. A hundred copies of the resolutions were printed and posted on the morning of July 5. The next day, Monday, July 6, the military, followed by several hundred citizens,

---

to "suppress gambling. Spirited resolutions have been drawn up, and committees appointed."

[43] *Vicksburg Register*, July 9, 1835.

[44] Ibid.

sought out and destroyed every faro table and other gambling apparatus they could find. When this posse or mob approached the house of a gambler named North, it was met with a volley of gun fire. Dr. Hugh S. Bodley, a much admired citizen, was killed. The mob stormed the house, seized five gamblers, including North, and shortly thereafter hanged them.[45]

The expulsion of the Vicksburg blacklegs was important enough, but even more significant were the repercussions. The steamboat *Freedom* carried news of the hangings to New Orleans, and word swiftly reached other cities, where outraged residents set about curtailing, in one way or another, gamblers in their midst. Clinton, Louisiana, posted the following notice: "All Gamblers found in Clinton after !2 o'clock will be used according to Lynch's Law. The importation from Vicksburg will look out." Natchez notified gamblers living under the hill to break up their establishments and leave within twenty-four hours. When the warning was not heeded, citizens destroyed gambling paraphernalia and ran the operators out of town. Several flat boats, filled with blacklegs, were seen on the river. Excited citizens thronged the wharf at New Orleans to hear the latest news brought down by the steamers *Scotland* and *Washington.*[46]

So disturbed were citizens of New Orleans and of Mobile, Alabama, that they hastily endorsed resolutions disapproving of gamblers and gambling, but declaring that the type of justice meted out in Vicksburg was "unconstitutional, illegal, tyrannical, cruel, and inexpedient." New Orleans, indeed, resolved not to adopt or resort to any violent measures against the gamblers lately expelled from Nashville, Tennessee, for there also irate residents had driven them out.[47] Cincinnati, Ohio, mustered up a hundred special policemen to assist five hundred citizens to support measures deemed necessary to protect inhabitants from the lawless depredations of gamblers and others who flout the law. Many blacklegs had fled to Cincinnati after being driven out of Louisville, Kentucky, which, said an editor, was "too hot for them." Antigambling meetings were held, among other places, in Danville, Kentucky; Rich-

[45] Ibid. See also James Elbert Cutler, *Lynch Law: An Investigation into the History of Lynching in the United States* (New York: Longmans, Green, & Co., 1905), p. 99; *Washington Daily National Intelligencer*, July 29, 1835; *Niles' Weekly Register*, July 25, August 8, 1835.

[46] *Vicksburg Register*, July 9, 30, 1835; *New Orleans Bee*, July 13, 14, 16, 1835; *Daily National Intelligencer*, July 25, 29, 1835.

[47] *Daily National Intelligencer*, July 25, 29, August 5, 1835; *Niles' Weekly Register*, August 8, 22, 1835.

mond and Petersburg, Virginia; and Charleston, South Carolina. "The Gamblers will soon have no abiding-place in South Mississippi," said the Vicksburg *Register*. "Where will their headquarters be!" [48]

"The tremendous explosion which took place in Vicksburg not long since," wrote an Alabama editor, "has dissipated the professional gamblers which infested the State of Mississippi, [and] all over the South and West it seems." Professional gamblers, he continued with some heat, "have rode rough shod in open day, and at public places, over the peaceful community, shooting, dirking, and damning, and no one to step forward and face the insolent outlaws in their high career of insult and outrage. But there is a point beyond which insolence cannot with safety go." He urged strict enforcement of gaming laws. [49]

The purge of gamblers spread in ever-widening circles, forcing the professionals to flee well-entrenched establishments, not only along the Mississippi and Ohio rivers but also in inland hamlets. It caused communities to revise and tighten existing ordinances and, at least, to make token gestures of enforcing the law. In August, 1835, for example, a public meeting in St. Louis passed several resolutions, not only in support of a stringent antigambling ordinance approved in May but also a warning to all gamblers—many of whom arrived after the Vicksburg affair—that they were unwelcome and would be prosecuted if they remained. Ward committees were appointed to hunt out and report all gaming establishments. The mayor and city council were requested to pass an ordinance requiring all professional gamblers to vacate the city within twenty-four hours. If, said the meeting, gamblers did not heed proper warnings, then all means, forcible or otherwise, would be taken against them. Several were jailed. [50]

The hold of gamblers upon middle-western society was broken, even though Columbus, Mississippi, in the autumn of 1838 used troops to dispel and expel a gang of gamblers who sought to control the town. [51] Unwanted and hounded out of a score of communities, gamblers continued to work river boats, to move quickly in and out of river towns, to make brief sojourn in county seats, and, of course, to remain in New Orleans. Some followed the frontier wherever it might

---

[48] *Niles' Weekly Register*, August 8, 1835; *Daily National Intelligencer*, August 6, 1835; *Vicksburg Register*, August 10, 13, September 24, 1835.

[49] *Huntsville Democrat*, quoted in *Vicksburg Register*, August 27, 1835.

[50] *St. Louis Argus*, June 5, August 14, 1835; J. Thomas Scharf, *History of St. Louis City and County*, 2 vols. (Philadelphia: Louis H. Everts & Co., 1883), 2:1824.

[51] *Niles' Weekly Register*, November 10, 1838.

lead them. During the 1840s and 1850s, for example, they attempted, without much success, to take root in Dubuque, Iowa, but public opinion, grand juries, and local marshals made life too risky and profits too small. On one occasion, fifty gamblers were ordered to leave Dubuque.[52] A strong ordinance to prohibit gaming and gambling houses was passed in Winona, Minnesota, in 1857. The arrival of gamblers excited the town's righteous indignation, said the local newspaper. "The quicker they put up their helm when they catch sight of Winona's highlights, the quicker they save their craft from going to wreck totally. Winona may have a few failings, but she doesn't waste time and words in parleying with the villains in any such form."[53]

Gamblers followed the flag during the Mexican War, and, as their contribution to the war effort, introduced marked decks into Mexico City after its capture by General Winfield Scott. At the discovery of gold, they journeyed in droves to California,[54] where they also used "advantage" decks in glamorous establishments which, a young Englishman wrote, were never closed and always full. He saw tables covered with bets, and the bets of money surmounted with ornamental lumps of gold and bags of dust. Everybody, he said, was armed, "from the ruffian who transfers his treasures from the mines to the gamblers' tables to the frail, fair one who relieves the gambler's pocket for the benefit of her own."[55] Later, in the Civil War, many a soldier, in both the Federal and Confederate armies, gambled his pay away. Some, when mustered out, invaded Texas and the Southwest and the Far West with card and dice, and the wheel of fortune that might spin out death as easily as it whirled out wealth. Ed Chase, for example, left Denver to serve in the Third Colorado Cavalry. His military duties over, he returned to Denver where, with an associate, he opened the Palace, the city's finest gambling hall.[56]

For some reason, the notion has circulated that from Appomattox until the closing of the frontier in 1890, only the western country was a gambler's paradise. There, between sagebrush and mountain peak, faro, roulette, and Spanish monte ran endlessly, for in the words of a Colorado poet,

[52] *Dubuque Daily Express and Herald*, May 5, 6, 15, 29, 1856; October 27, November 15, 18, 1857; March 11, 25, 1858. *La Crosse National Democrat*, January 26, 1858.

[53] *Winona Argus*, May 21, 1857; *Winona Daily Republican*, October 13, 1868.

[54] Morris, *Wanderings of a Vagabond*, 427–28.

[55] *London Times*, May 16, 1851.

[56] For a sketch of Chase's career, see Parkhill, *The Wildest of the West*, pp. 64–67.

It's day all day in the daytime,
And there is no night in Creede.

And there every hand was aces and eights. Lady Luck was young and gay in spangles and long, black stockings. The impression persists that the back-East country was clean and pure, where Lady Luck had become a wrinkled granny, knitting in a rocking chair.

This is rubbish, for Knights of the Royal Flush bet and wagered and "took" the suckers in every state of the nation, and Lady Luck everywhere retained her youthfulness and her brashness. Fort Wayne, Indiana, after the Civil War, was noted as a gambling town, a gathering place for "slickers coming from all directions—New York, Chicago, Detroit, Cincinnati, St. Louis, Indianapolis, Cleveland, and Canada."[57] A Minneapolis editor said in 1872, "All our larger towns are filled with gambling places, where loaded dice, marked cards, and all the devices for cheating and robbery are used."[58]

No gaming establishments in the West were more elaborate than was the house owned by Richard Canfield from 1894 to 1906 in Saratoga Springs, New York. Myriads of less genteel houses, floating crap games, and hotel-room poker sessions the nation over continued to attract swarms of suckers, so that the role of Lady Luck and her henchmen at the turn of the century was little different from what it was decades earlier. To raise the ante, to caress the bones, to bet on the spin of the wheel, to put money on the ponies was an established American way—a fever coursing wildly through the national arteries for which there was no sure cure. And neither luck nor knowledge of games of chance could aid a pigeon at play with professional gamblers.

[57] For Fort Wayne as a gambling center, see Bessie K. Roberts, "Crime and Crinoline," *Indiana Magazine of History* 41 (December 1945):388.

[58] *Minneapolis Daily Tribune*, June 23, 1872, March 28, 1873, September 2, 1878, December 6, 1879. See also *Winona Daily Republican*, November 27, 1860, April 20, 22, July 11, 1867; October 13, 1868; July 13, 1870; *Minnesota* v. *H. L. Watkins*, Hennepin County Court, file 556.

CHAPTER FIVE

Bayonet, Bowie Knife, and Bloody Jack

Charles L. Fish, full of drink, but still thirsty and feisty, wandered late one May evening in 1861 into the Exchange Hotel in Winona, Minnesota. There, surrounded by the cultural ambience of a river-town saloon, he lurched up to the bar and engaged in what he believed to be light talk with a local character whose name appeared on the tax rolls as John Reynolds, but who was better known as Whiskey Jack. One word —as it so frequently does—led to another, with the result that Whiskey Jack attempted to evict Fish. Annoyed at the thought of being deprived of his drink and irritated that hands should be laid upon him, Fish resisted. Whiskey Jack persisted. Thereupon Fish drew a pistol from his pocket and shot Whiskey Jack, grievously wounding him in the left side near the heart.

No strenuous attempts were made to apprehend or arrest Fish by either the marshal or the sheriff, an oversight which a local editor thought woeful and caused him to say: "It has come to pass here that to shoot or stab a man is only a trifling breach of decorum, to be passed over without punishment, and soon to be forgotten." Be this as it may, Fish fled down the Mississippi River in a skiff. The sheriff, after due interval, started in sluggish pursuit. Fish was arrested by Wisconsin officers near La Crosse and returned to Winona authorities. In time-honored manner, he pleaded self-defense and was committed to jail to await trial at the coming term of the district court. In early August, weary of life without amenities, he broke jail, never to return. "We understand," said the editor, who was somewhat testy about the entire affair, "that this man Fish has enlisted and is now ready to do battle for the North, so the county is relieved of a large bill of expense and contributes one more person for the war."[1]

[1] *Winona Daily Republican*, May 15, 17, 22, 25, August 8, September 19, 1861.

Unfortunately, the record does not show whether or not Fish fought, bled, or died, but the incident is typical of numerous disturbances and lawless acts related to the Civil War. A soldier in a community artillery company met up in La Crosse with a gentleman of secessionist persuasion. The two quarreled, and the soldier was stabbed seriously. "The 'secesh,' " said a brief newspaper account, "who prided himself upon being a Kentuckian, was arrested and put in jail."[2] A few days later a goodly number of the same artillery company avenged the stabbing of one of their number by riddling the saloon where the assault occurred.[3]

In Jackson County, Wisconsin, a dozen members of a rifle company completely gutted Specht's saloon.[4] And, to further demonstrate the zeal of men fighting on the home front, an officer with men from the Black River Rangers, Jackson County, drank themselves into a frenzy, murdered and robbed a lumberjack, and escaped.[5] Fortunately, the officer, a man who unhappily bore the name of Lincoln, was apprehended.[6] A discharged soldier, Courtney Clement, knifed a fellow Irishman, Hugh Finegan, near La Crosse.[7] One Saturday night, rollicking members of the Third Minnesota Infantry raided a Minneapolis saloon, destroying the liquor stock and breaking windows. During the course of this unhappy event, Warren P. Lincoln, a twenty-eight-year-old youth, sustained brain damage and died.[8]

It would indeed be pointless to recite the litany of crimes committed by soldiers against civilians. They forged notes, vandalized stores, raised hell in bawdy houses, fought in the streets, committed burglary,

[2] Ibid., September 23, 1861.
[3] *La Crosse Weekly Democrat*, September 27, 1861.
[4] Ibid., October 11, 1861.
[5] Ibid., November 22, 1861.
[6] Ibid., December 6, 1861.
[7] *Winona Daily Republican*, October 11, 1862.
[8] *Minnesota State News* (St. Anthony and Minneapolis), December 20, 1862; November 4, December 2, 1863. For Lincoln's service record, see Board of Commissioners, *Minnesota in the Civil and Indian Wars, 1861–1865*, 2 vols., 2d ed. (St. Paul: Pioneer Press Co., 1891), 1:179. He enlisted October 10, 1861, in A Company. The Third Infantry left Fort Snelling on November 17, arriving at Louisville, Kentucky on December 6. In July, 1862, at Murfreesboro, Colonel Henry C. Lester surrendered the regiment. Later it was engaged in putting down the Sioux Uprising in Minnesota, participating in the battle of Wood Lake in October, 1862. Lincoln was with the regiment during the entire period and was killed only a few weeks before the regiment again was ordered south. It left Fort Snelling on January 16, 1863.

and assaulted peaceful residents.[9] Private A. Taunt got drunk, beat up a gentleman who happened to get in his way, and was arrested. When released, Taunt took "his line of march for Fort Snelling, swearing that a town that could not tolerate a wee bit of knock down was very small potatoes." A Minneapolis newspaperman suggested that he "better bottle his bloodthirsty desire until an opportunity is given to vent it on the satellites of rebeldom."[10]

So disruptive of peaceful society did the military become that the provost guard patrolled Minneapolis streets.[11] Even such supervision did not prevent larceny by soldiers. Joel E. Eastwood, for example, was tried and convicted on a larceny charge and sentenced to a fine of two hundred dollars or imprisonment in the county jail until the fine was paid. Upon petition from the county commissioners, a judge released Eastwood on the grounds that the "military service may be benefitted and the public interests will suffer no prejudice" if the prisoner were turned over to military authorities.[12]

That young men, full of adolescent beans, should drink and fight and chase the gals, whether in uniform or out, is no surprise. Nor is the fact that troops, far away from home and mother, stole, swore, carved one another up with bowie knives, and tippled, whored, and gambled any cause to consider such deportment atypical. It may well be true, as a private in the Nineteenth Michigan wrote in 1863, that "the army is the worst place in the world to learn bad habbits of all kinds. there is several men in this Regt when they enlisted they were nice respectable men and belong to the Church of God, but now where are they? they are ruined men." [13]

[9] *Winona Daily Republican*, December 26, 1862; January 19, October 27, 1863; *State Atlas* (Minneapolis), February 11, 25, 1863.

[10] *State Atlas*, April 8, 1863.

[11] Ibid., February 10, 1864. Troops at Fort Snelling always were a thorn in the flesh to St. Paul, St. Anthony, and Minneapolis. See, for example, *Minnesota Pioneer* (St. Paul), January 20, 1853; *Minnesota Democrat* (Minneapolis), September 19, 1857. For intemperance at the fort in the 1830s, see Marcus L. Hansen, *Old Fort Snelling, 1819–1858* (Iowa City: State Historical Society of Iowa, 1918), pp. 89–90.

[12] *Minnesota* v. *Joel A. Eastwood*, file 204, Hennepin County District Court, April 30, 1864.

[13] No one has written better accounts of the personal sins of omission and commission of the Civil War soldier, both North and South, than Bell I. Wiley in his *The Live of Johnny Reb* (Indianapolis: Bobbs-Merill Co., 1943), chap. 3, and his *The Life of Billy Yank* (Indianapolis: Bobbs-Merrill Co., 1951, 1952), chap. 10. The quotation is from *Billy Yank*, p. 247. For army crime and vice during the Indian wars, see Don Rickey, Jr., *Forty Miles a Day on Beans and Hay* (Norman: University of Oklahoma Press, 1963), chap. 9.

Drinking and gambling, of course, were escape mechanisms. Whiskey blotted out both past and present and opened the door to a befogged future where no Minié balls tore comrades and no bayonet ripped into guts. Poker, played in bivouac far behind front lines or dealt when the enemy was only a voice throw away, eased tensions. The slap of cards on drumhead pushed the war farther away. Neither Johnny Reb nor Billy Yank knew why play with spades, hearts, diamonds and clubs brought relief, for they were innocent of both the psychology and the history of the deck. They were unaware that the red suits symbolized rebellion, that the bloody jack represented the amorous male (in the distant past the jack of hearts carried a phallic symbol), that poker was mostly a man's game and represented a peer group.[14] Each player was equal in the eyes of Lady Luck—the corporal no better than the private the sergeant no better than the corporal, the lieutenant no better than the sergeant. It is doubtful that a soldier learned bad habits—however they be defined—unless he subconsciously desired to do so or unless a feeling of inferiority compelled him to compensate by adjusting to group habits.

Moreover, army life mirrored, to an astonishing degree, civilian life. The soldier entered the army from a society which was lawless, criminally inclined, and violent. For thirty-odd years before the outbreak of war, the nation was plagued by counterfeiters and horse thieves, so that at least one state put a bounty on the latter; was bullied by gamblers, who eventually were purged by irate citizens of Vicksburg, Mississippi, and other river towns; was thrown into confusion by one mob action after another; and was constantly threatened not only by bands of adult vagrants but also by groups of rough, tough juvenile delinquents.[15]

Judge Lynch was the patron saint of the day. Men wore weapons, drew them, and used them as unconcernedly and as naturally as they glanced at their watches or saddled a horse.[16] Life was cheap, not only on the various frontiers but also in city and rural regions. Many a man, considering himself immune from the criminal code, killed and justified

[14] For an analysis of a pack of playing cards, see Robert D. Herman, *Gambling* (New York: Harper & Row, 1967), pp. 136–52.

[15] For more specific statements, see "The Derringer and the Ace of Spades: Reflections on Middle Border Law and Order," "The Mississippi River—Spillway of Sin," and "Lincoln and Mob Rule," pp. 23, 99, and 38 respectively, of this volume. For bounty on horse thieves, see *Minnesota General Laws* (St. Paul: Pioneer Press Co., 1875), 17:121, and ibid, (St. Paul: Ramaley & Cunningham, 1877), 19:104–5.

[16] See "The Wearing of Weapons in the Western Country," p. 1 of this volume.

the slaying on the basis of a "higher" law—a law that came from the heart and not from the statutes.

"Almost every day furnishes some new and melancholy exhibition of that spirit which sets Law at defiance," said the *Philadelphia Public Ledger* on October 29, 1840, "and pursues its mischievous purpose, regardless of consequence to itself and others." The editorial continued: "We witness an attack upon a religious and literacy school on one day, upon a citizen's house upon another, upon a mercantile warehouse on a third, upon a debating hall on a fourth, upon a charitable institution on a fifth, upon a printing office on a sixth, upon a railroad on a seventh." Nor was that all. "Today," continued the *Ledger*, "a citizen is tied to a tree and scourged, tomorrow another is hoisted upon a tree and hanged, on the next a dozen are hanged all together, on a fourth an editor is shot, on a fifth a man is burned alive. In short every day exhibits some portion of the *sovereign* people in arms against the laws of God and the country, and against their own rights and the rights of others." [17]

Perhaps it would be well to state here that no section of the country was any more, or any less, lawless than were other sections.[18] The quaint notion of the efficacy of a Puritan ethos depended for result, as in the case of Drake's Plantation Bitters, more upon faith than upon any healthful properties.[19] In short, Yankees failed, although they tried, to make the nation over into the image and likeness of New England. Conscience fled before appetite, and stability before lawlessness.

[17] This is only one example among many which appeared in the national press.
[18] See, for example, Clement Eaton, *The Growth of Southern Civilization* (New York: Harper & Row, 1965), chap. 12; Francis S. Philbrick, *The Rise of the West* (New York: Harper & Row, 1966), pp. 356–60, particularly p. 360: "There seems to be no evidence that in any of these nine incidents of southwestern history the people of the West, otherwise than in a very local sense, exhibited lawlessness, violence, or turbulence in a special degree; and as respects such of the incidents as affected public opinion in both East and West, there appears to have been in its expression nothing to distinguish western from eastern society." W. H. Masterson, reviewing Philbrick's book (it does have its faults) in the *Journal of American History* 53 (June 1966):118–19, wrote that Philbrick regarded the "cherished tradition of a peculiar western lawlessness as historically untenable." I most emphatically agree with Philbrick.
[19] Of great cogency is Edmund S. Morgan, "The Puritans and Sex," *New England Quarterly* 15 (December 1942):591–607. For other views, see Louis T. Merrill, "The Puritan Policeman," *American Sociological Review* 10 (December 1945):766–76; Paul H. Boase, "Moral Policemen on the Ohio Frontier," *Ohio Historical Quarterly* 68 (January 1959):38–53; Mabel A. Elliott, "Crime and the Frontier Mores," *American Sociological Review* 9 (April 1944):185–92.

In a sense, then, the war was only an extension of the social upheaval and violence which operated and worked its dreadful will long before Fort Sumter was fired upon. But the conflict also gave opportunity to the ignorant to learn the heady lesson of murder and to be instructed in the finer arts of vice. This is true of all wars. George Rogers Clark's militiamen not only behaved in a "very disorderly manner," but also broke into the quartermaster's stores to filch lead and liquor and to steal even the pads from pack saddles.[20] American troops introduced advantage decks, marked cards, and crooked dice into Mexico during the 1840s. They called the mestizo or Indian girls with whom they lived *cholas*.[21] An army camp, like a penal institution, can be a training school for the inexperienced and a graduate academy for proficient professionals, but it need not be if an individual rejects instruction. Only a fatuous person accepts undiscriminatingly each and every invitation offered.

The army, however, was not the only breeding place of lawlessness and vice. Who taught the ambivalent guerrillas and bushwhackers, who sometimes gave loyalty to the South and other times to the North, their trade? What stimulated the Jayhawkers of Kansas to lawlessness? What prompted contractors to supply troops with shoddy shoes? What brought fear and terror not only to the battlefield but also to families which never knew the horror of war except by reading newspapers or by trudging down to telegraph offices to see posted the names of the dead and wounded? It is true, of course, that violence may occur without terror, but not terror without violence.[22] Finally, did the Civil War cause an epidemic of crime? To put the question more specifically, Did the federal and the Confederate veteran return home to live peaceably or did he wander elsewhere to thwart and break the law, to act in a violent manner, to turn to crime rather than to adjust to a nonmilitary, civilian behavior pattern? Crime, it is true, fell off during the war and shot to new highs afterward.

[20] James A. James, ed., *George Rogers Clark Papers, 1781–1784* (Springfield: Illinois State Historical Library, 1926), pp. 172–73.

[21] See, for example, John Morris, ed. [pseud.], *Wanderings of a Vagabond: An Autobiography* (New York: The Author, 1873), p. 427; Ronald D. Miller, *Shady Ladies of the West* (Los Angeles: Westernlore Press, 1964), p. 29.

[22] Leo E. Huff, "Guerrillas, Jayhawkers and Bushwhackers in Northern Arkansas during the Civil War," *Arkansas Historical Quarterly* 24 (Summer 1965):127–48; see also E. V. Walter, "Violence and the Process of Terror," *American Sociological Review* 29 (April 1964):248–57. For a discussion of crime as a product of the general culture, see Donald R. Taft, *Criminology: A Cultural Interpretation*, rev. ed. (New York: Macmillan Co., 1950), chap. 15.

Immediately after the return of mustered-out troops of the Mexican War, the *St. Louis Daily Reveille* ran a short paragraph captioned *War Veterans*. It read: "License, recklessness and crime—these are the demoralizing attendents upon war, conduct it as we may; and that the Mexican War have let loose these evils upon society is but too plain."[23] Much the same opinion was expressed after Appomattox. A writer, discussing the increase of crime in Fort Wayne, Indiana, in the two-year period of 1865 to 1867, said: "The Civil War was over, but the spirit of adventure was still in the air. Young sports who had mastered poker, casino, chuck-a-luck, while sitting in on the game by torchlight on the skirmish line, were still just about as reckless as upon the eve of battle."[24]

Boston, Massachusetts, to offer one example, enjoyed a high rate of major crime before the war. A decrease was noticed during the campaigns, but major crimes rose after the war to reach an all-time high in the years from 1875 to 1878. The murder rate in Boston showed the same tendencies—high before, low during, and a new high after the war. The peak was reached about 1869, so that the Panic of 1873 cannot possibly be responsible. Forcible rapes in Boston also peaked about the same year. Robberies increased from about 1866 to 1869, but then fell and continued to fall until 1880, when they began to climb. Assaults fell during the war years, but increased markedly immediately afterward. Between 1863 and 1865, for example, the assaults per 100,000 population were somewhat less than 600, but about 1875 they reached more than 900 per 100,000 population.[25]

The decrease of crime during the war was explained by the fact that there was not less crime, but there were fewer convictions. This means, in part, that sentences were set aside provided a culprit enlisted. Few scholars dispute the fact that, no matter what the criminal activities of

[23] November 2, 1848. The first troops returning from the war to St. Louis, according to the *Reveille* of February 23, 1848, landed on that date. On July 9, 1848, the *Reveille* noted that detachments of Illinois troops arrived in rags, although they wished to make a respectable appearance, but the "government under pretence of paying off the soldiers as near home as possible, but, in reality, to save mileage, refuses to advance the means of a change of garb even—and are sent home in all their Mexican glory."

[24] Bessie K. Roberts, "Crime and Crinoline," *Indiana Magazine of History* 41 (December 1945):388–94.

[25] Theodore N. Ferdinand, "The Criminal Patterns of Boston Since 1849," *American Journal of Sociology* 73 (July 1967):84–99. See also Paul Dolan, "The Rise of Crime in the Period 1830–1860," *Journal of Criminal Law and Criminology* 30 (March–April 1940):857–64.

adults were, there was an increase in juvenile delinquency. The reasons were obvious: disturbance of home conditions, absence of male members of the family, employment of the mother in other than domestic pursuits, and interruption of school attendance. One other fact stands out clearly: a good many veterans were in prison. It was estimated that in 1866 "two thirds of all commitments to state prisons in loyal states were men who had seen service in the army or navy. In 1867, the figure was put at nearly half of the existing prison population." [26] It was evidence such as this which caused a researcher to state:

> Immediately after the establishment of peace, however, there was a great increase in crime and disorder not only in the south where conditions were abnormal, but throughout the north as well. And a very large proportion of the new offenders in the northern states were men who had "worn the blue." To some, the large numbers of soldiers and sailors in prison was a "new occasion for denouncing the war and those who carried it on." [27]

Of the 126 convicts in the Kansas State Penitentiary in 1867, 98 had served a full term in the federal army and 6 in the Confederate. For the period between November, 1864, and April, 1865, the commitments to the prison in Charlestown, Massachusetts, "increased at the geometrical ratio of more than two to one." The increase at the penitentiary in Auburn, New York, was nearly six to one. The figures released in 1866 for the Western penitentiary showed that about three-fifths of those committed were returned soldiers. These figures were revised the following year, when it was said that throughout 1866 nearly 70 percent of the prisoners committed were army and navy veterans. Of, for example, 179 male convicts in the Connecticut prison, 97, or 54 percent, had seen service. It was believed that not less than five or six thousand veterans were confined to state prisons in addition to those who were sitting out jail sentences. "But we cannot look with unconcern," said a commentator, "upon the thousands of veterans now lying in our prisons, though their crimes may have been heinous and their punishment deserved. A man who lost one arm in defence of the nation, working with the other at the convict's bench, is not an agreeable spectacle; nor do we smile to see '*les habits bleus par la victoire usés*' exchanged for the prison jacket." [28]

[26] Betty B. Rosenbaum, "The Relationship between War and Crime in the United States," *Journal of Criminal Law and Criminology* 30 (January–February 1940):725, 929. For a general discussion of juvenile activities, see Victor H. Evjen, "Delinquency and Crime in Wartime," ibid. 33 (July–August 1942):136–46.

[27] Edith Abbott, "Crime and War," ibid. 9 (May 1918):39.

[28] Edith Abbott, "The Civil War and the Crime Wave of 1865–70," *Social Service Review* 1 (June 1927):225, 228; "American Prisons," *North American Review* 103

A word of caution is necessary. No researcher of the nineteenth century can even begin to trust statistical information in almost all areas, but this is particularly true when dealing with statistics relating to the broad field of crime. A baffled and vexed worker in the field spoke in 1928 to all researchers:

> Certainly there is nothing very encouraging in the history of social statistics during the last twenty-three years. If progress in the future is to be at the same rate of speed as in the past . . . our children's children will all be dead and gone, perhaps swept away by recurrent crime waves, before we have the kind of criminal statistics which plain common sense now dictates we should have.[29]

If statistics are, indeed, a frail reed, they, at least, are suggestive, for a frail reed is not necessarily the last straw. Many a veteran did graduate from camp to cell, but just how many made the march will never be known with certainty. Nor is it possible to learn whether or not those committed to state prisons or county jails were criminally inclined before they entered service, were corrupted while in the service, or fell into evil ways after discharge from the service. One thing is certain: soldiers got into trouble with the law.

They were suspected of robbing clothing stores, were known to assault and rob citizens, and were believed to tipple overmuch.[30] So

---

(October 1866):409–10; E. C. Wines and Theodore W. Dwight, "The Reformation of Prison Discipline," ibid. 105 (October 1867):581.

[29] Louis N. Robinson, "The Need for Adequate Criminal Statistics," *Journal of the American Statistical Association* 23 (Supplement, March 1928):125. See also Leon E. Truesdale, "The Problem of Collecting and Standardizing Statistics of Crime in Forty-eight Sovereign States," ibid. 23 (Supplement, March 1928):128: "From 1850 to 1890, therefore, the available statistics include little more than the prison population, and even these figures involve considerable variations in definitions." Also E. H. Sutherland and C. C. Van Vechten, Jr., "The Reliability of Criminal Statistics," *Journal of Criminal Law and Criminology* 25 (May–June 1934): 10–20; and Arthur C. Hall, *Crime in Its Relationship to Social Progress* (New York: Columbia University Press, 1902), pp. 280–81: "Of course the judicial statistics of crime, whether dealing with the number of persons held for trial before the courts, with the number of convicted, or the number of prisoners, do not and cannot give any *exact* information as to the total amount of criminality in the nation. This would require the entire number of those acts which the society intends to punish as wrongs against itself, and for which it inflicts a penalty when it discovers and convicts an offender. Many crimes remain hidden, and others, although known, remain unprosecuted and unpunished. Such do not appear in the statistics."

[30] *La Crosse Weekly Democrat*, April 5, 1864; *St. Paul Pioneer*, May 31, 1865; *Minneapolis Daily Tribune*, September 5, 1879.

strong, indeed, was the impression that soldiers were sots that a song
which parodied "Just before the Battle, Mother" and entitled "Bourbon
on the Brain" became popular:

> Just before the battle, mother, (hic)
> I was thinking least of you,
> While upon the field we're spreeing, (hic)
> With the enemy in view.
> Filled with bitters made by Dod,
> For well they know that on the morrow
> Some will lie drunk on the (hic) sod.
>
> Oh, I long to have, dear mother,
> A demijohn sent me from home; (hic)
> First thing at morn I like my bitters
> Ere to picket post (hic) I roam.
> Tell the traitors all around you,
> That (hic) their cruel deeds we know,
> In every instance, kill our soldiers
> With the stuff called "Kill (hic) me slow,"[31]

Patrick Calloon liked his liquor and relished his fun. At the age of
nineteen, he was mustered into the Second Minnesota Infantry and
assigned to H Company. This all happened on January 21, 1865. The
regiment was already in the field near Savannah, Georgia. Young
Patrick, as a member of two detachments of recruits, joined his outfit
at Goldsboro, North Carolina. He marched with it during the campaign
of the Carolinas and he marched with it during the grand review in
Washington of the Army of the Potomac and he marched with it at the
final dress parade at Fort Snelling. He was mustered out on July 11,
1865, and received his final pay on July 20. Whether he demonstrated
valor in the field is problematical. His officers did not think of him as an
exemplary defender of the Union. Discharged and with spending money
burning his pocket, Patrick, with all deliberate speed, hied himself
from Fort Snelling to St. Paul, where, with little difficulty, he found a
whorehouse. During his period of rest, refreshment, and relaxation, he,
for some reason or other, was not content to enjoy only the comforts of
the establishment.

---

[31] From the author's collection of nineteenth-century music, as sung by Harry
Vandemark, the English comic. Equally popular was "Grafted into the Army."
See Philip D. Jordan and Lillian Kessler, *Songs of Yesterday: A Song Anthology of
American Life* (Garden City: Doubleday, Doran, & Co., 1941).

Forgetting momentarily the military injunction that once an objective is determined nothing should deter one from taking it, Patrick allowed himself to be diverted by the sight of a fat wallet belonging to a comrade in C Company. Its owner, Henry Lee, was a hardened veteran who had enlisted in 1861 and reenlisted in 1863 and who should have known enough, if not to keep away from palaces of pleasure, at least to keep his money out of sight. Anyway, Patrick robbed Henry of $170, causing somewhat of a disturbance in the recreational area. Henry swore out a warrant for Patrick, and he was arrested and committed, in default of bail in the amount of $500, to jail to await trial at the next term of the district court. When tried, he was found guilty and sentenced.[32]

The sad saga of Patrick Calloon obviously is not unique. If fame was denied him on the battlefield, at least he now has earned a measure of it as a symbol representing hundreds of others unknown, unwept, and unsung. Among these are the army captain arrested for horse stealing; the returning soldier who was robbed of $400 in La Crosse, Wisconsin, a town "now cursed with a surplus of pimps, thieves, and prostitutes"; the veteran of the First Minnesota who got into a row with a neighbor over a cow and almost had his head blown off; the recruit who gave his name successively as Johnson, Thomas, and Moore, and who attempted to steal a horse and buggy; and the soldier who tried to sell in a saloon a gold watch belonging to a captain.[33] Troops, after pay day, at Ft. Snelling turned Minneapolis into such bedlam that, said a local newspaper, "The blue coats of the police force were actively engaged . . . in running in their brother blue coats of the military service, and twenty well soaked soldiers pulled up in the lock-up. A group of guards came up from the fort this morning, and have been raiding the drinking saloons and house of ill-fame in search of the 'brave boys' who still linger in the city."[34]

In July, 1865, only a few months after the successive surrenders of Confederate forces during April and May, editors were warning readers against terrorism of returning troops. Crime, violence, and ruffianism appeared to be on the increase not only in eastern cities but also every-

[32] *St. Paul Pioneer*, July 27, December 9, 1865; *Minnesota in the Civil and Indian Wars*, 1:129, 140.

[33] *St. Paul Pioneer*, August 29, 1865; *La Crosse Weekly Democrat*, September 11, 1865; *Winona Daily Republican*, September 28, 1865; *Minneapolis Chronicle*, September 15, 1866; *Minnesota* v. *Peter Summers*, file 453, Hennepin County District Court.

[34] *Minneapolis Tribune*, May 9, 1878.

where. Much of the violence, it was believed, came from the fearful schooling of the war, the worst demoralizer of virtue and good order ever known. The carrying of concealed weapons was blamed for numerous assaults. "This is done to an extent fourfold, perhaps tenfold more than formerly," commented an editor, "as so many discharged soldiers have retained the side arms carried by them in service, or sold them to others, thus greatly multiplying weapons, and when crazed with liquor or excited by some quarrel, the weapons are drawn and bloodshed follows. There have been more cases of this nature during the past six months than for as many years prior to that period." Although the sentence structure leaves something to be desired, the sentiments are sound.

In August the same editor wrote: "There is no use disguising the fact, that so great has been the demoralization produced by the war, the classes of persons ready to commit crime, and who are now subsisting by crime, is increased many fold." He, being a cautious and prudent individual, exempted St. Paul veterans. "The evil to be apprehended," he warned, "is from persons not citizens [of St. Paul] who have always been low and brutal, have been rendered four fold worse by the riot and license of passion in the army, and who are now, or soon will be discharged from the service, to pick up a living as they can."[35]

Similar warnings, printed in towns throughout the Middle West and along the Mississippi River, were rooted in fact. Springfield, Illinois, for example, in 1865 was so thronged with blacklegs, burglars, garroters, and male and female harlots come to rob soldiers being mustered out, that General John Cook ordered two additional companies to act as provost guard. Among the Springfield soiled doves was Martha (Mattie) A. Silks, who retreated from that city to operate a house of ill fame in Johnson County, Kansas. Mattie's proud boast was that she never was a prostitute, except for a brief period when she was in the freighting business. "I was a madame," she was proud of saying, "from the time I was nineteen years old in Springfield. I never worked for another madame. The girls who work for me are prostitutes, but I am, and always have been, a madame."[36]

[35] *St. Paul Pioneer*, July 27, August 1, 1865.

[36] See, for example, *Fort Madison* (Iowa) *Democrat*, April 3, 1878; *Warsaw* (Illinois) *Bulletin*, October 5, 1878; *Keokuk* (Iowa) *Daily Constitution*, October 5, 1877; July 25, 1879. Arthur C. Cole, *Centennial History of Illinois*, quoted in Forbes Parkhill, *The Wildest of the West* (New York: Henry Holt & Co., 1951), pp. 214–15.

The decade following the Civil War was characterized by as much social disturbance and general violence as was the decade before the war and the war years themselves. The draft riots in New York City in 1863 were not, of course, equaled in ferocity by the New Orleans riot of 1866, but it must not be forgotten that Confederate veterans, some of whom were police officers, played a major role in New Orleans. A witness testified before a congressional hearing that police officers shouted: "We have fought for four years these God damned Yankees and sons of bitches in the field and now we will fight them in the city." [37] Each of these riots, although it seems unnecessary to underscore the fact, was rooted in the war.

Both the Panic of 1873 and the railroad strike three years later not only disrupted the economy but also threatened the nation's peace and security. At Baltimore, Maryland, a mob placed the state armory under siege, fought with militiamen, and attempted to put a torch to the building. Five hundred federal troops were dispatched to Martinsburg, West Virginia, where railroaders had halted freight cars of the Baltimore and Ohio Railroad. Both panic and strikes, which spread with epidemic speed, resulted in unemployment, and many a veteran who lacked stamina hit the road as a tramp.

After all, the ex-infantryman had learned to move on foot, to sleep in the open, and to forage for himself. There was little, if any, difference between the technique of robbing a chicken coop in Georgia and that of robbing one in Ohio. "The temptations to a tramping life is aggravated in such circumstances as ours," said a social worker in 1877, "where a state of war has taught to a large number of laboring men, the methods of the bivouac, and its comforts, not to say luxuries, such as they are. To the old soldier, the hardships of a tramp's life are not more severe than he has borne, perhaps cheerfully, in the line of his duty." [38]

---

[37] For participation of Confederate veterans, see U.S. Congress, House Select Committee, *Report on the New Orleans Riots*, 39 Cong., 2 sess., rpt. no. 16 (Washington: G.P.O., 1867), pp. 19, 32, 67, 199. Also, Donald E. Reynolds, "The New Orleans Riot of 1866, Reconsidered," *Louisiana History* 5 (Winter 1964):5–28; for an earlier period, see Clement Eaton, "Mob Violence in the Old South," *Mississippi Valley Historical Review* 29 (December 1942):351–70. For the role of the Negro in the New York draft riots and the New Orleans riot, see Allen D. Grimshaw, "Lawlessness and Violence in America and Their Special Manifestations in Changing Negro–White Relationships," *Journal of Negro History* 44 (January 1959):52–72.

[38] Edward E. Hale, "Report on Tramps," National Conference of Charities and Corrections *Proceedings, 1877* (Boston: A. Williams & Co., 1877), p. 103.

A Yale professor stressed the military like organizations of tramps in Massachusetts, telling delegates to a National Conference of Charities and Corrections there was reason to believe that tramps were formed into organized groups, that they were directed by skillful leaders, and that they operated from a general headquarters where their plunder was deposited and divided.[39] Again and again social workers gave war as a cause of trampery.[40] How many restless, discontented, and lawlessly inclined veterans enlisted in the informal brotherhood of tramps is impossible to determine, for once again the lack of records thwarts the researcher. Nevertheless, the war, in part, stimulated trampery, and trampery was adopted as a temporary or semipermanent way of life by veterans.

"The first appearance of tramps as a professional class," reported the Minnesota commissioner of statistics in 1877, "dates from the suppression of the rebellion. They gradually made their appearance then. . . . The disbanding of our armies, for a long time removed from the restraints of friends and society, accustomed to scenes of violence, bloodshed and barbarism, unused to labor and giving no thought to care and thrift, occasioned infinitely less political difficulty, in fact, than anxiety in its anticipation." Then the commissioner said: "After the demoralization of the country incident to the war had measurably ceased, and the necessity of application to peaceful art and labor was realized, the avenues to these were choked by a rushing throng." Then came the Panic of 1873, paralyzing both labor and capital. The result was that some men "would not work if they could, many more could not if they would, and so the vagrant class was born."[41]

[39] Francis Wayland, "The Tramp Question," ibid., p. 117.

[40] W. L. Bull, "Trampery: Its Causes, Present Aspects, and Some Suggested Remedies," ibid. (Boston: G. H. Ellis Co., 1886), p. 194. Also, Morton Ellis, "The American Tramp from an Historical Standpoint," *Americana* 5 (January 1910): 63–66. The term *tramp* did not appear in the statutes of any state before the Civil War.

[41] *Minnesota Executive Documents, 1877* (St. Paul: Pioneer Press Publishing Co., 1878), 3:260. See also *Report of the Chief Detective [of Massachusetts]*, Public Document No. 37 (January 1878), p. 17, quoted in John D. Seelye, "The American Tramp: A Version of the Picaresque," *American Quarterly* 15 (Winter 1963): 543: "This tramp system is undoubtedly an outgrowth of the war; the bummers of our armies could not give up their habits of roving and marauding, and settle down to the honest and industrious duties of the citizen, as did most of our volunteer soldiers, but preferred a life of vagrancy." For a discussion of the veteran who returned to normal life, see Frank H. Heck, *The Civil War Veteran in Minnesota Life and Politics* (Oxford, Ohio: Mississippi Valley Press, 1941).

The outrages committed by armies of tramps—it is astonishing how many newspaper accounts refer to the military organization of tramps —included practically all the crimes in the criminal code—arson, rape, burglary, larceny, mayhem, homicide, assault, drunkenness, seizure of property, rioting.[42] They scared housewives, put torch to stores and burned agricultural machinery, fouled public parks, snatched vegetables from gardens, and waylaid and beat innocent citizens.[43] These deeds, however, were mere pranks when compared with other activities. During 1875 and 1876, tramps rode freight trains, climbing like swarms of grasshoppers. They seized trains in Illinois, Iowa, Minnesota, and Wisconsin. The governor of Iowa issued a proclamation urging the peace officers to be prompt and diligent in keeping the peace. In Minnesota, the governor sent fifty guns and sufficient ammunition to Faribault to equip a company of citizens hastily organized to deal with tramps.[44] In Davenport, Iowa, a company of volunteers composed of "veterans of the War to Preserve the Union" was asked to patrol the city both by day and by night. At Moline, Illinois, a posse of citizens, led by the town marshal, met trains. In the posse were men in uniforms with muskets.[45]

The tramp-veteran and the hobo were, of course, immortalized in bathetic verse and song. Joaquín Miller's "The Tramp of Shiloh" is unbelievably bad verse and, if possible, even worse plot. The poem tells of a Confederate veteran who lost a brother on the field of blood and sorrow, and who not only turns to trampery but also goes north—a double misfortune. He begs one day for bread from a curt Yankee, but is refused, and so to gain meal and favor, the tramp spins his sad tale, lost brother and all. Suddenly the two men recognize one another:

[42] See, for example, *New York Times*, November 12, 1874; June 13, 1875; January 10, August 2, 1876; September 14, 15, November 17, 18, 21, 1877; July 12, 28, 1878; April 26, 27, June 6, July 9, 1879; January 31, 1880.

[43] For activities in Minnesota, see *St. Paul Pioneer Press*, April 10, 15, June 18, 23, 28, July 3, 6, 9, 1880; also *Minneapolis Daily Tribune*, July 3, 15, 1876; May 15, 29, June 20, November 12, 1877; July 1, 30, 1878; January 18, March 12, 19, 22, April 16, August 29, October 8, 9, 1879. The *Minneapolis Tribune*, January 8, 1879, reported that the St. Paul jail lodged 1,384 tramps in 1878, an increase of 200 over the previous year. Also [A. E. Costello], *History of the Fire and Police Departments of Minneapolis* (Minneapolis: Relief Association Publishing Co., 1890), pp. 257–59, 263, 265–66.

[44] *Minneapolis Daily Tribune*, July 28, 30, 1877; July 12, 1878; *Keokuk* (Iowa) *Daily Gate City*, June 22, 25, July 7, 12, 21, 1878; April 2, July 20, 1879. See the *New York Times*, July 13, 1878, for the Iowa governor's proclamation.

[45] *Davenport* (Iowa) *Democrat*, July 7, 1876.

My brother! My own! Never a king on his throne
  Knew a joy like this brought to me.
God bless you, my life; bless your brave Northern wife,
  And your beautiful babes, two and three.[46]

The symbolism, if any, escapes me.

Romantic interpretations, however, may be balanced with realism. The fictional tale of the tramp who found his brother who he thought had died on the battlefield is insipid and as shallow as a ghost's breath when contrasted with the vigorous vitality of Ed Chase, ace of all Denver gamblers. A blood-and-guts man, Chase arrived in Colorado a year or so before the war. He was well on his way to fame when the war intervened. Chase took enough time out from his faro and his poker and his blackjack to enlist in the Third Colorado Cavalry and become captain of F Company. He took part in the Sand Creek Massacre of November 29, 1864, when Cheyenne and Arapaho women and children were murdered. At war's end, Chase calmly and coolly returned to open and operate the Palace, Denver's finest gambling hall.[47]

The war's impact upon the nation's lawless life gave a new meaning to the word *gunboat*. This term, in its true naval sense, had been in common use since small, heavily armed vessels were first used during the Barbary wars of the early nineteenth century. Such ships were relied upon extensively in river operations during the Civil War. After the war, for obvious reasons which need not be laid bare, *gunboat* came to mean, not a fighting ship, but a floating bawdy house, plying inland waters, especially the Mississippi River. Structurally, gunboats were large flats upon which cabins were built. Some gunboats were large enough for a downstairs and an upstairs.

One of these boats, remembered a river captain, was anchored at one time or another, near every large town. Young men and women, he said, were "enticed to these dens of iniquity and brought to ruin. The boats, indeed, were schools of crime and the hiding place of criminals."[48]

[46] *Frank Leslie's Illustrated Weekly Newspaper* 49 (January 3, 1880):324. For tramp songs, see Vance Randolph, ed., *Ozark Folksongs*, 4 vols. (Columbia: State Historical Society of Missouri, 1946–1950), 4:843 for "The Tramp," and pp. 844–45 for "The Tramp's Story." The first stanza of the former goes like this: "I'm a broken-down man without money or friends, / My clothes are all tattered and torn, / Not a friend have I left in this wide world to roam, / I wisht I had never been born."

[47] Parkhill, *Wildest of the West*, pp. 64–66.

[48] *Saturday Evening Post* (Burlington, Iowa), October 28, 1911.

River boats, pandering to appetites for vice and gambling, were nothing new on the Ohio, Mississippi, and Missouri rivers, but in the prewar era they were relatively few in number and, if referred to at all in polite society, generally were called "disorderly" river craft. After the war, they increased rapidly, and the new coinage *gunboat* came into the language.[49]

From 1865 through the next decade and on into the 1880s, river towns were plagued not only by gunboats but also by their inmates, who, when not rollicking in vice on board, went ashore to steal, rob, assault citizens, and, what perhaps was worse, to compete with land-locked whores. A gunboat, anchored for two years and more off Winona, Minnesota, sent its "flaunting denizens" to parade the streets clad in "gaudy clothes to attract, allure and debase those who are susceptible of their temptations."[50] Near Red Wing, Minnesota, the owner of a gunboat shot and killed a customer.[51] Inmates of floating pleasure palaces believed themselves immune from arrest if their boats were anchored beyond state boundaries, but peace officers of Red Wing took into custody occupants of a vice raft tied up on the Wisconsin side of the Mississippi, justifying their action on a provision in the state constitution which provided for concurrent jurisdiction in cases of crime committed on the river.[52] In March, 1868, a father in Winona swore out a warrant for the arrest of his own daughter who had slipped away to begin professional life on a "floating hell."[53]

Now and again the sword of retribution was swung not by lawmen but by irate patrons. A group of disgruntled raftsmen in 1869 went aboard a gunboat, drove out the bartender, drank up all the whiskey, and then doused the establishment with kerosene and burned it to the water's edge. On another occasion a gang of toughs, swearing they

[49] Evidence for the procuring of girls for prostitution is difficult to come by, but, now and again, glimpses of the trade are found. See, for example, the *Valley Whig* (Keokuk, Iowa), May 3, 1858, which relates actions of local police, who "overhauled a flat boat, which was floating down the [Mississippi] river, with two men and a young woman on board. An old horse, seventeen carpets old and new, and one or two trunks, said to be stolen property, were taken. . . . It was reported that the girl also was stolen. Her father was after her. . . . One of the men, named Rankin, had en-ticed away the girl, named Hall, sister of his wife."

[50] *La Crosse Weekly Democrat*, August 7, 1865; *Winona Daily Republican*, November 13, 22, 27, 1866.

[51] *Winona Daily Republican*, August 17, 1867.

[52] For the Red Wing arrests, see ibid., March 28, 1868. For gunboat arrests generally, see ibid., February 18, March 24, 25, 26, 27, 1868.

[53] Ibid., March 30, 1868.

would kill a gunboat's manager, swarmed aboard, seriously wounded the manager, threatened to slash the throat of one of the girls with a razor, and were about to fire the craft when a posse arrived.[54]

Perhaps the most spectacular, vicious, and bloody gunboat murder was the slaying of Jessie McCarty, soiled dove, by Bill Lee. Lee, proprietor of the boat, was believed by some to have served in the Confederate forces and by others to have been in the Union army. He spoke with a soft accent and frequently spun yarns of his heroic military exploits.[55] He employed on his gunboat four males who mingled pimping with gambling and four ladies of such easy virtue that it is possible they never comprehended the full meaning of the term. Among the girls was a comely lady of the evening—although she was on call twenty-four hours a day—who was deaf and dumb. Her closest friend was a co-worker by name of Jessie McCarty.

In November, 1875, Lee's bagnio barge lay at anchor near the Illinois shore between Burlington, Iowa, and Oquawka, Illinois. One evening, for reasons wholly known only to himself, Lee stormed into the crib cabin shared by the deaf-and-dumb Mary Magdalene and Jessie. Lee seized Jessie by the hair, the better to pull her from bed, dragged her downstairs, and then, to quote the record, broke both her back and neck, stamped out an eye, crushed her temple, and so disfigured her face that it was unrecognizable. He then carted the body to the river bank and hid it until such time as it could be tossed into the stream. A few days later one of the pimps squealed to the Burlington police. By the time the gunboat was raided by Iowa and Illinois officers, the body had disappeared. A few weeks later it was found floating by some small boys. Meanwhile, the boat's inmates were arrested and eventually corroborated the pimp's account. Lee was lodged in the Oquawka jail.

Lee was indicted and brought to trial. A jury, deliberating only fifteen minutes, returned a verdict of murder in the first degree. He was sentenced to be hanged on June 16, 1876. When that day arrived, Lee was escorted from the jail to the gallows by a German band and a military

[54] Ibid., May 6, 1869; June 5, 1870; *La Crosse Daily Republican*, June 28, 1870; *Minneapolis Daily Tribune*, June 21, 1870.

[55] Interview with John W. Murphy, Burlington, Iowa, June 20, 1930. Murphy for many years was editor of the *Saturday Evening Post*, published in Burlington, and was considered an authority on river history and crime. He was the author of *Outlaws of the Fox River Country: A Tale of the Whiteford and Spencer Murders* (Hannibal, Missouri: Hannibal Printing Co., 1882). The author of this article feels that the belief that Lee served in the Confederate army is an apocryphalness.

company. Before the trap fell, the condemned man made a ten-minute speech—he had asked for three hours—during the course of which he, with excessive piety, confessed that his fall from grace was due to prostitutes and whiskey. Finally, he gave thanks to his military escort for the "honor they had paid him as a soldier." [56]

A throng, come to see Lee "jerked to Jesus," thought it good riddance. Perhaps some, caught in the postwar crime wave, echoed the sentiment of a wagonmaster on the western plains. Exasperated beyond endurance by the antics of troops supposed to protect his outfit from the tribes, he burst out: "God preserve us from the soldiers, we can take care of the Indians ourselves." [57]

[56] The account of the Lee affair is based upon the *Keokuk Gate City*, November 25, 27, 1875; February 27, 29, March 1, June 16–18, 1876.

[57] Quoted in Henry P. Walker, *The Wagonmasters* (Norman: University of Oklahoma Press, 1966), p. 266.

CHAPTER SIX

"*Gimme a Hoss I Kin Ride!*"

The horse thief sneaking a pinto from a corral, cutting a branded roan from a free-running remuda, or stealing a mount from a hitching post in front of a frontier saloon came by his larceny dishonestly enough. Judge and jury and vigilante committee might charge such a rascal with all manner of lawless conduct, but they never could say truthfully that their victim had not comported himself in the American tradition. This, of course, did not deter lawmen or impromptu preservers of property from hanging the guilty—and sometimes the innocent—from the nearest tree.

But "jerking to Jesus" a horse thief was also traditional. It satisfied justice, and, so far as anyone knew, was fairly final. But the silhouette of a body swaying from lonesome limb somewhere in the far-western country after the Civil War symbolized the close, not the beginning, of a practice old as the nation was old. This account traces the early days and decades of the illegal taking of horses and not the end of a shady, but lucrative, practice of making away, without benefit of purchase, of animals belonging to others and then galloping hell-for-leather on stolen steeds toward the setting sun.

Like the common law, Shakespeare, and brussels sprouts, statutes forbidding and prescribing penalties for horse theft were imported into the American colonies. Blackstone, in his widely read *Commentaries*, cited a statute from the reign of George IV: "That if any person shall steal any horse, mare, gelding, colt, or filly . . . every such offender shall be guilty of felony, and, being convicted thereof, shall suffer death as a felon."[1] Colonial barristers, turned legislators, aped this statute and enacted it, or something akin to it, throughout the English settlements in America.

---

[1] William Blackstone, *Commentaries on the Laws of England*, ed. with an introduction and notes by George Sharwood, 2 vols. (Philadelphia: J. B. Lippincott & Co., 1872, 1873), vol. 2, bk. 4, p. 236, n. 20.

Massachusetts, for example, obliged clerks in every seaport town to keep a toll book in which were registered all horses brought for exportation. Clerks entered not only names of horses, but also color, distinguishing marks—both natural and artificial—age, and place of dwelling and the names of owners and shippers. The purpose of the act, in case anyone is in doubt, was to prevent the stealing of horses and clandestinely conveying them away.[2]

Charles Woodmason, a wildly moralistic preacher, sputtered that the South Carolina backcountry on the eve of the American Revolution was infested with "Gamblers Gamesters of all Sorts—Horse Theives Cattle Stealers, Hog Stealers . . . All in-a-manner useless to Society, but very pernicious in propagating Vice, Beggar, and Theft."[3] Indeed, a rather established alliance of horse thieves cooperated with one another throughout the colonies. In the South Carolina Broad River District, the fraternity was so strong and bold that it, in June, 1767, struck at an expedition led by Governor William Tryon of North Carolina and rode off on some of the governor's horses.[4]

Such ruffians, skilled at muffling hooves with cloth strips and adept at severing picket ropes, were among the forefathers of later generations of horse thieves. After the colonists won their independence, state after state sought by legislation to end the spiriting away of livestock, or at least to cripple the practice. One does not necessarily have to eat an entire buffalo in order to savor the taste of the tongue; neither is it obligatory to cite every statute in order to convey their common characteristics.

Louisiana statutes of 1804 offer a certain piquancy, for mule and horse stealing were tied together in the same act with slave stealing. Five years later, Georgia reinforced an earlier law by stipulating that a convicted thief be punished, for the first offense, with thirty-nine lashes

[2] General Court, *Acts and Resolves, Public and Private, of the Province of Massachusetts Bay, 1692–1786*, 21 vols. (Boston: Wright & Potter, 1869–1922), 1:444: Act for tolling horses that are to be exported, February 26, 1700/1.
[3] Richard J. Hooker, ed., *The Carolina Backcountry on the Eve of the Revolution: The Journal and Other Writings of Charles Woodmason, Anglican Itinerant* (Chapel Hill: University of North Carolina Press, 1953), p. 121.
[4] Richard M. Brown, *The South Carolina Regulators* (Cambridge: Harvard University Press, Belknap Press, 1963), pp. 32–33, 35. For Virginia, see Arthur P. Scott, *Criminal Law in Colonial Virginia* (Chicago: University of Chicago Press, 1930); for a general discussion of criminal codes in colonial New England, see Louis T. Merrill, "The Puritan Policeman," *American Sociological Review* 10 (December 1945):766–76.

on his back on three separate days, stand in the pillory for one hour for three days, and be imprisoned not less than twenty days nor more than one month. A second conviction brought the death sentence without benefit of clergy.

Alabama, not to be unduly influenced by any humanitarian motives in the Louisiana and Georgia statutes, set as punishment a fine not to exceed five hundred dollars, plus thirty-nine lashes on the bare back, well laid on, and branding on the face or right hand with the letter T, and imprisonment for a term not exceeding twelve months. Some twenty years later, Alabama revoked the harsh act of the 1820s, substituting for the physical punishment imprisonment in the state penitentiary for not less than three nor more than seven years. But—and this is interesting—the law said that in an indictment for such larceny, "it shall not be necessary to designate the particular sex or character of the animal stolen, but it shall be enough to describe it by such general designation, as, in common understanding of mankind, embraces it."[5]

There appears to be reason for the harsh penalties written into the codes of states south of the Ohio River. This vast region, during the 1790s, was a haven for horse thieves. Indeed, Governor William Blount, of the Southwest Territory, said categorically that the major markets for stolen horses were Swannano in North Carolina, settlements at the foot of the Ocunnee Mountain in South Carolina, and Tugelo in Georgia. He was horrified by the extent of horse stealing, declaring it the one great source of hostility with the Cherokees.[6]

The passions engendered by the crime are obvious in the preamble of a North Carolina act of November 18, 1786, which spoke of horse stealing as "inconsistent with the policy of a well regulated government" and, even more wrathfully, said the crime should be subject to a "punishment as severe as that which is inflicted for the most atrocious

[5] Meinrad Greiner, comp., *Louisiana Digest, 1804–1841* (New Orleans: Benjamin Levy, 1841), p. 120, this act passed in 1804; Augustin S. Clayton, comp., *A Compilation of the Laws of the State of Georgia, Passed by the Legislature Since the Political Year 1800, to the Year 1810, Inclusive* . . . (Augusta: Adams & Duyckinck, 1813), p. 536, passed December 12, 1809; Harry Toulmin, comp., *Digest of Laws of Alabama* (Cahawba: Ginn & Curtis, 1823), p. 208; *Alabama Acts, 1839–1841* (Tuscaloosa: Hale & Eaton, 1840), p. 137, passed January 9, 1841. Mississippi, like Alabama, used the lash, the brand iron, fine, and imprisonment; see *Revised Code of the Laws of Mississippi* (Natchez: Francis Baker, 1824), pp. 299–300.

[6] Clarence E. Carter, ed., *The Territorial Papers of the United States*, 24 vols. (Washington: G.P.O., 1936–1962), 4:365 (Territory South of the River Ohio), Blount to Secretary of War, November 10, 1794.

offense of which human nature is capable." The penalty, in this statute, was the usual whipping, and standing in the pillory. To these certain refinements were added: the ears were nailed to the pillory and cut off, and the culprit was branded on the right cheek with the letter H, three-quarters of an inch high and half an inch wide, and on the left cheek with the letter T of the same dimensions in a plain and visible manner. A second conviction brought death without benefit of clergy.[7]

Throughout Arkansas and Tennessee, shaggy men whose skins ranged in hue from Indian browns to pale-face white plundered mounts from one another. Settlers in the Territory of Arkansas, to offer one example among many, became so wrought up over the spiriting away of their horses by the tribes—Cherokees, Choctaws, Osages—that a grand jury in Hempstead County, in April, 1820, returned a present-ment which fairly stammered in its haste to tick off the many instances of theft:

> In Septem. 1817 at one sweep were stolen from Joseph English & others fifteen horses.... In the year 1819 the Cado Indians stole at one time fourteen horses.... In the Winters of 1818 and 1819 the Cherokees stole a horse from Mr. Amos Kuykendall.... A few days since two valuable horses were stolen.... Also two other horses ... have been missing for some time & supposed to be stolen by the Cherokees.... Also two other horses missing belonging to Mr. Silas Rowls & have been seen with the Cherokees.[8]

A distraught resident of Near Memphis, Tennessee, a decade and half later, complained that he and his neighbors were in "perpetual fear" of losing slaves and horses at the hands of a lawless band of white freebooters squatting on public lands in Arkansas. "There is little law, and less Justice in this quarter," he wrote, "and if you were as well acquainted with the circumstances as are those in whose behalf I now address you, you would *shudder* at the attrocities so often per-petrated."[9]

If one, provided his horse was not stolen en route, headed into the territory north of the Ohio, one would have faced the same dismal

---

[7] Edward Scott, comp., *Laws of the State of Tennessee ... 1715–1820*, 2 vols. (Knoxville: Heiskell & Brown, 1821), 1:366; also 1:648 for act of October 23, 1799, and 1:1056 for act of December 3, 1807.

[8] Carter, *Territorial Papers*, 19:196, Territory of Arkansas.

[9] Ibid., 21:1059, Charles D. McLean to Elijah Howard, July 28, 1835.

problem. The Treaty of Fort Harmar—if, indeed, it was a treaty—was negotiated between the United States and the Wyandot and other tribes in 1789. An entire article of the treaty concerned itself with horse theft. Indian and white man pledged themselves to forgo the luxury of swiping one another's ponies, but, unfortunately and normally, the pledge was honored more in the breach than in the pious promise.[10]

Although the governor and judges of the Northwest Territory passed no legislation specifically referring to horse theft, it may be presumed that the crime was covered by the law of robbery, which provided punishment for those who, unlawfully and forcibly, stole money, goods, or chattels.[11] After Ohio entered the Union, it passed a general act respecting crimes and punishments, and this statute included a section on horse theft. Indeed, in some ways the penalty was harsher than some prescribed earlier by other states. A first offender received no more than fifty-nine stripes on the bare back, a second offender no more than a hundred. The second offender was liable to a fine not exceeding five hundred dollars and imprisonment for not more than a year.[12]

[10] Ibid., 2:176, Northwest Territory: "And whereas, The practice of Stealing horses has prevailed very much, to the great disquiet of the Citizens of the United States, and if persisted in cannot fail to involve, both the United States of America and the Indians in endless animosity, it is agreed that it Shall be put an entire Stop to on both sides, Nevertheless should some individuals in defiance of this agreement, and of the laws provided against such offenses continue to make depredations of that nature; the person convicted thereof shall be punished with the utmost severity the Laws of the Respective States, or Territory of the United States, North West of the Ohio, where the offence may have been committed, will admit of. And all horses so Stolen, either by the Indians from the Citizens or Subjects of the United States; or by the Citizens or Subjects of the United States from any of the Indian Nations; may be reclaimed, into whose possession soever they may have passed and upon due proof Shall be Restored; any Sales in Market Ouvert; notwithstanding. And the Civil Magistrates in the United States Respectively, and in the Territory of the United States, Northwest of the Ohio, Shall give all necessary aid & protection to Indians claiming Such Stolen horses."

[11] Salmon P. Chase, comp., *Statutes of Ohio, 1788–1833*, 3 vols. (Cincinnati: Corey & Fairbank, 1833–1835), 1:98–99. Art. 3 of the Northwest Ordinance did say that Indians' lands and property shall never be taken from them without their consent.

[12] Ibid., 1:441. Passed January 15, 1805, this act was softened considerably on January 27, 1813, when the General Assembly altered the punishment to imprisonment in the penitentiary, at hard labor, for a period of not less than three years nor more than fourteen years. For the full text, see *Ohio Acts, Sixteenth General Assembly, 1817* (Columbus: P. H. Olmsted, 1818), pp. 175–76.

The illegal taking of horses was prevalent throughout Indiana. Both white men and Indians were guilty. John Gibson, acting governor of the Territory of Indiana, wrote as early as September 2, 1812, that everything was quiet at Fort Harrison, except that two horses had been delivered up by the Indians and two others "belonging to the Inhabitants, were lately stolen by two potawatomies & One Kickapoo Indian."[13] Whether such horses were worth the snatching is a moot question, for one writer said contemptuously that pioneer horses were of inferior quality and described them as small, scrawny, and ungainly looking.[14] But regardless of the quality or beauty of the beasts, they were in demand.

As settlement edged westward and territories were divided and subdivided into more and more new states, the larceny of horses increased. Harried legislators hurried to impose new strictures, bindings thought as tight as a taut lariat, but which, in practice, were slippery as a granny's knot. Illinois, whose western edge bordered the Mississippi River, a major highway for criminals of all types, took notice of illegal altering or defacing marks and brands. The act included not only horses, jacks, and jennets but also neat cattle, sheep, goats, and hogs. This statute was similar to a Missouri prohibition, but with one significant exception. The penalty in the Sucker State was imprisonment; that of Missouri included whipping.[15]

As steamboats plied the Upper Mississippi, villages took root, and prairies were plowed into farms, a great unrest agitated the area. The murderer, the counterfeiter, the burglar, and the robber preyed, almost at will, upon storekeeper, steamboat passenger, professional man, and settler. To many, the Mormon stronghold at Nauvoo, Illinois, was a gathering place and a citadel for the lawless. The return of veterans from the Mexican War resulted in an increase of crime of all types. River cities, like St. Louis, witnessed a constantly increasing rate of

[13] Carter, *Territorial Papers*, 8:198, Territory of Indiana.

[14] R. Carlyle Buley, *The Old Northwest: Pioneer Period, 1815–1840*, 2 vols. (Indianapolis: Indiana Historical Society, 1950), 1:191–92.

[15] *Revised Laws of Illinois, 1832–1833* (Vandalia: Greiner & Sherman, 1833), p. 183, in force July 1, 1833; *Missouri Laws, Revised and Digested* (St. Louis: E. Charles, 1825), p. 289. For general discussions of illegal activities throughout the Mississippi Valley, see "The Derringer and the Ace of Spades: Reflections on Middle Border Law and Order," and "The Mississippi—Spillway of Sin," pp. 99 and 23, respectively in this volume. The St. Louis *Missouri Argus*, May 26, 1837, announced the execution of John Wright for horse stealing on March 31, "in pursuance of the sentence of the St. Francis Circuit Court." See John L. Harr, "Law and Lawlessness in the Lower Mississippi Valley 1815–1860," *Northwest Missouri State College Studies* 19 (June 1, 1955):51–70.

crime. By the 1850s it was clearly apparent, throughout this western country, that law enforcement had broken down.[16]

The horse thief took advantage of the times, and, obviously, helped shape them. Statute law, strict and rigid as it might be, was bent out of shape for the simple reason that there always is great difference between the law as it is written and the law as it is enforced. Yet enforcement cannot be understood or discussed without some knowledge of what the law prescribed. Peace officers—constables, marshals, and sheriffs— were largely self-trained. Constables and marshals were either appointed or elected, and, as the nineteenth century wore on, county sheriffs were elected. Elected peace officers normally desired reelection, and usually were careful not to offend their constituents. In addition, law enforce- ment was only one among many duties. In reality, peace officers were jacks of all trades—they kept council chambers clean, collected taxes, supervised the lock-up or jail, inspected warehouses and lumber mills, shooed hogs from streets, performed political favors, and enforced the law as they could. Some peace officers were utterly unfit, others com- petent, and a few outstanding.[17]

No wearer of a star, however, need worry if he pursued a horse thief, for he could be sure that public opinion was squarely behind him. Indeed, in unorganized counties, citizens themselves took the law into their own hands. At times, irate men thwarted both sheriff and justice

[16] Countless newspapers, national journals, foreign travelers, clergymen, politi- cians, and plain citizens testified to the breakdown of law and order. One example, among many in my files, comes from Brigham Young: "The ranklings of violence and intolerance, and religious and political strife, that have long been waking up in the bosom of this nation, together with the occasional scintillations of settled ven- geance, and blood guiltness cannot long be suppressed" (*The Latter Day Saints Millennial Star* [Manchester, England], December 1, 1845; see also *St. Louis Reveille* for the period).

[17] No satisfactory general account of the sheriff and his office has yet been written. See, for example, Bruce Smith, *Police Systems in the United States* (New York: Harper & Brothers, 1949) and his *Rural Crime Control* (New York: Columbia Uni- versity Press, 1933); William A. Jackson, *The Office of Sheriff in Iowa* (Cedar Rapids: Torch Press, 1924); Raymond Moley, "The Sheriff and the Constable," *Annals of American Academy of Political and Social Science* 146 (November 1929):28–33; George E. Howard, *Introduction to the Local Constitutional History of the United States*, 2 vols. (Baltimore: Johns Hopkins University, 1889). For background, see Cyrus H. Harraker, *The Seventeenth-Century Sheriff: A Comparative Study of the Sheriff in England and the Chesapeake Colonies, 1607–1689* (Durham: University of North Carolina Press, 1930); *Abridgement of the Laws in Force in Her Majesty's Plantations of Virginia, Jamaica, Barbadoes, Maryland, New-England, New-York, Carolina* (London: R. Parker, R. Smith, & Benj. Tooke, 1704).

by shoving a peace officer aside and dispensing justice according to the dictates of Judge Lynch. On one occasion at least, a thief masquerading as a solid citizen whose horses had been stolen approached a sheriff who had the mounts in custody and demanded their return. "Show me the man who bought the horses," he said, "and I will rid the country of him, and put him where he can steal no more." [18] Jackson County, in northern Iowa, was a hotbed of organized horse theft during the 1830s. The gang pillaged the area from Dubuque south to Keokuk, and from Davenport to Cedar County. [19] This fraternity of ruffians, led by W. W. Brown, during the next decade extended its activities into portions of Wisconsin, northern Illinois, and down the Mississippi River into Missouri. [20]

For three long, bloody years, the Brown gang passed counterfeit money and stole horses. Finally a sheriff's posse, armed with pitchforks and guns, cornered a portion of the outlaws, killed three, and took thirteen prisoners. Seven escaped. Four of the sheriff's men were killed and several were wounded. Still horse theft increased. In May, 1840, a settler of Linn County appealed to the governor to restore peace. "I lay before you," he wrote, "the distressed situation of the people of that vicinity, we are constantly alarmed by riotous bodies of armed men, without lawful authority, without discipline and I may add without principle, parading through our country and threatening violence to all who do not countenance their unlawful conduct." [21]

Aroused citizens in Linn and Benton counties formed the Iowa Protection Company, whose object was to protect the property of their members and "particularly their horses" from the depredations of robbers and thieves, to rescue and restore property stolen, and to assist in the faithful administration of law and society. The company did manage to discourage the stealing of horses, but in no wise was it able to stamp out the practice. [22] Indeed, the number of men at the "wrong end of the halter" increased. In July, 1842, for example, leaders

[18] *History of Jackson County, Iowa* (Chicago: Western Historical Co., 1870), p. 361. For further information on the Bellevue War, see Harvey Reid, *Thomas Cox* (Iowa City: State Historical Society of Iowa, 1909), pp. 122–67.

[19] *History of Jackson County*, 356.

[20] Edward Bonney, *The Banditti of the Prairies . . . A Tale of the Mississippi Valley*, intro. by Philip D. Jordan (Norman: University of Oklahoma Press, 1963).

[21] John C. Parish, "White Beans for the Hanging," *Palimpsest* 1 (July 1920):24.

[22] John Ely Briggs, "Pioneer Gangsters," ibid. 21 (March 1940):84. Not all protection associations were impromptu. Michigan, for example, in 1859, passed an act providing that any number of persons, not less than ten, were authorized to form themselves into a company for the purpose of detecting and apprehending horse

of a gang of sixty counterfeiters and horse thieves were arrested in Linn County.

About the same time, just to keep the record straight, considerable hell-raising was going on in the California country. Mountain men, after the decline of the Rocky Mountain fur trade, put aside their traps to trade for buffalo robes or to raid California horse herds. A trader wrote from the Green River in January, 1840, that mountain men had returned from their traps and that "horse thieves about 10 or 15 are gone to California for the purpose of Robbing and Steeling. Such thing never has been known until late." The Mission San Gabriel was robbed of three bands of tame mares. Other thieves raided ranches eastward to San Bernardino and southward to Mission San Juan Capistrano. Pegleg Smith and Wakara, a Ute chief, struck at the Mission of San Luis Obispo, running off an entire herd. Although the prefect of Los Angeles organized a posse to pursue the thieves, the effort was embarrassingly unsuccessful, for the mountain men not only whipped the Californians in a lively skirmish but also snitched their mounts, so that the posse was obliged to trudge home on foot. Similar raids continued throughout the Mexican War and did not stop until about 1855, when Chief Wakara died.[23]

Although the making away of horses throughout the Mississippi Valley was not as picturesque as were the California escapades, it, following the sturdy entrepreneurial spirit, managed to sustain itself. Victimized citizens, dozens of newspapers reported, were hard after horse thieves, and captions, in bold, black type, warned: "Horse thieves about! Lock your stables." Two thieves were arrested in Davenport, Iowa, and four in Rock Island, Illinois, during September, 1852. Not infrequently editors spoke of sheriffs taking convicted thieves to prison. "T. G. Drippes, sheriff of Clayton County," read a typical news item from Dubuque, Iowa, "passed through our city yesterday morning, having in charge David Harrison, convicted of horse stealing and sentenced to the Penitentiary for six months."[24]

---

thieves and other felons (Andrew Howell, comp., *Michigan General Statutes*, 2 vols. [Chicago: Callaghan & Co., 1882], 1:1235–36).

[23] This account is based upon LeRoy R. Hafen and Ann W. Hafen, *Old Spanish Trail: Santa Fé to Los Angeles* (Glendale: Arthur H. Clark Co., 1954), pp. 227–57. For Indian stealings, see Walker D. Wyman, *The Wild Horse of the West* (Caldwell, Ida.: Caxton Printers, 1945), pp. 53–54, 74–78.

[24] *Dubuque Miners' Daily Express*, October 1, 1851; *Dubuque Observor*, November 3, 1854; *Iowa Democratic Enquirer* (Muscatine), October 15, 1852; *Democratic Banner* (Davenport), July 16, September 3, 1852.

Toward the close of the 1850s and the first years of the Civil War, the rate of horse thefts leaped alarmingly. The reasons were two: some newly arrived settlers, needing horse flesh desperately to help work farms, were not above purchasing purloined steeds, and the war itself increased the desire for horses to be used as cavalry mounts and whooped the prize. Farmers, livery stablemen, doctors, and deacons reported missing horses. During July, 1857, a vigilante committee of some two hundred broke up a gang of Iowa horse thieves, hanged three, and shot to death a fourth. Another was hanged a few days later, and a young boy, caught in the act of taking a horse, received seventy lashes. When fifteen horses valued at three thousand dollars were stolen within ten days in Grant County, Wisconsin, a waggish editor suggested that the thieves should incorporate as the Great Western Incorporated Horse Thief Association.[25]

That horse thieves "are prowling around and good horses have to be watched" was no exaggeration, for, time and again as the North built its armies for the long struggle with the Confederate States, evidence that organized horse stealing was increasing continued to mount. In October, 1861, the number of horses spirited away in the vicinity of Winona, Minnesota, was "extraordinarily" great, and it was presumed some were driven to Illinois and there sold for cavalry horses, "for which the demand is great, and prices good." Scoundrels, representing themselves as government buyers, traveled the country, stealing when they were able.[26] Now and again, boys in blue uniforms snatched time from military duties to make away with a horse. One enterprising individual, a member of a Captain Bennet's company stationed at Fort Snelling, not only stole a fine mare but also forged discharge papers and separated himself from the service forever.[27]

The close of the war mustered out an army of men accustomed to violence. Some were hardened by those ubiquitous sins so common to army posts and battlefield bivouacs throughout time, and most came

[25] *La Crosse Independent Republican*, September 13, 14, 1859, July 8, 28, 1857; *Winona Weekly Republican*, July 8, 1856, August 25, 1857; *Winona Democrat*, March 26, May 9, 1859.

[26] See, for example, *Winona Daily Republican*, October 11, 17, 1861, May 15, 22, 1863. On October 31, 1863, the *Republican* said: "An organized band of thieves exists, the members of which carry on their operations in the river towns of this State. This fact was ascertained by the arrest of their leader, who is now in jail at Red Wing, and who, since his capture, has confessed to the existence of the gang and the objects for which they are associated."

[27] Ibid., November 11, 1861.

home to start a new life. Others, finding civilian chores dreary, wandered elsewhere in search of crime's excitement.[28] They exchanged the carrying of arms for the wearing of weapons. Homicide, counterfeiting, larceny, gambling, burglary, and horse stealing reached peaks previously unknown. Indeed, the Far West, during the turbulent postwar decades, was no wilder than was the Middle West. Some veterans, both northern and southern, turned to vagrancy and others hit the road as tramps. How many became horse thieves is difficult to say with assurance, but one fact is clear: the taking of horses increased markedly.[29]

An "epidemic of savagery," said a historian of an Iowa county, ravaged the area in the late 1860s.[30] He might well have added that the epidemic, like cholera, swept not only Minnesota, Wisconsin, and Illinois but also the Missouri–Iowa border. In this bucolic and apparently peaceful agricultural area lay the Missouri hamlets of Kahoka and Luray. Stolen horses were run through this country from states of the Upper Mississippi on into Kansas. It was rumored that some stolen steeds reached Texas.[31] To curb such annoying interstate commerce and to protect their own livestock, a few residents of Clark County, in

[28] Among the better studies describing the drinking, gambling, and chasing of whores are Louis Pelzer, *Marches of the Dragoons in the Mississippi Valley* (Iowa City: State Historical Society of Iowa, 1917), pp. 2–5; Bell I. Wiley, *The Life of Billy Yank* (Indianapolis: Bobbs-Merrill Co., 1951), chap. 10, and his *The Life of Johnny Reb* (Indianapolis: Bobbs-Merrill Co., 1943), chap. 3. See also, for the postwar period of the Indian wars, Don Rickey, Jr., *Forty Miles a Day on Beans and Hay* (Norman: University of Oklahoma Press, 1963), chap 9. Also, Edith Abbott, "The Civil War and the Crime Wave of 1865–70," *Social Service Review* 1 (June, 1927):212–34; and Betty B. Rosenbaum, "The Relationship between War and Crime in the United States," *Journal of Criminal Law and Criminology* 30 (January–February, 1940): 722–40.

[29] Outlawry increased in all sections of the West after the Civil War. See Wayne Gard, *Frontier Justice* (Norman: University of Oklahoma Press, 1949), p. 200: "Some of the bandits were former soldiers who turned to outlawry to prolong the sectional conflict or to offset unpopular Reconstruction measures. A larger group of bandits were local bushwhackers or guerrillas who had used the war as an excuse for terrorism and dared not to return to civil life in their own homes. . . . Other vandals robbed to recoup gambling losses or were tempted by the ease of cattle rustling on the unfenced plains." One ranchman, quoted by Gard, estimated that in the twenty years before 1873 some 100,000 cattle were driven from Texas by thieves.

[30] Ellery M. Hancock, *Past and Present of Allamakee County, Iowa* (Chicago: S. J. Clarke Publishing Co., 1913), p. 197.

[31] *Penal Code of State of Texas* (Galveston: News Office, 1857), p. 150, provided, as the penalty for horse theft, not less than two nor more than seven years' confinement in the state penitentiary.

which Kahoka was situated, looked to precedent for a remedy. Anti-horse thief associations were not unfamiliar. Such an organization was organized in Minneapolis during the summer of 1866. A Horse Thief Protection Society had been initiated in Clinton County, Iowa, on the eve of the Civil War and another, to mention only a few among many, was the Sioux Rapids Vigilance Committee, organized in Clay County, Iowa, in 1870. The latter took a no-nonsense point of view. It scattered handbills throughout the countryside, reading: *"Horse Thieves, Beware!"* Then followed a simple statement saying that thieves when caught would be dealt with promptly and properly.[32]

The Clark County Anti–Horse Thief Association was the brain child of David McKee, a pepper-and-salt transplanted Kentuckian who might have come straight from a picaresque novel. McKee moved to Clark County in 1848, where, according to reports, he now and again became a sort of private detective, even to disguising himself so cleverly that his own family did not recognize him. He had been a justice of the peace and township assessor. He was a Mason and a member of the Congregational church. He once attempted to sell a pair of elk, broken to harness, to P. T. Barnum, but whether or not the deal was consummated is uncertain. During the Civil War, he raised the Seventh Missouri Cavalry and was elected major. In July, 1863, he resigned his commission because of disabilities and returned home. He and Hugh Allen Stuart had gone to California in 1849, and one story has it that the two adventurers got the idea of a protective association from vigilante activities in the mining camps. Such may be the case, but it seems strange that McKee should not have known of regional associations long before his trek to the gold fields.[33]

[32] *Minneapolis Chronicle*, June 30, 1866; Patrick B. Wolfe, *Wolfe's History of Clinton County, Iowa* (Indianapolis: B. F. Bowen, 1911), p. 267; James E. Parker, "Pioneer Protection from Horse Thieves," *Annals of Iowa*, 3 ser., 6 (April 1903): 59–63.

[33] Unless otherwise indicated, this and subsequent material pertaining to McKee and his association is drawn from "History of the A. H. T. A.," *Missouri Historical Review* 18 (October 1923): 114; Minnie M. Brashear, "The Anti–Horse Thief Association of Northeast Missouri," ibid. 45 (July 1951): 341–48; *History of Lee County, Iowa* (Chicago: Western Historical Co., 1879), pp. 551–52; H. C. Gresham, *The Story of Major David McKee* (Cheney County, Kans.: The Author, 1937). For a few other selected accounts of other such organizations throughout the region, see James A. Rose, "The Regulators and Flatheads in Southern Illinois," *Illinois State Historical Society Transactions, 1906* (Springfield: Illinois State Journal Co., 1906), pp. 108–21; Orville F. Grahame, "The Vigilance Committees," *Palimpsest* 6 (October 1925): 359–70; William C. Bek, "The Followers of Duden," *Missouri Historical Review* 17

Although McKee's Anti–Horse Thief Association was formed in 1854, the organization was not particularly effective until 1863, when it was reorganized in Luray. A year later, both a charter and a constitution were adopted. The first annual meeting of the Grand Order was held in Memphis, Missouri, in October, 1864. Membership was secret, and no records were kept of cases investigated. In theory, the association was opposed to mob violence in any form and described itself as a "fraternal, protective and detective organization." Its motto was "To protect the Innocent and bring the guilty to Justice." It did not declare, as did the Vigilance Committee of Jackson County, Iowa, that it would be governed by a state penal law "so far as is convenient," but such was to be the case in at least one horrible incident.[34]

With a rapidly increasing membership, with generous support from area editors, and with belly bloated with success, McKee's association tried its hangman's hand at apprehending and bringing to justice the murderer of the Spencer family.[35] The action was rationalized on the

---

(October 1922):28–31; A. M. Haswell, "The Story of the Bald Knobbers," ibid. 18 (October 1923):27–35; Lucille Morris, *Bald Knobbers* (Caldwell, Ida.: Caxton Printers, 1939); Gladys H. Du Priest, "The Waseca County Horse Thief Detectives," *Minnesota History* 13 (June 1932):153–57. Space does not permit the listing of similar organizations in the trans-Missouri area and the Far West. That California vigilance committees might have exerted some influence is glimpsed in a letter from San Francisco to a New York merchant and reprinted in part in the *Minnesota Democrat* (Minneapolis), October 3, 1857: "In consequence of the reform brought about by the Vigilance Committee, this city has been governed during the past year at an expense of $250,000, against an average expense the previous year of *over one million five hundred thousand* dollars—six times as much as it now costs. Aside from the great benefits arising from the repression of outrage, tumult, violence and robbery, the saving of one and a quarter million of dollars per year to our city, is worth all it has cost to bring about the desirable results, and speaks loudly for the necessity of such reforms." During the late 1890s, the White Caps were organized in Tennessee to control lewd characters, especially women. In their first raid, members, wearing masks and white caps, whipped some half-dozen women and warned them to leave the county. An opposition group, the Blue Belles, soon caused even more disturbance. See E. W. Crozier, *The White Caps: A History of the Organization in Sevier County* (Knoxville: Bean, Warters & Gaut, 1899), pp. 11, 20. McKee once apparently toyed with the same idea of enforcing moral codes. Not until 1909, when a ladies' auxiliary was formed at Sedan, Kansas, did the association concern itself with such welfare activities as protecting girls from the white slave traffic and teaching boys to avoid the drug and liquor habits.

34 For the objectives of the Jackson County Vigilance Committee, see *Winona Argus*, June 11, 1857.

35 The *Keokuk Daily Gate City*, August 15, 1877, gave the membership as over 4,000, but this was exaggerated, for in 1885 the association itself reported only 4,973

slim premise that perhaps horse thieves were involved, and that, anyway, the mission of the association was to bring the guilty to justice.
The homicide which brought the pristine sense of justice of the Anti–
Horse Thief Association and its sensitive regard for maintaining the
purity of the moral atmosphere of Clark County into play was fairly
simple in its details.

One morning in early August, 1877, the slain bodies of Lewis Spencer,
his two adolescent daughters, and two young sons were found on the
family farm about seven miles from Luray. Soon after the discovery of
the mutilated corpses, crowds of curious citizens, horrified by the
bloody scene but anxious not to miss a single stain, pawed through the
house and trampled any physical evidence that might have existed
outside. After them came newspaper reporters whose hemorrhagic
adjectives graphically changed a sordid killing into a sort of gala
spectacle. They wrote that "the only reception given us was the cackling
of five geese," of the "mournful surroundings," of a "ghastly pile of
blood-stained clothing."[36] All this not only inspired local peace
officers but also raised to fever pitch public opinion. During the course
of the investigation, suspects were arrested and released. Finally, perhaps as much by a left-handed throw of Fate's dice as anything else,
and with the aid of the association, William J. Young was arrested and
brought to trial.

Bill Young, although perhaps no paragon of virtue, was not on trial
for his life because of his morality or lack of it. He had been brought to
court largely because the Anti–Horse Thief Association had hired
Frank Lane, a double-crossing, good-for-nothing private detective.
One of the main witnesses against Young was a slattern by the name of
Laura Sprouse. Fortunately, despite cries of injustice by some of the

members. Membership increased to 10,191 in 1900 and to 50,000 in 1916. The term
Horse was dropped in the 1920s, and membership decreased to 8,000 in 1932.
Probably the *Fort Madison Democrat*, April 3, 1878, was more nearly correct when
it estimated a membership of 2,370. Newspaper support was lavish. "As a means of
detecting and punishing, as well as suppressing crime," said the *Keokuk Daily
Constitution*, October 16, 1878, "we believe that no organization in the U.S. can
show as good a record as the AHTA, composed as it is of men who have suffered
and are liable to suffer from the depredations of the boldest and worst thieves in the
country, the men, who, in the dead hour of night when the farmer is sleeping in
fancied security, rob him of his most valued possessions." See also *Warsaw* (Illinois)
Bulletin, October 18, 1879; *Clark County* (Missouri) *Democrat*, February 1, 1879;
Edina (Missouri) *Sentinel*, June 5, 1879.
[36] *Keokuk Daily Constitution*, August 17, 1877.

association, a jury found Young innocent. After his release, he, paying slight attention to rumors that he might be lynched, married a woman who had stood by him throughout his trial and took her home.

Their reception was scarcely a rollicking, old-fashioned shivaree. Instead, a mob surrounded the house, exchanged gunfire with Young wounded him once in the arm and four times in the breast, and then dragged him out and hanged him from his orchard gate. The mob, it was said, was composed of the most respectable men in the community. The Sheriff, although present, was "unable" to prevent either the shooting or the lynching.[37] Young went to his death protesting his innocence. He may have been telling the truth, for even today whispers in Clark County hint with sly obliqueness of the identity of the "real" murderer. When the hue and cry subsided, Clark County enjoyed a reputation as a New Orleans at its worst and a Gomorrah at its best, and this appears to be somewhat less than complimentary.

The troublous Middle Border, before the official closing of the frontier in 1890, witnessed a decline in horse stealing. Anti–horse thief associations dwindled away from lack of lynch business, became purely social conclaves, or, like McKee's organization, sought, as a catharsis, to purge society of its evils. Gangs, once powerful, splintered, their power broken. Old-timers, dipping into the mildew of memory, cackled of the excitement of the old days, when news of the theft of a neighbor's horse inflamed the countryside. So far as horse stealing was concerned, the Mississippi Valley had pretty well settled down. Now and again a farm animal disappeared. But the taking of a work horse for sale to a fire department or to be used to pull a streetcar became increasingly risky. More profit was to be had with less danger, during the 1890s, in driving off some farmer's oxen and selling the steady beasts to lumber companies for use in Minnesota's pineries. Such larceny, however, was a humdrum affair, scarcely keeping a thief of taste in pocket money.

Most of the states, by 1890, had provided punishment for horse thieves

---

[37] Although details of the trial are not pertinent to this account, they may be found in John W. Murphy, *Outlaws of the Fox River Country* . . . (Hannibal, Mo.: Hannibal Printing Co., 1882); Paul Rowe, ed., *The Trial of Bill Young* (Kahoka, Mo.: Kahoka Herald-Gazette, 1965); Patrick B. Nolan, "Outlaws of the Fox River Country: A Study in the Validation of Source Materials," (M.A. thesis, University of Minnesota, 1967). Vivid, but not always consistent, accounts of the hanging were printed at length in, for example, *Burlington Daily Hawkeye*, October 30, 1879; *Burlington Daily Gazette*, October 31, 1879; *Warsaw* (Illinois) *Bulletin*, November 1, 1879; *Quincy Weekly Whig*, November 6, 1879; *Fort Madison Democrat*, October 29, November 5, 1879.

either under the laws covering larceny or grand larceny, or by special statutes.[38] These, of course, in the farther west, were supplemented with the vigilante's noose and the marshal's six-gun. If an ambitious, red-blooded young buck from the Middle West was determined to carve for himself a career as a horse thief, his best opportunity lay in the Southwest, or—tossing a coin—in Montana, Nebraska, or Kansas.[39] Wichita and Dodge City were likely spots, but the swaggering young caballero would have found the law operating fairly effectively.

Yet it was still possible, although hazardous, to sneak off with a good riding horse, or, if stealth failed, to hold a gun on a victim with the demand: "Gimme a hoss I kin ride!" With this gesture and these words, he not only perpetuated a tradition but also possibly sealed his fate. Had he been wise enough, before he was dropped to eternity, he would have forsaken the stealing of horses and taken to tending cows.

Appendix

LARCENY OF HORSES
STATUTES OF THE SEVERAL STATES
IN 1890

North Atlantic Division

		Min.	Max.	
1	Maine	None	5 yrs.	Punishable as larceny.
2	New Hampshire	None	7 yrs.	
3	Vermont	None	10 yrs.	Or fine not exceeding $1,000 or both such fine and imprisonment.
4	Massachusetts	None	5 yrs.	Punishable as larceny.
5	Rhode Island	None	5 yrs.	Punishable as larceny.
6	Connecticut	2 yrs.	10 yrs.	
7	New York	—	—	

[38] See "Statutes of the Several States regarding Larceny of Horses in 1890," appended to this article. The schedule was compiled from Frederick H. Wines, "Report on Crime, Pauperism, and Benevolence in the United States," *Eleventh Census, 1890* (Washington: G.P.O., 1896), vol. 3, pt. 1, pp. 396, 398–411.

[39] See, for example, the delightful volume by Nyle H. Miller and Joseph W. Snell, *Great Gunfighters of the Kansas Cowtowns, 1867–1886* (Lincoln: University of Nebraska Press, 1963) and the equally fascinating study by Joe B. Frantz and Julian Ernest Choate, Jr., *The American Cowboy: The Myth and the Reality* (Norman: University of Oklahoma Press, 1955).

8	New Jersey	None	10 yrs.	Punishable as larceny.
9	Pennsylvania	None	10 yrs.	And fine not exceeding $500.

South Atlantic Division

10	Delaware	None	5 yrs.	And fine not exceeding $20, 1 hour in the pillory, and 20 lashes.
11	Maryland	2 yrs.	14 yrs.	And the offender must make restitution or pay to the owner the value of the property taken.
12	Dist. of Columbia	2 yrs.	7 yrs.	
13	Virginia	3 yrs.	18 yrs.	
14	West Virginia	None	10 yrs.	Punishable as larceny.
15	North Carolina	5 yrs.	20 yrs.	
16	South Carolina	1 yr.	10 yrs.	And fine, at the discretion of the court.
17	Georgia	4 yrs.	20 yrs.	
18	Florida	None	5 yrs.	Punishable as larceny.

North Central Division

19	Ohio	1 yr.	15 yrs.	
20	Indiana	None	14 yrs.	Punishable as larceny.
21	Illinois	3 yrs.	20 yrs.	
22	Michigan	3 yrs.	15 yrs.	In case of first offense the court may sentence to the state house of correction for not more than 2 years.
23	Wisconsin	2 yrs.	15 yrs.	
24	Minnesota	None	10 yrs.	Punishable as larceny.
25	Iowa	None	5 yrs.	Punishable as larceny.
26	Missouri	2 yrs.	7 yrs.	
27	North Dakota	—	—	Punishable as larceny.
28	South Dakota	—	—	Punishable as larceny.
29	Nebraska	1 yr.	10 yrs.	
30	Kansas	None	7 yrs.	

South Central Division

31	Kentucky	2 yrs.	10 yrs.	
32	Tennessee	3 yrs.	10 yrs.	
33	Alabama	1 yr.	10 yrs.	Punishable as grand larceny.

34	Mississippi	None	5 yrs.	Punishable as larceny.
35	Louisiana	1 yr.	5 yrs.	
36	Texas	5 yrs.	15 yrs.	
37	Arkansas	5 yrs.	15 yrs.	

Western Division

38	Montana	1 yr.	14 yrs.	Punishable as grand larceny.
39	Wyoming	None	10 yrs.	Punishable as larceny.
40	Colorado	None	10 yrs.	Punishable as larceny.
41	New Mexico	1 yr.	10 yrs.	
42	Arizona	1 yr.	10 yrs.	Punishable as grand larceny.
43	Utah	1 yr.	10 yrs.	Punishable as grand larceny.
44	Nevada	None	14 yrs.	Punishable as larceny.
45	Idaho	1 yr.	14 yrs.	Punishable as grand larceny.
46	Washington	1 yr.	10 yrs.	Or imprisonment in county jail not more than 1 year, or fine not exceeding $100, or both such fine and imprisonment.
47	Oregon	1 yr.	10 yrs.	Or by imprisonment in county jail not less than 3 months nor more than 1 year, or fine not less than $50 nor more than $1,000.
48	California	1 yr.	10 yrs.	Punishable as grand larceny.

The Derringer and the Ace of Spades: Reflections on Middle Border Law and Order

Ever since Cain clobbered Abel and Peck's bad boy tried to do away with his pa, sin and crime have scarred society, pocking it with mob vengeance, sapping its economic vitality with the long green of bogus currency, and strewing city street and rural lane with butchered bodies. Those lilting lines from the theme song of Car 54, "there's a holdup in the Bronx and Brooklyn's broken out in vice," are applicable not only to New York's bothered boroughs but also to every American community.

Crime, in proportion to population, always was larger than it might have been. Each successive frontier was marked by lawlessness. The so-called "Wild West" of the post-Civil-War era was no more wild and woolly than were previous frontiers. There was about as much disaster, vice, crime, and social upheaval and unrest in practically every segment of the Union prior to the Mexican and Civil wars as in the decades which followed. Today the rate of crime climbs annually.

The American carried his peculiar concept of justice with him as he traveled from one frontier line to the next. He took along his weapons and instruments with which to rob and murder. He toted well-established, useful techniques both to commit crime and to punish the criminal. In other words, the nature of illegal acts, the methods of the man outside the law, the character and quantity of criminal activities were, all factors considered, just about the same in Texas, the Dakotas, and California during the later decades of the nineteenth century as they had been on the Middle Border (those territories and states bordering the Mississippi River from New Orleans to St. Paul) during the middle decades.

The crime picture on the Middle Border was little different from what it had been in the Ohio country a decade or so earlier. And the pattern of the Ohio area varied only slightly from that which characterized the Atlantic seaboard states and cities—Philadelphia, Baltimore, New York—at the close of the eighteenth century. Counterfeiting, for example, was an established and lucrative business among the colonists. What may be the first instance of bogus-making occurred when sturdy Puritans forged wampum, the better to swindle the Indian.[1] The illegally drawn hangman's noose, fashioned by vigilantes, was commonplace long before the term "Lynch Law" became a vogue.

America, from its inception, most certainly was a nation in which every category of crime flourished, but this does not necessarily imply that the country was without law in that it lacked criminal codes, peace officers, courts of justice, and penal institutions. It does not mean that the population at large was criminally inclined or even that public opinion approved and supported nefarious conduct more than it endorsed law and order. Yet even these generalizations must be refined. Certain types of offenses, in particular periods and localities, generally were endorsed. Gambling and duelling are obvious examples. Lynching was looked upon with favor in instances where men took the law into their own hands either because a community was unorganized legally or because peace officers, particularly sheriffs, shunned their duty. Judge Lynch frequently was not rebuked when he punished a man whose color was other than white.[2] During the early decades of the nineteenth

[1] See the following works by Kenneth Scott, published by the American Numismatic Society: *Counterfeiting in Colonial New York* (New York, 1953); *Counterfeiting in Colonial Pennsylvania* (New York, 1955); *Counterfeiting in Colonial Connecticut* (New York, 1957); as well as his *Counterfeiting in Colonial America* (New York: Oxford University Press, 1957); and *Counterfeiting in Colonial Rhode Island* (Providence: Rhode Island Historical Society, 1960). See also Don Taxay, *Counterfeit, Mis-Struck, and Unofficial U.S. Coins* (New York: Ace Publishing Co., 1963); "Letters of Nathaniel Cox to Gabriel Lewis," *Louisiana Historical Quarterly* 2 (April 1919):179; "Progress of American Counterfeiting," *Banker's Magazine and Journal of the Money Market* (London) 22 (October 1862):621–24.

[2] For a history of lynching, see James E. Cutler, *Lynch-Law* (New York: Longmans, Green, & Co., 1905); for a study of the legal aspects of lynching, see James H. Chadbourn, *Lynching and the Law* (Chapel Hill: University of North Carolina Press, 1933); for semi-popular approaches, see Walter White, *Rope and Faggot: A Biography of Judge Lynch* (New York: Knopf, 1929), and Jack K. Williams, *Vogues*

century, the term "lynching" was not restricted to the stringing up and death of an individual. Lynching covered any type of physical punishment: whipping, scalping, tar and feathering, bodily mutilation, or even the setting of a suspected or convicted person adrift in a skiff on the broad bosom of the Mississippi River.

If Lynch law is defined, as it was during the Jacksonian period, as "extra-legal infliction of punishment or exercise of correctional power which resulted in personal injury," then in Iowa, from 1834 to 1908, there were at least 161 lynchings involving 216 persons.[3] Lynching increased rapidly on the Middle Border after 1830. Contrary to general belief, lynching was not confined to the Lower Mississippi (from New Orleans to St. Louis) nor were the servants of Judge Lynch more active on the lower river than they were in the stretch of water from St. Louis north to St. Paul. Mobs and vigilantes worked their dreadful will the entire length of the river.

The Mississippi has long been delineated and painted with idyllic strokes and pleasing nostalgic hues by both novelists and historians, yet the Father of Waters was more than a leisurely stream winding its romantic way between wooded shores and among verdant islands. The river was more than the freshly painted sternwheeler and the echoing calliope. The Mississippi, and the basin its tributaries drained, was also a sewer of social pollution, a rendezvous for thugs, a convention place for gamblers and prostitutes, a harbor for horse thieves, robbers and murderers, a home of organized criminal bands who traveled a water highway easily and without much fear of apprehension.

To the scholar interested in law and lawlessness, the Mississippi River is one of the major routes of inland rascality. On the river and along its shores, liberty, equality, and fraternity did battle with arson, arsenic, and assassination. The river proffered women, royal flush, and planter's punch. The derringer and the ace of spades were as valid symbols of Middle Border life as were the post digger and the ax. Raftmen and river pilots knew all too well that southern bayous and

in Villainy: Crime and Retribution in Ante-Bellum South Carolina (Columbia: University of South Carolina Press, 1959); for an account which was challenged, see Lynn White, Jr., "The Legacy of the Middle Ages in the American Wild West," *American West* 3 (Spring 1966): 77–78; for origin of the term and for the life of Charles Lynch, see "Lynch's Law," *Southern Literary Messenger* 2 (May 1836):389; "Lynch Law," *Harper's Magazine* 18 (May 1859):794–98, and "Uses and Abuses of Lynch Law," *American Whig Review* 11 (May 1850): 459–76.

[3] Paul W. Black, "Lynchings in Iowa," *Iowa Journal of History and Politics* 10 (April 1912):151, 159.

northern sloughs were as dangerous to life and property as were snags and sawyers, for bayou and slough concealed banditti and pirates. Indeed, pirates operated between New Orleans and St. Louis before the close of the eighteenth century. The infamous James Colbert, for example, on May 2, 1782, seized a vessel bound for St. Louis and carried off gifts intended for Indian tribes and 4,500 pesos.[4]

Piracy and robbery increased with the spread of settlement. Both steamboats and river towns were looted not only by individuals but also by organized bands of desperados. The Chicester and Murrell gangs operated on the Lower River, and the Timber Wolves and the Brown Gang terrorized residents in Iowa, Illinois, and Missouri. Nauvoo, the Mormon stronghold, was thought by many to be a center of Middle Border crime.[5] The steamer *Kentuckian* was robbed of

[4] For material on Colbert and other river pirates, see Louis Houck, *The Spanish Regime in Missouri*, 2 vols. (Chicago: R. R. Donnelly & Sons, 1909); John W. Gaughey, *Bernardo de Galvez in Louisiana, 1776–1783* (Berkeley: University of California Press, 1934); Firmin A. Rozier, *History of the Early Settlement of the Mississippi Valley* (St. Louis: G. A. Pierrot & Son, 1890); Frederic L. Billon, *Annals of St. Louis in Its Early Days Under the French and Spanish Dominations* (St. Louis: G. I. Jones & Co., 1886), and his *Annals of St. Louis in Its Territorial Days from 1804 to 1821* (St. Louis: Nixon-Jones Printing Co., 1888); Wilson Prim, "History of St. Louis," *The Early Histories of St. Louis* (St. Louis: St. Louis Historical Documents of Foundation, 1952), pp. 105–31; Henry E. Chambers, "Early Commercial Prestige of New Orleans," *Louisiana Historical Quarterly* 5 (October 1922): 451–61; D. C. Corbitt, "James Colbert and the Spanish Claims to the East Bank of the Mississippi," *Mississippi Valley Historical Review* 20 (March 1934): 537–49; Francis A. Sampson, "Glimpses of Old Missouri by Explorers and Travelers," *Missouri Historical Review* 1 (July 1907): 247–67; J. Thomas Scharf, *History of St. Louis City and County*, 2 vols. (Philadelphia: Louis H. Everts & Co., 1883), 2: 1091–93.

[5] *Niles' Register*, August 8, 1835; Harvey Reid, *Thomas Cox* (Iowa City: State Historical Society of Iowa, 1900), pp. 122–67; Kent and Margaret Lighty, *Shanty-Boat* (New York: Century Co., 1930); H. R. Howard, *The History of Virgil A. Stewart* (New York: Harper & Bros., 1836), and his *Life and Adventures of Henry Thomas, the Western Burgular and Murderer, and the Thrilling Narrative of Mrs. Whipple and Jesse Strang* (Philadelphia: T. B. Peterson, 1848); Lester B. Shippee, ed., *Bishop Whipple's Southern Diary, 1843–1844* (Minneapolis: University of Minnesota Press, 1937), p. 128; Edward Bonney, *The Banditti of the Prairies*, ed. Philip D. Jordan (Norman: University of Oklahoma Press, 1963); Juanita Brooks, ed., *On the Mormon Frontier: The Diary of Hosea Stout*, 2 vols. (Salt Lake City: University of Utah Press, 1964); John Ely Briggs, "Pioneer Gangsters," *Palimpsest* 21 (March 1940): 73–90; James C. Parish, "White Beans for Hanging," ibid. 1 (July 1920): 9–28; J. W. Murphy, *Outlaws of the Fox River Country: A Tale of the Whiteford and Spencer Murders* (Hannibal, Mo.: Hannibal Printing Co., 1882); Kahoka Gazette-Herald, *The Trial of Bill Young, the Accused of Murdering the Spencer Family* (Kahoka, Mo.: Kahoka Gazette-Herald, 1965); John L. Harr, "Law and Lawlessness in the Lower

$37,000 in September, 1831, and a few months later a passenger on the *Peruvian* was robbed of a trunk containing $2,500. Such thefts could be multiplied many times over. St. Louis newspapers, as the decades advanced, regularly reported steamboat robberies. Thus, on June 1, 1845, a passenger aboard the *White Cloud* was robbed of $300, and nine days later a judge on board the *Di Vernon* had $5,000 in gold lifted. "Our city," said the *St. Louis Reveille*, "was never so infested with scoundrels as at the present time."[6] Robbery and piracy continued after the Civil War. In 1878, for example, James Coyle who secreted plunder on Ward's Island was shot and seriously wounded before capture by a sheriff's posse.[7]

All types and conditions of men broke the law. Gentlemen of quality gambled, duelled, and frequented houses of ill-fame. The Westerner was no different from his Yankee cousin of the East. Tanners, curriers, mechanists, masons, and riggers marched in Satan's legions with cartmen, dock workers, diggers, stage drivers, and clerks. A comparison of the trades or occupations of criminals in New York City with those along the Mississippi River in the 1830s shows little variation.[8] The vagabond, regardless of age, was a vagabond wherever found. Except for dress and speech, he might have come fleeing straight from England's vagabond act of 1572 or from Bridewell's where gathered "the bawd, the rogue, and whore." If the vagrant were a juvenile, he disturbed the peace in the same manner whether he lived in the East or on the Middle Border, for delinquency on the part of the young was a social problem everywhere.[9]

St. Louis, Louisville, and Cincinnati, during the 1840s, were watersheds for truant, runaway lads of the Mississippi Valley. These young scoundrels hired on boats as waiters and cabin boys for the specific purpose of stealing from passengers. Up and down the river, said the *St. Louis Daily Reveille* on February 4, 1848, "hundreds of youth are

---

Mississippi Valley, 1815–1860," *Northwest Missouri State College Studies* 19 (June 1, 1955):51–70.

[6] *New York Evening Post*, October 1, 1831; *New Orleans Bee*, April 5, 1831; *St. Louis Daily Reveille*, May 23, 29, June 25, September 11, October 1, 1844; March 20, June 1, 29, 1845; May 5, 17, June 24, October 6, December 13, 1846. Other papers, up and down the river, reported similar incidents.

[7] *Quincy Weekly Whig*, April 18, 1878.

[8] See, for example, *New York Evening Post*, March 24, April 12, December 30, 1830; May 26, June 23, 1831; September 27, 1832; also, January 18, April 16, May 11, 1830; August 6, 1831; February 27, 1832.

[9] Ibid., April 24, 1830; February 14, May 9, 1831; July 19, 1832.

roaming through these cities, without parental control, and becoming versed in every vice which leads to degradation and vice." They appeared in court clothed in rags and with bare feet and they ranged in age from six years well into the teens.[10] J. S. Buckingham, like other English travelers, criticized American youth, saying they were untaught by precept or example, lacked parental control, and, as a result, "riot in unrestrained career." [11]

From the close of the Mexican War until well past the Civil War, young hoodlums swelled a growing army of tramps. These wayfarers, a breed of jungle cat, commandeered freight trains, disrupted railroad traffic, frightened housewives, and engaged in all manner of pillage and petty crime with now and then a foray into assault and murder. Local police and county sheriffs feared them and governors not only called the people to watchfulness but also dispatched arms to be used against them.[12]

Ladies of easy virtue, like tramps, followed advancing frontiers. Bret Harte's Cherokee Sal operated either individually or as a loose corporation throughout the Middle Border. During 1858, deprived lumberjacks sprung from the St. Anthony, Minnesota, jail a favorite girl known only as "the Norwegian." A few days later irate citizens marched to Lumber Joe's emporium and then on to Water's house to expel several "soiled doves" and to remove furniture.[13]

Of all river communities, New Orleans and St. Louis were the most vice ridden. Records of the St. Louis Criminal Court, for the 1840s and 1850s, list a monotonous recital of cases involving disorderly and bawdy houses. Now and again, one catches in newspapers a brief, but illuminating, glimpse of energetic entrepreneurs who occupied cribs,

[10] *St. Louis Daily Reveille*, April 21, September 12, 1846; August 22, 29, 1847; February 4, May 24, June 14, August 30, 1848.

[11] J. S. Buckingham, *The Eastern and Western States of America*, 3 vols. (London: Fisher, Son & Co., 1842), 2:81.

[12] *Keokuk Daily Constitution*, April 2, 1879; also June 22, 25, July 7, 21, 1878; July 20, 1879.

[13] William L. Sanger, *The History of Prostitution* (New York: Harper & Brothers, 1858); *Minnesota Republican* (St. Anthony), July 9, 23, 1858; for a foreign traveler's account of New York's "nymphs of the pave," see Alexander Majoribanks, *Travels in South and North America* (London: Simpkin, Marshall, & Co., 1853), pp. 404–5; also Ward Stafford, *New Missionary Field: A Report to the Female Missionary Society for the Poor* (New York: J. Seymour, 1817), pp. 13–15; for New Orleans, see *New Orleans Picayune*, September 26, 1840, quoted in E. Merton Coulter, ed., *The Other Half of Old New Orleans* (Baton Rouge: Louisiana State University Press, 1939), p. 30.

rooms, and houses that were not homes. A group of four drove in a cab to St. Louis' Third Street to quarrel, fight, and hallo to such a degree they promptly were arrested.[14] During 1871, 2,684 prostitutes were arrested. There then were in St. Louis 136 bawdy houses, 6 assignation houses, and 6 keepers of single rooms. An ordinance of March 31, 1872, required the registration of prostitutes living in single rooms, so that they would be "within reach of the police and the Medical Examiners at all times."[15]

The tenth federal census of 1880 attempted to enumerate houses of ill-fame in cities of 5,000 or more inhabitants. New Orleans reported 365; St. Paul, seven; Minneapolis, four; Winona, Minnesota, three; Muscatine and Keokuk, Iowa, five and four respectively; and Rock Island, Illinois, two. St. Louis made no return. Indeed, so many communities either listed no houses at all or refused to make a return that a census official wrote, "If these towns are as virtuous as they claim to be they are indeed fortunate; if not, the police are blind."[16]

When, in 1891, Belle Breezing inaugurated in Lexington, Kentucky, what has been described as the most orderly of disorderly houses, she imported girls—some wearing sorority badges—from Memphis, Nashville, Cincinnati, Louisville, and St. Louis. Belle Breezing, of course, was the inspiration for the character Belle Watling, Margaret Mitchell's madame in *Gone With the Wind*. The real Belle left a unique historical document—a journal listing in detail specific items relating to her business. When Belle died, she was buried under a granite shaft upon which is inscribed "Blessed be the pure in heart."[17]

The defiance of social mores was not alone in blemishing the Middle Border and earning it a reputation as a wildly lawless area. Counterfeiting, theft, vagrancy, and prostitution, although threats to the economic and social structure, generally did not result in bloodletting.

[14] *St. Louis Daily Reveille*, January 5, February 6, 10, April 9, May 5, July 15, 1850.

[15] St. Louis City Council, *Mayor's Message with Accompanying Documents* (St. Louis: St. Louis Times Co., 1872), pp. 38, 94–96.

[16] Frederick H. Wines, *Report on the Defective, Dependent, and Delinquent Classes . . . as Returned to the Tenth Census . . . June, 1880* (Washington: G.P.O., 1880), p. liv, table 136; for a discussion of prostitution in Minnesota, 1870–1948, see Philip D. Jordan, *The People's Health* (St. Paul: Minnesota Historical Society, 1953); for the Northwest Territory, see R. Carlyle Buley, *The Old Northwest: Pioneer Period, 1815–1840*, 2 vols. (Indianapolis: Indiana Historical Society, 1950), 1:377; for the post-Civil War period in Ohio, see Jordan, *Ohio Comes of Age, 1873–1900* (Columbus: Ohio State Archaeological and Historical Society, 1943), pp. 192, 194, 197, 257–58.

[17] William H. Townsend, *The Most Orderly of Disorderly Houses* (Lexington: Privately Printed, 1966); for obituary, see *Time* 36 (August 26, 1940):56.

Duelling, although illegal in many states, was tolerated, if not approved. Gambling, like tippling, brought no particular censure if the play was honest and if professional card sharks did not disturb the peace over much. The one crime in the bloodless category that instantly provoked immediate hostile reaction was grave robbing. But body snatching by medical students and physicians turned resurrectionists was not confined to the Mississippi Valley. It followed the frontier from East to West.[18]

What agitated both natives and foreigners were acts of violence—murder, lynching, mob rule. It was the taking of the law into one's own hands, the administration of justice by rule of thumb, the contempt of legal procedure. Such actions and attitudes were no more prevalent on the Middle Border than they had been in earlier settled areas or as they were to be in later ones. It is true, of course, that recurrent crime waves marked all areas. Their causes were many and varied. During the 1830s mobs of New Yorkers rioted because they disliked an ordinance restricting hogs running loose on the streets and because anti-Jacksonians thought it proper to destroy ballot boxes; Philadelphia citizens rioted because they opposed an election; New Bedford men rioted because they wished to destroy two tenement whore houses; Hudson inhabitants rioted because they disagreed with the teachings of a Methodist minister. In Charlestown and Philadelphia and along the Baltimore and Washington Railroad, mobs rioted for so many reasons that state governments considered passing laws to prevent such action. Citizens of the nation's capital patrolled streets in 1835 to stop mob action. Rioting resulting in mob law most certainly was not uniquely characteristic of the Middle Border or of the Old South.[19]

[18] "Scalpel and Science," *MD* 10 (July 1966):205–15; A. G. Ross, "The Fine Art of Body Snatching," *Medical Economics* 21 (March 1944): 64–68, 103, 107, 109; "Scenes in a Medical Student's Life—Resurrectionizing," *Scalpel* 7 (April 1855):93–100; *Cincinnati Enquirer*, May 31, 1878; June 1–4, 1867; Scharf, *History of St. Louis City and County*, 2: 1835–36; *Gate City* (Keokuk, Iowa), February 27, October 11, November 5, 1878.

[19] *New York Evening Post*, July 2, October 15, 23, 1830; October 28, 1831; November 8, 1832; *Washington Daily National Intelligencer*, March 27, 1835. Clement Eaton makes clear that mob violence was not a sectional phenomenon in his "Mob Violence in the Old South," *Mississippi Valley Historical Review* 29 (December 1942):351–70. See also Wayne Gard, *Frontier Justice* (Norman: University of Oklahoma Press, 1949); Hubert H. Bancroft, *Popular Tribunals* (San Francisco: History Co., 1887); James M. Hiatt, *Murder and Mob Law in Indiana* (Indianapolis: Indianapolis Printing & Publishing House, 1872); *The Facts in the Case of the Horrible Murder of Little Myrtle Vance and Its Fearful Expiation at Paris, Texas, Feb. 1, 1893 . . .*

Among the many riots and mob actions in river communities from St. Paul to New Orleans were: the medical college riot and the election riot of 1844 in St. Louis; the riot between fire fighters and citizens in 1849 in St. Louis; the nativist election riot of 1852 in St. Louis and the election riot of 1852 in St. Louis in which ten persons were killed and about thirty wounded; the railroad riot of 1877 in St. Louis.[20] Violent anti-gambling riots, resulting in loss of life, occurred in Vicksburg, Natchez, Louisville, Mobile, and New Orleans in 1835.[21] A particularly nauseating act was the burning to death by a mob of a live Negro in St. Louis in 1836, an event which foreign travelers to America frequently cited to demonstrate that this nation was, indeed, lawless.[22]

A twenty-eight-year-old Lincoln, addressing the Young Men's Lyceum in Springfield, Illinois, in 1838, described the growing disregard for law which pervaded the country. He spoke of the hanging of the Vicksburg gamblers and the burning of the St. Louis Negro. "Accounts of outrages committed by mobs," he said, "form the every-day news of the times. They have pervaded the country from New England to Louisiana. . . . Whatever then their cause may be, it is common to the whole country."[23]

Hezekiah Niles, in his *Register*, wrote even more pungently and bitterly. He said he had in one week clipped more than five hundred articles concerning violent crime. "Society," wrote Niles, "seems everywhere unhinged, and the demon of 'blood and slaughter' has been let loose upon us." He spoke of kidnappings and manstealing in relation to slave uprisings. He talked of "the proscription and prosecution of gamblers, with mobs growing out of local matters—and a great collection of acts of violence of a private, or personal nature, ending in death." He exclaimed that "we have executions and murders, and riots

---

(Paris: P. L. James, 1893); Duluth Publishing Company, *Mob Violence, A Photographic Review and Descriptive Account of the Appalling Lynching of Three Negroes by a Revengeful Mob* . . . (Duluth: Duluth Publishing Co., 1920); Thomas J. Dimsdale, *The Vigilantes of Montana* . . . (Virginia City, Mont.: D. W. Tilton, 1882); George F. Robeson, "Justice in Early Iowa," *Palimpsest* 5 (March 1924): pp. 102–13.

[20] Scharf, *History of St. Louis City and County*, 2: 1835–49.

[21] *Washington Daily National Intelligencer*, July 25, 29, August 3, 5, 6, November 21, 1835; *Niles' Register*, July 25, August 1, 8, 22, November 21, 1835; Captain Frederick Marryat, *A Diary in America*, 3 vols. (London: Longman, Orme, Brown, Green, & Longmans, 1839), 3:240–52.

[22] Scharf, *History of St. Louis City and County*, 2:1824–25; *Niles' Register*, June 4, 1836; Buckingham, *The Eastern and Western States*, 3:196–97; Marryat, *Diary*, 3:238–40.

[23] John C. Nicolay and John Hay, eds., *Complete Works of Abraham Lincoln*, new and rev. ed. (New York: Francis D. Randy Co., 1905), 1:37–44.

to the utmost limits of the union. The character of our countrymen seems suddenly changed, and thousands interpret the law in their own way . . . guided apparently only by their own will." [24]

Most rural communities and urban centers deplored prevailing lawlessness and licentiousness and attempted, in bungling fashion, corrective measures. A major difficulty, of course, in cities was the poorly organized and inept night watch which attempted to patrol streets and to maintain a semblance of order before police departments, as we know them, existed. The idea of the watch was imported directly from England, where it operated not too well in London in the eighteenth century before the London Police System was established in 1829. A perceptive student commented upon the watch of New York City: "And look at their style of dress; some with hats, some with caps, some with coats like Joseph's of old, parti-colored. If they were mustered together, they would look like Falstaff's Regiment." [25]

Cincinnati established a short-lived night watch in 1806, but an organized police force was not to come for decades. St. Louis did not have a regular force in 1830. Boston ended a watch system in 1854. New Orleans organized its force under a single head in 1854. Chicago did not maintain a satisfactory force until 1861. Law enforcement in St. Anthony, Minnesota, began with the election of a constable and the building of a watch-house in 1855, and Minneapolis established a police force in 1872. The police badge possibly came into existence in New York City about 1844 when it was stipulated that every member of the watch "shall wear a medal inside his clothes, suspended around his neck, both day and night when on duty, and shall expose the same when about restoring peace, or on making an arrest, or when performing any duty of that kind." [26]

[24] *Niles' Register*, September 5, November 28, 1835; January 30, 1836; *New Orleans Bee*, quoted in *Washington Daily National Intelligencer*, August 6, 1835; *New Orleans Bee*, July 1, 1830.

[25] J. W. Gerard, *London and New York: Their Police and Crime* (New York: William C. Bryant & Co., 1853), pp. 6, 17–18.

[26] Ibid. For an editorial on the inefficiency of the Philadelphia police, see the *Public Ledger*, August 11, 1836; Richard C. Wade, *The Urban Frontier: The Rise of Western Cities, 1790–1830* (Cambridge: Harvard University Press, 1959), pp. 89, 220; Bessie L. Pierce, *History of Chicago, 1848–1871*, 2 vols. (New York: Knopf, 1940), 2:310; A. E. Costell, *History of the Fire and Police Departments of Minneapolis* (Minneapolis: Relief Association Publishing Co., 1890), pp. 236, 248–49; *St. Louis Daily Reveille*, May 10, June 5, 1846; October 13, 1847; May 10, June 24, September 27, October 1, 21, 1848; see also Philip D. Jordan, "The Stranger Looks at the

The county sheriff system, again having its roots in England, seldom functioned effectually during the middle decades. All too frequently the sheriff was totally ignorant of police methods of his day and almost always he was subjected to the whims of local politics. The sheriff simply was not equipped to deal satisfactorily with crime at a time when distances were long and communication was slow. On every hand the nation was undergoing dramatically rapid growth, stretching itself with seven-league boots across the face of the land. Patterns of social conduct and personal behavior were in flux. A system of state and private banks stimulated counterfeiting. Slavery provided excuses to break the law. Too many individuals felt themselves obligated to a higher law—a law superior to criminal codes.

A defense attorney in the famous trial of the Louisville Galt House murder of 1839 summarized this concept of the higher law:

Sirs, there are sins against individuals as well as sins against heaven, which can only be expiated by blood—and *the law of Kentucky* is, that the man who is attempted to be cowhided, not only may, but must, if by any possibility he can, *at the time*, kill the man who attempts thus to degrade him. I do not refer to a law of Kentucky, enacted by the Legislature of the State; I mean a law paramount to any enacted by the Kentucky Legislature, a law that emanates from the *hearts* of the people of Kentucky, and is sanctioned by their *heads*—a law that is promulgated in the *os ad coelum* of every Kentuckian, and proclaimed in the sparkling of every eye of *both* sexes and *all* ages—a law, the force of which, every one feels, the import of which every one perceives by intuition. It is the law of *Kentucky instinct*— none are so ignorant as not to know this law; few are so dastardly as to deny its injunction.[27]

If such a concept did not stimulate crime, it did little to deter it. Yet other factors accounted, at least in part, for increase in lawlessness. Among these were economic unrest as evidenced by the panics of 1837 and 1857, actual or alleged Mormon activities, the character and disposition of immigrant groups, and a nativist, anti-foreign prejudice.

Yankee," in Henry Steele Commager, ed., *Immigration and American History* (Minneapolis: University of Minnesota Press, 1961), p. 60.

[27] Buckingham, *The Eastern and Western States*, 3:31–33; T. Egerton Browne, *Trial of Judge Wilkinson, Dr. Wilkinson, and Mr. Murdaugh, on Indictments for the Murder of John Rothwell and Alexander H. Meeks* ... (Louisville: T. E. Browne & Co., 1839); A. B. Carlton, *The Law of Homicide Together with the Trial for Murder of Judge Wilkinson, Dr. Wilkinson, and Mr. Murdaugh* ... (Cincinnati: Robert Clarke & Co., 1882).

Slavery and slave uprisings certainly stimulated lynchings. Both the Mexican and Civil Wars were followed by crime waves. Epidemic disease throughout the Middle Border was a contributing factor. Finally, it is not unreasonable to suggest that crime begets crime, that lawlessness is contagious. The Nativist viewpoint was put succinctly in *Harper's Magazine:* "The extraordinary number of immigrants who have landed in our country . . . begins to produce the effect upon our criminal statistics which was to be apprehended." [28]

It is a fact that shortly after the first steamboat of troops returned on February 23, 1848, from the Mexican War that crime increased greatly. "Our city," wrote an editor, "is literally at the mercy of the swarms of criminals—they have found the weakness of the police." Ten months later—in October—the *St. Louis Daily Reveille* said categorically that veterans were the first cause of crime's upturn. After the Civil War the crime rate increased in Massachusetts, New York, Ohio, and Michigan and also throughout the Middle Border. One example must suffice: "Of the 126 convicts in the Kansas State Penitentiary in 1867, 98 served a full term in the Union Army and 6 in the rebel army." [29]

"The condition of the social relations of this country within the past five years," said the report of the Eastern Penitentiary of Pennsylvania, "has had a very marked effect on the character of a large number of our people. Growing out of this condition, familiarity with deeds of violence to persons and property has been produced. . . . It has become a cause of crime." [30] It was estimated in 1867 that nearly 70 per cent of men committed to penal institutions had seen service and that, in the total prison population, nearly half the inmates were veterans.[31] Confederate veterans, some of whom were police officers, played a major role in the

[28] "Progress of Crime," *Harper's New Monthly Magazine* 3 (September 1851):557; "Editor's Table," ibid. 6 (December 1852):125–28.

[29] *St. Louis Daily Reveille*, February 23, May 12, October 21, 1848; Edith Abbott, "The Civil War and the Crime Wave of 1865–70," *Social Service Review* 1 (June 1927):212–34.

[30] Ibid., p. 228.

[31] Ibid., E. C. Wines and Theodore D. Dwight, "The Reformation of Prison: Discipline," *North American Review* 105 (October 1867):580–81; "American Prisons," ibid. 103 (October 1866):383–412; see also Betty B. Rosenbaum, "The Relationship Between War and Crime in the United States," *Journal of Criminal Law and Criminology* 30 (January–February 1940):722–40; Paul Dolan, "The Rise of Crime in the Period 1830–1860," ibid., 30 (March–April 1940), 857–64; *St. Louis Daily Reveille*, November 2, 1848: "War Veterans: License, recklessness and crime—these are the demoralizing attendants upon war, conduct it as we may; and that the Mexican War have let loose these evils upon society is but too plain."

ghastly New Orleans riot of 1866. A witness testified before a congressional hearing that officers shouted, "We have fought for four years these God damned Yankees and sons of bitches in the field and now we will fight them in the city."[32]

Climate and disease also influence crime. Vagrants and tramps laid low, hibernating in flop houses and finding their daily bread in soup lines during the dark, cold months. When spring came and the grass was up, they, once again, became peripatetic. And when ice closed the Upper River, light-fingered cabin boys and burly roustabouts had slight opportunity to pick pockets or fights. Yet the winter season generally witnessed an increase in urban crime. During the days when temperature fell and snow mantled the North Country, the lawless frequently migrated with the birds to warmer climates. The hot months in the South saw those who lived by their wits and muscle forsake the Lower River to pursue their roguery in cooler, more congenial climate. In other words, there was a regular, seasonal pattern of criminal migration.[33]

The southern states of the Middle Border had long been ravaged by one epidemic disease after another—smallpox, yellow fever, typhoid, and most deadly of all, the dreaded Asiatic cholera. Men of every class fled these plagues. The criminally inclined scurried to the safety of upriver communities, there to resume their predatory practices. Editors

[32] For participation of Confederate veterans, see U.S., Congress, House, Select Committee, *Report on the New Orleans Riots*, 39th Cong., 2d Sess., H. Rept. 16, pp. 19, 32, 67, 199.

[33] *St. Louis Daily Reveille*, October 2, 1849: "This is about the time when the light-fingered fraternity, who infest our city during the summer months, commence their preparations to emigrate south." On March 26, 1850, the *Reveille* said, "With the return of warm weather our city is visited with the return of our efficient corps of the *gens de industrie*. Among them are John Hawkins, alias John Hall, just out of the workhouse . . . Marcus Bennett, a daring and skilled hotel thief; Butcher Fred, and many more." For Minnesota, see John Stevens, *Personal Recollections of Minnesota and Its People, and Early History of Minneapolis* (Minneapolis: Tribune Job Printing Co., 1890), p. 269: ". . . in these early days [1854], the prosperous cities away up north were infested, during the summer, with persons known in New Orleans as wharf-rats, who came up the Mississippi early in the spring and returned late in the fall"; also *Minneapolis Daily Tribune*, August 15, 1782; "From a reliable police source, we learn that there is now in Minneapolis a larger number of thieves, burglars, and pickpockets than has ever before cursed the city. They are most of them from New Orleans and other large Southern cities, and they have probably followed in the wake of numerous wealthy gentlemen and their families from the South. . . . Our people should look well to securing their doors and windows, and be prepared with powder and ball for cases of emergency"; ibid., March 23, 1875.

stated frequently and bluntly that epidemics in New Orleans and other southern cities forced criminals to move north.[34] Yet not even the cholera, striking St. Louis with great force in 1849, halted crime, although the rate did fall off. Once the epidemic had worked its will, the crime pattern returned to normal.[35]

The scholar who seeks to bring into focus patterns of law and lawlessness should be cautious. He realizes early in the search that he must not put faith or trust in nineteenth-century criminal "statistics." There were none until well past the turn of the century. In addition, county court records were lost or destroyed; municipal archives were poorly kept and are incomplete; reports of police chiefs tend to favor the department; federal and state records are inconsistent with themselves and with one another. Published stories of illegal activities vary in detail from one newspaper to another, and reporters whose daily beat included courts and jails at times published items based more upon imagination than fact. Foreign travelers, upon occasion, were less than accurate, objective observers of the American scene. But, above all else, it must constantly be borne in mind that there existed no science of statistics such as is relied upon today.[36] Yet, despite all difficulties with evidence and source, it is possible to reach plausible conclusions.

[34] Ibid., October 21, 1848; for general accounts of disease and epidemics, see John Duffy, ed., *The Rudolph Matas History of Medicine in Louisiana* (Baton Rouge: Louisiana State University Press, 1958), vol. 1; Lucius H. Zeuch, comp., *History of Medical Practice in Illinois* (Chicago: Book Press, 1927), vol. 1; J. S. Chambers, *The Conquest of Cholera* (New York: Macmillan, 1938); Scharf, *History of St. Louis City and County*, 1:1574–83; for the spread of disease upriver, see for example, *Burlington Tri-Weekly Telegraph*, July 6, 9, 13, 1850; *Burlington Hawk-Eye*, July 25, August 1, 22, 1850; *Minnesota Pioneer* (St. Paul), June 7, August 23, 1849; *Stillwater Messenger*, December 14, 1858.

[35] The total number of cases to be tried in the criminal court in St. Louis was unusually high in January, 1850; see *St. Louis Daily Reveille*, January 5, 1850, and January 6, February 2, 6, 19, May 5, June 11, July 4, 1850.

[36] Donald R. Taft, *Criminology: A Cultural Interpretation* (New York: Macmillan, 1950), chap. 2; Frederick H. Wines, "Report on Crime, Pauperism, and Benevolence in the United States," in U.S., Bureau of the Census, *Eleventh Census of the United States: 1890*, vol. 3, pt. 1, p. 126: "The increase in the number of prisoners during the last 40 years has been more apparent than real, owing to the very imperfect enumeration of the prison population prior to 1880"; E. H. Sutherland and C. C. Van Vechten, Jr., "The Reliability of Criminal Statistics," *Journal of Criminal Law and Criminology* 25 (May–June 1934): 10–20; for the gathering of statistics by both the states and the federal government, see Louis N. Robinson, *History and Organization of Criminal Statistics in the United States* (Boston: Houghton, Mifflin, 1911).

Obviously, a few citizens were criminals all of the time, more were lawless some of the time, and most were law abiding all of the time. The core of society, as a pioneer editor in the Black Hills pointed out, was sound and wholesome, "composed as it was of fine men and women who stood for personal and civic virtue against the surge of wickedness, and whose influence was the leaven that eventually brought regeneration." [37] Satisfying as is this affirmation, it still fails to explain why crime flourished to the degree it did; how it perpetuated itself so effectively from one frontier line to another; why it, like disease, periodically assumed epidemic and even pandemic proportions; and how concepts of lawlessness and law enforcement affected and conditioned the American character. It does not explain how the crime rate in proportion to population has consistently been higher than in any country of Western Europe. On the other hand, it must not be assumed that sin, vice, and illegal force were indigenous either to the American experience or to the white race. Prostitution, gambling, theft, and murder are as old as man. Street gangs terrorized Roman streets during the Late Republic. [38]

The point to be emphasized is that the United States inherited vice and crime from the Old World and passed them and their techniques successively from one settlement line to another. Although criminal categories did not change, the methods, instruments, and weapons altered. Thus the grave robber's curved hook replaced the shovel; the Bowie knife superceded the dirk; the revolving pistol superceded the single-shot gun; new, mechanical processes made obsolete the crude hand tools of the forger and counterfeiter. But theft is theft, murder is murder, and bogus money is counterfeit regardless of the tools used. The spirit of a mob is the mob spirit everywhere. It makes slight difference whether a culprit's wrists are bound with a twist of vine, a piece of hemp, a length of lariat, or a pair of case-hardened, steel handcuffs. Stripped to basic motives, warfare between Chippewa and Sioux for hunting rights or between settler and miner in Minnesota is essentially the same as warfare between cattleman and sheepherder or between California gold digger and claim jumper. Anti-horse-thief associations in Missouri and Montana operated on the same principles.

[37] Richard B. Hughes, *Pioneer Years in the Black Hills* (Glendale, Calif.: Arthur H. Clark Co., 1957), pp. 199–200; for a physician's experiences in Deadwood, see F. S. Howe, "Deadwood Doctor," *South Dakota Journal of Medicine* 19 (July 1966): 36–39; 19 (November 1966): 57–58; 19 (December 1966): 47–50.

[38] The M.A. thesis by Gerald E. Kadish at the University of Chicago in 1962 was an account of Roman street gangs in the period of the Late Republic.

A man's neck broke with the same snap whether he was lynched in New England, the South, or the West.

Nothing in the evidence indicates that the national crime pattern was anything else than monotonous repetition the length and breadth of the nation. When it varied, it differed only in techniques and degree. These were less than is generally believed. Tombstone was not the only town too tough to die.[39] A score or more of towns far to the east and north of Tombstone had been too tough to die. The crimes of the "wild" Far West were no more abundant, no more dramatic than were the saloon brawls, the shootings and stabbings and murders and lynchings and riots which occurred elsewhere. Those who lived outside the law in the turbulent, passionate, reckless, uncouth, hell-for-leather Far West were no less dipped in red—costume, language, bravado— than were ruffians and desperados of the cotton and corn belts, of the highlands and lowlands, of the rural areas and of the cities. Indeed, the crime rate of the land of the rustler and the cowboy possibly was lower than it was in regions which always have been considered as settled down, civilized, and law abiding.

[39] Douglas D. Martin, *Tombstone's Epitaph* (Albuquerque: University of New Mexico Press, 1951).

CHAPTER EIGHT

"Come Back Soon, Honey!"

She was sloppy and slovenly, and she was voluptuous and lovely. She was both lady and slut. She was of all ages and colors and of every nationality. Her body was her stock in trade, and she bartered it and rented it and sold it for baubles or drink or dubious prestige. But most of all, she preferred cash—two bits in a cheap crib, two dollars in a bawdy house, and any amount from twenty to a hundred dollars if she were fortunate enough to operate in an elite and exclusive carriage establishment, where soft music soothed and champagne bubbled in tall-stemmed goblets.

Ubiquitous throughout the United States, she traced her lineage, back through the genealogy of sin, to the ancient world where sisters now long forgotten pandered to lust. Ladies of the evening in the United States were known by many names. They were called street-walkers, soiled doves, nymphs of the pavements, joy Elsies, chippies, hustlers, floosies, knock-around broads, biscuits, and, with Anglo-Saxon bluntness, harlots and whores.[1] She was part of the free-enter-

---

[1] Nyle H. Miller and Joseph W. Snell, *Great Gunfighters of the Kansas Cowtowns, 1867–1886* (Lincoln: University of Nebraska Press, 1963), pp. 12–13: "An interesting side study connected with this profession [prostitution] involves the names by which frontiersmen referred to the ladies in question. For the benefit of any future historian inclined to pursue research down these avenues (or alleys) here are a few samples: nymphs du prairie, nymphs du pave, fair Docinas (Dulcineas?), girls of the night, girls of the period, soiled doves, fancies, calico queens, painted cats, scarlet ladies, demi modes. And of course there were the more mundane appellations such as laundress, dancehall girl, and waitress by which many were shown on census records." See also Forbes Parkhill, *Wildest of the West* (New York: Henry Holt & Co., 1951), pp. 13–14, for brides of the multitude and sporting lady. Also Ronald D. Miller, *Shady Ladies of the West* (Los Angeles: Westernlore Press, 1964), pp. 29, 31 for Yankedos and girls of the cantinas, names given to mestizo or Indian girls who, during the Mexican War, lived with American soldiers. Miller, in his glossary, lists the following: bawd, broad, celestial female (Chinese prostitute), Chilena (Spanish

Spanish

115

prise system, and, in the opinion of a good many, filled as much of a need as did the local merchant or barber. Upon occasion, her sense of values and her ethical standards were no better or worse than those of lawyers, bankers, and doctors.

A strange aspect of the conquest of the Union by the prostitute is that, for some unaccountable reason—perhaps local pride—each geographic region and each frontier believed its painted cats to be different from their sisters in other portions of the country. Thus, the brides of the multitude of, say, San Francisco's Barbary coast, were thought wilder than those of Kansas cowtowns, and those of Kansas cowtowns more abandoned than those of the French quarter of wicked New Orleans, and those of New Orleans more colorful and more steeped in sin than those of Chicago, Philadelphia, or New York. No one seems to give a hoot about a calico queen in any section of the country other than his own.

The result of such parochial astigmatism has been to localize what, in reality, was a standardized national product and to distort a nation-wide public service into a series of regional specialities. Although the saga of the western and eastern ladies of the evening has been spun into what now is almost legend, the chronicle of the nymphs in negligee of the Middle Border has been largely neglected. This immense area—the heartland of America—embraces not only the states bordering both banks of the Mississippi River from St. Paul, Minnesota, south to New Orleans, but also the territory which fans inland from the river and its tributaries. There, as elsewhere, the prostitute made an impact upon the law, and the law made an impact upon the prostitute. The result, for a good many decades, was a stand-off, for morality by legislation seldom proved as effective as its champions wished. The curbing of the chippie was no exception. Little, if any, attention has been paid to the nature of this law, yet it is difficult to understand the legal status of those girls with beckoning eye in the Far West unless one knows that western codes

---

or mestizo prostitute), Chola (Spanish or Mexican girl of loose morals), Cyprian, fairy belle, hooker, Kate, kimono girl, and strange woman. Other names are given in Vern L. Bullough, *The History of Prostitution* (New Hyde Park, N.Y.: University Books, 1964), pp. 287–91, and in Hyman E. Goldin, ed., *Dictionary of American Underworld Lingo* (New York: Twayne Publishers, 1950). Also, Mitford M. Mathews, ed., *Dictionary of Americanisms on Historical Principles*, 2 vols. (Chicago: University of Chicago Press, 1951). Well worth reading is Joseph W. Snell, *Painted Ladies of the Cowtown Frontier* (Kansas City: Kansas City Posse of the Westerners, 1965), an essay of only twenty-four pages, but each page is helpful.

were aped from those of the Middle West, and those of the Middle West followed the pattern of codes drawn by eastern states, which, in turn, reflected colonial legislation.

From the nation's founding, state statutes and local regulations and ordinances sought to create and protect public morality. Indeed, the colonial period witnessed attempts, again without conspicuous success, to define and enforce moral codes. But the colonial American, despite what is generally believed, was no saint, for licentiousness was not unknown throughout the English settlements.[2] Courts were busy not only in New England but also in such areas as Virginia and South Carolina.[3]

Those men and women, some good and others bad, from both Yankeeland and southern states, who poured soon after the War of 1812 into the great trough of the Middle Border, came by various routes. They floated down the Ohio River, drove wagons and carts over the National Road, and took passage on Erie Canal boats. Some sank roots in the Middle West, but others, nagged by itching feet, tarried a brief spell and then joined movers headed for new frontiers in the Southwest and Far West. Newcomers carried with them not only ax and hoe but also common sense and practicality.

A wheat field, commented a shrewd observer, was more pleasing to their taste than a flower garden, and a well-plowed field more satisfactory to their eye than the most exquisite painting of a Raphael or a Claude. He thought westerners would prefer seeing a gristmill operating on their own land than the sight of the sculptured marble of the Venus or the Apollo.[4] They, upon occasion, refused to permit idealism to override materialism. Their way of life did not necessarily reflect the Ten Commandments nor did it mirror the idealized statutes they wrote into their legal codes, but this is only to say that almost always a gap exists between law as it is written and law as it is obeyed and enforced. Rudyard

[2] See, for example, "The Puritans and Sex," *New England Quarterly* 15 (December 1942): 591–607; George A. Billias, ed., *Law and Authority in Colonial America* (Barre, Mass.: Barre Publishers, 1965).

[3] See, for example, Hugh F. Rankin, "Criminal Trial Proceedings in the General Court of Colonial Virginia," *Virginia Magazine of History and Biography* 72 (January 1964): 50–74; Jack K. Williams, "Catching the Criminal in Nineteenth Century South Carolina," *Journal of Criminal Law and Criminology* 46 (July 1955): 264–71; Williams, "White Lawbreakers in Ante-Bellum South Carolina," *Journal of Southern History* 21 (August 1955): 360–73.

[4] James H. Lanman, "The Progress of the Northwest," *Hunt's Merchants' Magazine* 3 (July 1840): 39.

Kipling sensed this when he wrote that the American had a "cynic devil in his blood,

> That bids him flout the Law he makes,
> That bids him make the Law he flouts."[5]

The American's ambivalent attitude toward the law was based not only upon his utilitarian concept of life, but also upon self-interest and a demand for self-expression. He called the law's majesty to his aid when he needed protection, and he rejected the law when it interfered with or curtailed his activities and pleasures. In short, when purse, property, and person were threatened, the law was a noble handmaiden of justice, but when the law forbade gambling, drinking, and dallying with the girls, it became a tool of oppression. These conflicting views must be comprehended if the role of the prostitute not only throughout the Middle Border but also throughout the nation is to be understood.

Kimono girls, working their way west on the Erie Canal or establishing themselves in Detroit, Michigan, or Louisville, Kentucky, during the 1830s, occupied a curious legal position.[6] Neither the common law of England nor that of the United States regarded prostitution itself as an offense. The profession came into conflict with the law only when "it was associated with street soliciting or the operation of a bawdy house as to be annoying to the passerby. In other words, the test of the offense was the fact of annoyance." A girl could practice her profession legally, if she did not annoy neighbors, residents, or, as indicated, those passing by.[7] It was this fine distinction which gave rise in the United States to segregated "red light" districts, for houses "on the line" were

---

[5] Quoted in R. Carlyle Buley, *The Old Northwest: Pioneer Period, 1815–1840*, 2 vols. (Indianapolis: Indiana Historical Society), 1:367.

[6] For vice on the Erie Canal, see Ronald E. Shaw, *Erie Water West: A History of the Erie Canal, 1792–1854* (Lexington: University of Kentucky Press, 1966), pp. 221, 224–25. On p. 221, the author quotes from the *Rochester Observor*, which contended that for the "prostitution, gambling, and all species of vice practiced on our canals, the 'Big Ditch' should be called the 'Big Ditch of Iniquity.' " Buley, *Old Northwest*, which, in vol. 1, p. 377, quotes the *Detroit Daily Advertiser*, June 16, 1838, and the *Sangamo* (Illinois) *Journal*, August 11, 1832, concerning houses of ill fame. The first recounts the "beastly outrages that are rapidly degrading certain purlieus to the loathsome condition of the Five Points," and the second tells of a mob in Louisville burning two houses occupied by persons of ill fame.

[7] Willoughby C. Waterman, *Prostitution and Its Repression in New York City, 1900–1931* (New York: Columbia University Press, 1932), pp. 11–13.

removed from normal traffic and hence could not annoy righteous citizens. That, anyhow, was the argument. Girls could also be arrested and charged with disorderly conduct or vagrancy.

Vagrancy acts throughout the United States were inherited from English statutes. Their original purpose was to protect the English poor laws against abuse by wandering indigents or by undesirable persons such as palm readers, fortune tellers, minstrels, and jugglers. The Tudor period, 1485–1803, witnessed a series of such acts. Sir William Blackstone, whose *Commentaries* influenced to a great degree American law, said:

> In our own law, all idle persons or vagabonds, whom our ancient statutes describe to be "such as wake on the night and sleep on the day, and haunt customable taverns and alehouses, and routs about, and no man wot from whence they came nor whither they go" are divided into three classes, "idle and disorderly persons, rogues and vagabonds, and incorrigible rogues."

Disorderly persons, in this instance, were termed vagrants.[8]

Both during and after the colonial period legislators aped English vagrancy acts almost to the letter. An act of Massachusetts in 1699, for example, included as vagrants not only those who wandered about the country without means of making a living and fortune tellers, fiddlers, and common brawlers, but also persons wanton and lascivious in either speech or behavior. Georgia's law of 1788 spoke of "divers idle and disorderly persons, having no visible estate or lawful employment" who strolled from county to county, engaged in a disorderly life, and become a "pest to society." By 1819, a Georgia law included as vagrants persons leading an immoral, profligate way of life. A seventeenth-century Virginia act specifically included "whoredom."[9]

[8] Austin Van der Slice, "Elizabethan Houses of Corrections," *Journal of Criminal Law and Criminology* 27 (May–June 1936): 53–54; Arthur C. Hall, *Crime in Its Relation to Social Progress* (New York: Columbia University Press, 1902), p. 212; James F. Stephen, *A History of the Criminal Law of England*, 3 vols. (London: Macmillan & Co., 1883), 1:25; William Blackstone, *Commentaries on the Laws of England*, 2 vols., ed. with introduction and notes by George Sharwood (Philadelphia: J. B. Lippincott & Co., 1872, 1873), vol. 2, bk. 4, p. 169.

[9] General Court, *Charter and General Laws of the Colony and Province of Massachusetts Bay* (Boston: T. B. Wait & Co., 1814), pp. 334–38; General Court, *Laws of the Commonwealth of Massachusetts, 1780–1807*, 3 vols. (Boston: F. T. Buckingham, 1807), 1:411–13, additional acts were passed February 27, 1798, and June 23, 1802; Horatio Marbury and William H. Crawford, *Digest of the Laws of the State of Georgia, from Its Settlement as a British Province, in 1775, to the Session of the*

So all-inclusive were vagrancy laws that ladies of the evening found it difficult, indeed, to escape this sort of net. Unfortunately, vagrancy acts, as legislature after legislature formulated them during the nineteenth century, were so vague and general in nature that town marshals, city police, and county sheriffs far too frequently used the acts to arrest persons whom they only suspected of prostitution. In short, vagrancy laws provided authority to hold suspected persons for investigation when the police could not legally arrest them for other offenses. Such laws, as used from the early national period until today, were employed as a means of clearing streets of undesirable or unsightly persons, of driving such persons out of town, of aiding the police in detaining a suspected person during the investigation of a more serious crime, and of regulating street activities in marginal or slum neighborhoods. Persons caught under vagrancy laws, such as tramps, bums, and prostitutes, were obviously from the lowest economic and social levels.[10]

The very wording of state vagrancy acts underscores the fact that they were, indeed, designed for the underprivileged, and there was little, if any, essential difference between such an act passed by one state and a similar act passed by another. Thus, for example, a vagrancy act of the late nineteenth century in Arizona not only was first cousin to a law of the Tudor period in England but also was close kin to

---

General Assembly in 1800, Inclusive . . . (Savannah: Seymour, Wookhopter & Stebbins, 1802), 568–70; Augustin S. Clayton, *The Office and Duty of a Justice of the Peace, and a Guide to Clerks, Constables, Coroners, Executors, Administrators, Guardians, Sheriffs, Tax-Collectors, and Receivers, and Other Civil Officers, According to the Laws of the State of Georgia* . . . (Milledgeville: S. Grantland, 1819), p. 374. For Virginia, see William W. Hening, ed., *The Statutes-at-Large: Being a Collection of All the Laws of Virginia*, 13 vols. (New York: R. & W. & G. Bartow, 1823), 1:240: Act of March 2, 1642/43: "If any person or persons of what degree or condition soever shall abuse themselves with the high & foule offences of adultery, whoredome or fornication or with the loathsome sinne of drunkennes in the abuse of God's creatures, of those and every those to make a true presentment."

[10] For a discussion of the current use of vagrancy laws, see President's Commission on Law Enforcement and Administration of Justice, *Task Force Report: The Police* (Washington: G.P.O., 1967), p. 187: "Arrests for minor crime, such as vagrancy, disorderly conduct, use of obscene language, loitering, failure to move on, blocking the street or sidewalk, drunkenness, drinking in public, and curfew violations, constitute almost one-half of all the arrests made each year in the United States." Also President's Commission on Law Enforcement and Administration of Justice, *Task Force Reports: The Courts* (Washington: G.P.O., 1967), p. 103, for low economic and social groups. The findings of the several task forces are summarized in President's Commission on Law Enforcement and Administration of Justice, *The Challenge of Crime in a Free Society* (Washington: G.P.O., 1967).

statutes passed by other states within the Union.[11] Differences, if any, usually concerned the nature of punishment.[12] In short, Arizona's vagrancy law was much like that of Nebraska, Nebraska's much like that of Missouri, Missouri's much like that of New Jersey, and New Jersey's much like those of New York, Tennessee, Virginia, or Washington.

[11] Cameron H. King et al., eds., *Revised Statutes of Arizona* (Prescott: Prescott Courier Print, 1887), pp. 753–54: "Every person (except an Indian) without visible means of living, who has the physical ability to work, and who does not for the space of ten days seek employment, nor labor when employment is offered him; every healthy begger who solicits alms as a business; every person who roams from place to place without any lawful business; every idle or dissolute person, or associate of horse thieves, who wanders about the streets at late or unusual hours of the night, or who lodges in any barn, shed, shop, outhouse, lumber yard, vessel, or place other than such as is kept for lodging purposes, without the permission of the owner or party entitled to possession thereof; every lewd and dissolute person, who lives in and about houses of ill-fame, and every common drunkard is a vagrant." E. Estabrook, comp., *Statutes of Nebraska* (Chicago: Culver, Page & Hoyne, 1867), pp. 676–77: "All idle persons not having visible means of support and maintenance, and who live without employment, and all such persons wandering abroad and living in taverns, groceries, beer-houses, out-houses, market-places, sheds, barns, or in the open air, and not giving a good account of themselves, and all persons wandering abroad and begging, or who go about from door to door or place to place, or occupy public places for the purpose of begging and receiving alms, and all prostitutes, and all keepers, occupants, lessees, tenants, and pimps of houses used for prostitution or gambling, shall be deemed and are hereby declared to be vagrants." See also *Laws of the State of Missouri*, 2 vols. in 1 (St. Louis: E. Charles, 1825), pp. 783–86; *Laws of the State of New-Jersey* (Trenton: Joseph Justice, 1821), pp. 473–75; L. Bradford Price, comp., *General Laws of New Mexico* (Albany, N.Y.: W. C. Little & Co., 1880), 300–303; William P. Van Ness and John Woodworth, eds., *Laws of the State of New York, 1784–1813*, 2 vols. (Albany: H. C. Southwick & Co., 1813), 1:114–16; Edward Brown, comp., *Laws of the State of Tennessee . . . 1715–1820*, 2 vols. (Knoxville: Heiskell & Brown, 1821), 1:301–3; Hening, *Statutes-at-Large*, 2:298; *Code of Washington . . . 1881* (Olympia: C. B. Bagley, 1881), pp. 227–29. The author has similar citations for all the states up to 1890, the year which marked the official closing of the frontier.

[12] Punishments ranged from the laying on of lashes across the bare back during the colonial period and the early nineteenth century to fines or imprisonment in county jails or both in the middle and later decades of the nineteenth century. Frequently male vagrants were put to hard labor. Some states demanded that vagrants give surety for good behavior for time periods varying in length and others arranged for convicted vagrants to be hired out. See, for example, *Revised laws of Illinois* (Vandalia: Greiner & Sherman, 1833), p. 202, which authorized justices of the peace to permit peace officers to "hire out such vagrant within twenty-four hours to the best bidder, by public outcry, or on a notice given, for any term not exceeding four months; and such vagrant shall be subject to, and governed by, all the provisions of

Vagrancy acts caught up only the individual prostitute, the girl who did, indeed, wander from place to place and who operated from no bawdy house where she was the only occupant or where she was one among many. If she were one of a coterie of crimson damsels, she might or might not, depending upon the administrative ladder, have been a madam, for a nice distinction was drawn between management and labor. Of course, it was possible for a single individual to operate a one-Cyprian establishment and to function as both manager and worker. Generally, however, the term *house of ill fame* suggested several inmates, although this was not necessarily true. To augment vagrancy acts, states passed legislation aimed directly at bawdy houses. Most such acts, if not directly, at least in practice, distinguished between the keeper or manager of a house and its personnel. Indeed, with but few exceptions, most of the literature dealing with girls of the night concerns itself more with the corporate house than with the solitary demi-modes who solicited on their own or, perhaps, with one, two, or three companions.

Most of the houses in Nashville, Tennessee, in 1860, were either one-woman cribs, or, at most, were two- or three-woman operations.[13] The law, however, made no effort to distinguish between and among houses on the basis of the number of its practicing prostitutes. Bawdy houses were bawdy houses, and that was that! Illinois, in 1833, lumped together, in a single section of its criminal code, not only persons guilty of open lewdness and notorious acts of public indecency, but also those who maintained and kept lewd houses or common, ill-governed and disorderly houses. Wisconsin, by 1849, operated under a statute which prescribed imprisonment in the state prison of not less than six months nor more than a year, or a fine of not less than a hundred nor more than three hundred dollars for any person convicted of keeping a house of ill fame, resorted to for the purpose of prostitution or lewdness. This act, it will be noted, was directed against keepers of houses, not their inmates. Iowa's statute, under the code of 1850–1851, also was aimed at the keepers of houses. The penalty, upon conviction, in Iowa was imprisonment in the county jail for not more than one year, or a fine

---

the act regulating apprentices, during the time for which he has been so hired. The money for his hire shall, after deducting the costs, be, if he be without a family, paid into the county treasury; but if he have a family, the same shall be appropriated for their use and benefit."

13 David Kaser, "Nashville's Women of Pleasure in 1860," *Tennessee Historical Quarterly* 13 (December 1964):379–82.

not exceeding five hundred dollars. A Kansas act, in force in 1862, provided that persons who set up or kept a common gaming house or a bawdy house or brothel were subject, if guilty, to a fine not exceeding a thousand dollars.[14] These acts were fairly typical.

It was not uncommon for statutes concerning houses of ill fame to contain provisions which, as in the Texas law, defined any room or part of a building used for prostitution as a house of ill fame. The law of Iowa stated that when a lessee of a dwelling house was convicted of maintaining a bawdy house, the lease for letting the house was, at the option of the lessor, void. The lessor might then recover possession from the offending tenant. Furthermore, the statute made it perfectly plain that if any person rented a house knowing that the lessee intended to use it for the purpose of prostitution or lewdness or if the lessor knowingly permitted the property to be used for prostitution, he was subject, upon conviction, to a fine not exceeding three hundred dollars or imprisonment in the county jail not exceeding six months. It was not uncommon to find in state statutes a provision making it illegal for a person to inveigle or entice any female, "before reputed virtuous," into service in a brothel.[15]

[14] *Revised Laws of Illinois*, p. 199; *Wisconsin Revised Statutes* (Southport: C. Latham Sholes, 1849), p. 708; *Code of Iowa, 1850–1851* (Iowa City: Palmer & Paul, 1851), p. 374; *Kansas General Laws . . . in Force at the Close of the Session of the Legislature Ending March 6th, 1862* (Topeka: J. H. Bennet, 1862), p. 333. Every person "who shall be guilty of open, gross lewdness or lascivious behavior, or of any open and notorious act of public indecency, grossly scandalous, shall, on conviction, be adjudged guilty of a misdeameanor, and punished by imprisonment in a county jail, not exceeding six months, or by fine, not exceeding five hundred dollars, or by both (ibid., p. 331)." See also Meinrad Greiner, comp., *Louisiana Digest, 1804–1841* New Orleans: Benjamin Levy, 1841), p. 132: Act of 1818: "Whoever shall be guilty of keeping any disorderly inn, tavern, ale-house, tippling-house, gaming-house, shall suffer fine or imprisonment, or both, at the discretion of the court, and the offender may likewise lose license."

[15] *Penal Code of the State of Texas* (Galveston: News Office, 1857), p. 74; *Code of Iowa, 1850–1851*, p. 374; *Kansas General Laws . . . 1862*, p. 334. See also *Revised Codes of North Dakota* (Bismarck: Tribune Co., 1896), p. 1277, for statute covering bawdy houses. For the relationship between lessee and lessor in Wisconsin, see *Wisconsin Revised Statutes*, p. 708: "Whenever the lessee of any dwelling house shall be convicted of the offence [of keeping a house of ill fame] the lease or contract for letting such house, shall, at the option of the lessor, become void, and such lessor shall thereupon have the like remedy to recover the possession, as against a tenant for holding over after the expiration of his term." For Michigan, see Andrew Howell, comp., *General Statutes of the State of Michigan*, 2 vols. (Chicago: Callaghan & Co., 1882), 2:2249.

Local ordinances followed state statutes. Indeed, when legislatures chartered towns and cities, specific sanction was given members of the corporation or of councils to suppress vice. Thus, for example, when Mobile, Alabama, was incorporated under an act of December 17, 1819, the legislature gave the mayor and aldermen power not only to control vagrants, idle or disorderly persons, and all persons of evil life or ill fame, but also to suppress all those who were "grossly indecent, in language and behavior, publicly in the streets and all public prostitutes," The Illinois legislature, when it chartered the city of Quincy, February 3, 1840, gave the city council power to "tax, restrain, prohibit, and suppress tippling houses, dram shops, and gaming houses, and bawdy and other disorderly houses."[16]

Acting under such broad powers, communities throughout the Middle Border and elsewhere passed ordinances designed to curtail, if not stamp out, prostitution. A sampling of these shows that such ordinances differed from place to place and that some were rather curious. St. Louis, Missouri, during April and May, 1835, passed two ordinances. The first provided that net proceeds of all moneys arising from the licensing, regulating, restraining, or suppressing of bawdy houses should be used for the benefit of the St. Louis hospital. The second set a fine of ninety dollars for the first conviction on the charge of keeping a bawdy house and of five hundred dollars for each subsequent offense. In 1843, an ordinance listing misdemeanors included, in addition to

[16] Harry Toulmin, comp., *Digest of Laws of Alabama* (Cahawba: Ginn & Curtis, 1823), p. 787; see also An Act to restrain Idle and Disorderly Persons, December 5, 1801, ibid., pp. 377–78; *Illinois Laws, 1829* (Springfield: William Walters, 1840), p. 117. When the Kansas legislature incorporated the city of Elwood, February 8, 1859, it defined the powers of the corporate authorities which, in addition to specific powers, included the authority to make laws "for any purpose which may tend to the general good of the city." See *Kansas General Laws . . . 1862*, p. 405. In New Mexico, city councils possessed the authority to suppress gaming and gaming houses and houses of ill fame. See *General Laws of New Mexico*, pp. 183–86. Village trustees in Wisconsin had the right to suppress disorderly, lewd, and gaming houses. See *Wisconsin Revised Statutes*, pp. 294–96. In Iowa, village trustees had authority to provide against gambling and disorderly and indecent houses and conduct. See *Code of Iowa, 1850–1851*, pp. 106–7. When Albany, New York, was incorporated, April 6, 1813, the common council was authorized to pass ordinances for the suppression of vice and immorality and for the restraining and suppression of disorderly and gaming houses. See *Laws of the State of New York, 1784–1813*, 2:467. Michigan gave city corporations and village trustees the authority to prohibit and suppress disorderly houses and places of ill fame. See *Michigan General Statutes*, 1:660-722.

disturbing the peace generally and swimming naked in the Mississippi River, the keeping of houses of ill fame.[17]

Other Missouri towns bordering on the Mississippi River wrote ordinances of a similar character. Louisiana, Missouri, for example, in 1849 set a fine of fifty dollars for keeping a bawdy house. Cape Girardeau, in 1851, made it the duty of the city marshal to visit suspicious and disorderly houses. Later, in 1857, it prescribed a fine of not less than fifty nor more than a hundred dollars for anyone convicted of keeping a brothel. Two years later, Cape Girardeau city fathers, in a vagrancy ordinance, included persons who wandered about or lodged in bawdy houses and houses of bad repute.[18]

Fort Madison, an Iowa river town, in 1845, set a fine of not less than ten nor more than fifty dollars for keeping a disorderly house or house of ill fame. In 1866, the fine was increased to a hundred dollars.

Apparently Fort Madison, always a curious community, was troubled shortly after the close of the Civil War with ladies of the evening who plied their trade in the most convenient spot. An ordinance of 1866 provided a fine, not for the shady lady, but for her client, for the law said that any person found in any store, shop, saloon, or other place of business, after the close of the same for business, or in any room or apartment, or business not used as a dwelling, with a common prostitute was subject to penalty. A graveyard ordinance of 1866 said: "If any person should be found in the city cemetery in company with a common prostitute, at any time during the day or night, he and she shall be punished by imprisonment in the county jail for thirty days, and a fine of one hundred dollars and costs."[19] Both Burlington, Iowa, and Quincy, Illinois, set fines of not less than fifty dollars for persons convicted of running a brothel.[20]

[17] City of St. Louis, *Revised Ordinances . . . 1835–1836* (St. Louis: Office of the Missouri Argus, 1836), pp. 176, 233; City of St. Louis, *Revised Ordinances . . . Revised and Digested by the Fifth City Council* . . . (St. Louis, Chambers & Knapp, 1843), p. 300.

[18] Louisiana, Missouri, Ordinance Book, 1848–1854, holographic volume, city clerk's office, entry for September 5, 1849; Cape Girardeau, Missouri, Council Record Book, 1843–1875, holographic volume, city clerk's office, entries for June 10, 1851, June 19, 1857, May 23, 1859.

[19] Fort Madison, Iowa, Ordinance Book, 1845–1863, holographic volume, city clerk's office, entries for June 2, 1845; January 1, 13, 1866.

[20] Burlington, Iowa, Ordinance Book, 1852–1874, holographic volume, city clerk's office, entry for April 13, 1852; Quincy, Illinois, Ordinance Book, 1840–1856, holographic volume, city clerk's office, entry for April 8, 1851. On August 5,

Despite strict ordinances, enforcement was lax. Newspapers frequently called attention to an unchecked growth of vice. Typical of these was a warning from Minnesota which exclaimed: "Look to it, Citizens! Houses of ill-fame, regular hellish brothels are creeping into Minneapolis, if report be true. No wonder—they come along in due time to keep company with the rapidly increasing number of grog-shops."[21] Residents frequently took the law into their own hands, raiding and burning whorehouses. During 1857, mobs sacked houses in La Crosse, Wisconsin, and Minneapolis, Minnesota. In La Crosse, about two hundred men burned out business emporia frequented by "some fifteen or twenty public prostitutes, associated with nearly as many pimps and blacklegs." Two thousand dollars worth of property was destroyed, but those engaged in the destruction thought force was the "only effectual way of ridding the city of the characters" which infested the buildings.[22]

In Minneapolis, a committee of five waited upon the proprietor of a house of ill fame, warned him to leave town within twenty-four hours, and waited for his answer. When he, armed with a revolver and bowie knife, refused to comply with the committee's wish, he was carried to the door and thrown into the street. The Cyprians were driven from their rooms, and all their furniture was removed from the house. Now and again, a fallen angel found her patrons had not deserted her. A prostitute, known only as The Norwegian, was rescued by lumbermen from a St. Anthony jail.[23] In the spring of 1858, men "in high position" led a mob that raided a house in Peoria, Illinois. Mobs fired a house of ill repute in Kansas City, Kansas, in 1862 and three houses in Leavenworth the next year. A gang of men and boys pelted a Minneapolis bagnio so heavily with rocks and small boulders that its inmates, clad in the lightest of garments, fled.[24]

1861, a Quincy ordinance declared all bawdy houses and houses of ill fame to be nuisances and ordered the marshal to abate them.

[21] *Minnesota Republican* (St. Anthony), September 10, 1857.

[22] *La Crosse National Democrat*, June 9, July 7, 14, 1857, *La Crosse Independent Republican*, July 8, 14, 15, 22, 29, 1857.

[23] *Falls Evening News* (St. Anthony and Minneapolis), October 2, 1857; *Minnesota Democrat* (Minneapolis), October 3, 1857; *Minnesota Republican* (St. Anthony), July 9, 1858.

[24] The Quincy episode was reported in the *La Crosse Independent Republican*, April 28, 1858; the Kansas raid was reported in the Kansas City *Journal of Commerce*, December 27, 1862, April 25, 1863, and is quoted in Henry P. Walker, *The Wagonmasters* (Norman: University of Oklahoma Press, 1966), p. 51. See also *Minneapolis Daily Tribune*, July 23, 1870, May 29, 1876. See note 6 for earlier examples.

Both Minneapolis and St. Paul were natural centers for knock-around broads to congregate. Minneapolis was headquarters for the lumbering industry, and its Washington Avenue was lined with shops and saloons catering to lumberjacks. St. Paul was the head of navigation on the Mississippi River. Moreover, the two cities were the jumping-off place for the Dakotas and the Montana and Wyoming country to the west. Although not an easy trip, it was perfectly possible for soiled doves to work their way from the Twin Cities westward to Omaha and Denver. Some invaded Kansas by way of Omaha. From the Twin Cities, girls moved eastward through Wisconsin and into the iron-ore towns of Ishpeming and Marquette in upper Michigan. The river, of course, connected the two principal Minnesota cities with St. Louis and New Orleans. From these centers, nymphs moved easily in almost any direction.

One fact must be underscored: out from the land of the Middle Border spewed the bulk of characters who offered themselves willy-nilly to the cowboy at trail's end, to the red-shirted miner, to the eager railroad worker, to the jaded cavalryman at close of day. Of course, a few home-grown products went into the business, but the majority of the ladies came originally from the farms, small towns, and tenements of the states—Iowa, Illinois, Missouri—of the Middle Border.

An almost constant shifting of the whore population made it exceedingly difficult for authorities to control it. As near as can be ascertained, Matilda Waller, Nettie Connelly, and Kate and Sara Campbell not only were the outstanding madams in Minneapolis but also were the largest importers of girls.[25] Their business was reported fully in the press, and court records give ample evidence of their activities.[26]

[25] For Minnesota statutes and ordinances, see Moses Sherburne and William Hollinshead, comps., *Public Statutes of the State of Minnesota, 1849–1858* (St. Paul: Pioneer Printing Co., 1859), p. 729; City of St. Anthony, *The Charter, and Amendments Thereto, and Ordinances* (St. Anthony: Thomas and Clark, 1861), p. 10; Minneapolis City Council, *Proceedings* (Minneapolis: City Council, 1878), pp. 38–39. This Minneapolis ordinance, May 7, 1877, provided that keepers of houses of ill fame would, upon conviction, be subject to a fine of not less than twenty-five nor more than one hundred dollars plus costs, or imprisonment not exceeding ninety days, or both. It also set a penalty for persons found in such houses of a fine of not less than five and not more than ten dollars plus court costs, or imprisonment for thirty days or both. St. Paul had a similar ordinance. For the controversy over licensing houses of ill fame in St. Paul, see *St. Paul Daily Globe*, February 15, 1878; *St. Paul Pioneer Press*, July 26, August 8, December 4, 1883; April 6, 1884.

[26] For Matilda Waller, see *State* v. *Matilda Waller*, May 26, 1869, file 321, Hennepin County District Court; *State* v. *Waller*, November 29, 1869, District Court Minutes, Hennepin County; *Minneapolis Daily Tribune*, April 4, May 26, 27, June 1,

In St. Paul, the leading lights of night life were Henrietta Charles (Dutch Henrietta), who operated a house on the upper lévee; Kate Hutton, "the most notorious woman of her class"; and Fannie Schaffer, Hattie McBride, Lillie Davis, and Nellie Otis.[27] These were the madams who imported girls from St. Louis, Louisville, Chicago, and small Iowa towns, and who, after the Chicago fire of 1874, welcomed prostitutes fleeing from the blaze. More than five hundred prostitutes lost "costly fittings and wardrobes" in the fire.

When a Chicago nymph du pavé was picked up by St. Paul police, she exclaimed bitterly: "Burned out in Chicago and jailed the first night in St. Paul!"[28] It was Mattie Waller and Dutch Henrietta who supplied lumbering centers such as Brainerd, Minnesota, with girls. Now and again the young ladies, weary of both uncultured lumbering towns and uncouth lumberjacks, slipped away to enjoy Minneapolis. "Ellen Lofoy and Jennie Ward," said the *Minneapolis Tribune*, "street-walkers down from Brainerd, were run in for vagrancy."[29] Their respite was, indeed, short-lived.

23, September 19, 30, December 7, 9, 29, 1869; January 14, 1870; June 16, July 7, 1871; and *State* v. *Waller*, July 5, 1871, file 367, Hennepin County District Court. For Nettie Connelly, see *State* v. *George Finn and Nettie Connelly*, April 12, 1873, file 416, Hennepin County District Court; *Minneapolis Daily Tribune*, May 24, June 10, 15, 1873; May 2, 1874; March 21, April 11, 1876; November 13, 1878; June 26, October 29, 1879; *State* v. *Nettie Connelly*, January 22, 1876; file 82, Hennepin County Court of Common Pleas. For Kate and Sara Campbell, see *State* v. *James Wagner*, August 15, 1875, file 51, Hennepin County Court of Common Pleas; *State* v. *Kate Campbell*, March 14, 1876, file 93, Hennepin County Court of Common Pleas; *Minneapolis Daily Tribune*, November 30, 1875; July 12, 1876; January 2, 1877; January 3, 28, March 8, 9, June 4, 5, 26, July 6, August 6, September 12, October 22, November 7, 18, 1878; June 14, 16, October 10, 16, 21, 1879. The earliest Minnesota court case involving prostitution may be that of *United States* v. *Old Sal*, September 10, 1853, Records Territorial Court Minutes, Hennepin County District Court, in which a grand jury indicted "Old Sal for keeping a house of ill-fame."

[27] For Henrietta Charles, see *St. Paul Daily Pioneer Press*, January 25, 26, 1875. For Kate Hutton, see *St. Paul Pioneer Press*, February 24, 1880, August 26, 27, 28, 1881. For the others, see *St. Paul Pioneer Press*, February 3, 1881.

[28] *St. Paul Daily Press*, July 19, 20, 1874.

[29] June 28, 1879. For general survey of prostitution in Minnesota, see Philip D. Jordan, *The People's Health: A History of the Public Health Movement in Minnesota to 1948* (St. Paul: Minnesota Historical Society, 1953), chap. 13. Kate Campbell's place was a favorite resort of lumberjacks and those in the business. "A number of fellows of questionable morals, about to leave for up river this morning," said the *Minneapolis Daily Tribune*, July 12, 1876, "assembled at Kate Campbell's place last night and indulged in a little row among themselves. One of the party received a pretty good thrashing, but no serious injury was sustained. They all skipped out of

On one occasion, Kate Campbell brought from Chicago two girls to become inmates of her house, and she thoughtfully advanced the railroad fare. The girls were dissatisfied, stating that Kate's place was altogether too tough a hole for them, and prepared to return to the Windy City. Kate demanded the return of the ticket money. The girls refused. Whereupon Kate clapped, so the report goes, a garnishee on the Milwaukee and St. Paul Railroad for the amount of the fare. The railroad's lawyer laughed at this tactic. The girls returned home, and Kate was out both the fare and three days' board. The episode was reported in the local press under the caption: A RATHER PECULIAR CASE: A WHORE-HOUSE KEEPER USING THE LAW.[30]

Twin City brothels circulated girls of the period to the "gunboat" trade which grew rapidly on inland waters, especially the Mississippi River, after the Civil War. A gunboat was a raft with a cabin whose interior was designed for gambling and whoring. These boats were anchored off river towns, and they were numerous. The Fort Madison, Iowa, city council, as did other communities, defined a gunboat as "any flat boat, keelboat, or scow, or any other watercraft of any kind, within the limits of the city, and used for the purpose of prostitution, lewdness, dancing, fiddling, and drinking."[31]

Frequently, the "vagabonds, harlots, and pimps" that St. Louis drove out went upriver, stopping at "nearly all the larger towns."[32] Some of these must have entered the gunboat trade after the war. Floating palaces of pleasure were anchored, at one time or another, below St. Paul, at Red Wing and Winona, Minnesota, near La Crosse, Wisconsin, and, among other places, near Oquawka, Illinois, and Clinton and Burlington, Iowa.[33]

---

the city this morning." Activities at Kate's house always made good newspaper stories. The *Minneapolis Daily Tribune*, September 12, 1878, reported: "Four of the girl clerks at Kate Campbell's and four male prostitutes went up to the Lake Crystal house just outside the city limits on the river road going north. Emma Keyser, a sylphlike Cyprian of two hundred and fifty pounds of avoirdupois, and a hardened face, drew her slipper and made a charge on the window glass, Birdie Smith, a compatriot in sin, followed the assault by firing a beer keg through the window."

[30] *Minneapolis Daily Tribune*, June 14, 16, 1879.

[31] Ibid., May 26, 1869, for the arrest of Thomas Osborn, of "gun-boat" fame, and "keeper of a low bagnio at Nigger Hill," who was turned over by Minneapolis police to the deputy sheriff of Mankato, Minnesota, in answer to an indictment by the grand jury of Blue Earth County (City of Fort Madison, Iowa, Ordinance Book, 1865–1873, holographic volume in city clerk's office). The gunboat ordinance was passed January 13, 1866.

[32] *Winona Weekly Republican*, June 22, 1859.

[33] Ibid., November 22, 27, 1866; August 17, February 18, March 24, 25, 26, 27,

A boat wintered near Winona for some two years, and, said an editor, visited in the summer other cities and towns to "sow its corruptions." Then, waxing moral, he went on to complain that "numbers of young men, and even boys, have been drawn on to ruin from our very midst, by means of this infernal crew," which paraded Winona streets in gaudy clothes to "attract, allure, and debase."[34] Gunboats were all he described and more. Fights occurred, gambling was crooked, whiskey was rotten, and murder was not infrequent.

During November, 1875, a gunboat managed by Bill Lee was moored between Oquawka, Illinois, and Burlington, Iowa. Its occupants included a deaf-and-dumb prostitute, a pimp named Dan Brazier, a girl of the line who went by the name of Jessie McCarty, and several other soiled doves of each sex. One evening, for reasons known only to himself, Lee burst into Jessie's crib-cabin, yanked her from bed, broke both her back and neck, stamped out an eye, smashed her temple, and disfigured her face beyond recognition. He then hid the body, wrapped in a blanket, near the bank of the Mississippi. Later, with the help of Brazier, he placed the body in a skiff, rowed into the middle of the channel, and tossed it into the water. Somewhat later, plagued by conscience, Brazier squealed to authorities.

Peace officers from Illinois and Iowa then raided the gunboat, arresting all on board. Under pressure, the girls corroborated Brazier's account. Lee was lodged in the Oquawka jail, was indicted, and eventually came to trial. Meanwhile, Jessie's mangled body was found floating in the river. A jury found Lee guilty, and the judge sentenced him to be hanged on June 16, 1876. A crowd of merrymakers witnessed the hanging.[35]

Denizens of gunboats, as well as inmates of joy-houses on land, came and went, for madams considered it good business to offer new wares from time to time. The migration of girls was determined by the seasons, by the occupation of their customers, and by demand for their services in certain places and at certain times. Thus, many worked states with a warmer climate during the winter months and, to escape the heat,

---

28, 1868; April 22, 28, May 6, 1869; May 24, June 5, 30, 1870. *La Crosse Weekly Democrat*, August 7, 1865; *Minneapolis Daily Tribune*, June 21, 1870. For gunboat activities in Illinois and Iowa, see the *Saturday Evening Post* (Burlington, Iowa), October 28, 1911, in which a steamboat captain writes of gunboats.

[34] *Winona Daily Republican*, November 13, 1866.

[35] For the Lee affair, see *Keokuk Daily Gate City*, November 25, 27, December 1, 1875; February 29, March 1, April 30, June 16, 17, 1876. For the shooting of a marshal by a keeper of a gunboat, see ibid., July 24, 1872.

journeyed northward during the summer. Minneapolis and St. Paul houses increased their staffs just before crews of lumbermen went into the woods in the autumn and shortly before they returned from the pineries in the spring.

In much the same fashion, nymphs of the prairie followed the annual cattle drives on the plains "like vultures follow an army, and disappear at the end of the cattle driving and shipping season." Cowtowns of Kansas and Colorado, before the arrival of the first longhorn herds from Texas, said one account, were "invaded by a horde of desperadoes, gamblers, saloonkeepers, and filles de joy, most from the underworlds of St. Louis, Kansas City, and Memphis."[36]

When, during the early decades of the twentieth century, Oklahoma's oil boom attracted men and women of every description, gamblers, highjackers, and prostitutes swept into the state, resulting in confused lawlessness.[37] The rush of ladies to Oklahoma is reminiscent of the influx of women from China, European countries, and the states of the Union to the California gold fields.[38] Far on the other side of the country in Michigan's northern peninsula, rich iron-ore deposits were beginning to be exploited toward the close of the nineteenth century. This was wild country, and miners were not averse to relishing the pleasures of the flesh. They were not disappointed, for canny madams and the girls made the most of each new market, moving in with astonishing swiftness. Just as the broad Middle Border furnished prostitutes to stock Belle Breezing's "most orderly of disorderly house" in Lexington, Kentucky, and just as the same fruitful area sent pioneer whores and reinforcements to California, the cowtowns of the Southwest and West, and the pineries of Wisconsin and Minnesota, so did it supply hustlers to Michigan's ore fields.[39]

[36] *Pueblo Chieftain*, 1878, quoted in Miller and Snell, *Great Gunfighters*, p. 14; Parkhill, *Wildest of the West*, pp. 216–17; see also Ronald L. Davis, "Soiled Doves and Ornamental Culture: Kansas Cowtown Entertainments," *American West* 4 (November 1967):20–21.

[37] Stephen B. Oates, "Boom Oil: Oklahoma Strikes It Rich," *American West* 5 (January 1968):11. For Oklahoma's early statutes relating to houses of ill fame and their keepers, see Will T. Little, L. G. Pitnam, and R. J. Barker, comps., *Statutes of 1890* (Guthrie: State Capital Printing Co., 1891), pp. 484–85. Note that the act, in part, hinges upon the element of "annoyance," as indicated earlier in this article.

[38] Herbert Ashbury, *The Barbary Coast: An Informal History of the San Francisco Underworld* (New York: Garden City Publishing Co., 1933), pp. 33–34.

[39] For Belle Breezing, see William H. Townsend, *The Most Orderly of Disorderly Houses* (Lexington: Privately Printed, 1966); for her obituary, see *Time* 36 (August 26, 1940):56.

The migratory habit of birds of brothels need not be surprising, even though little attention has been paid it. Yet evidence to support the moving from place to place of girls is abundant. Beginning in the 1830s and continuing until the turn of the century, editors, city officials, and peace officers spoke, in one way or another, of the travel of those outside the law. To offer only four examples among many, in 1834, New Yorkers were warned of the arrival of a set of desperate villains from the South; in 1859, the mayor of St. Louis, said bluntly that rogues of every description were becoming more and more migratory; in 1875, a Minneapolis newspaper told its readers that, as spring opened each year and the river afforded means for migration, there was more thieving in river towns; in 1888, Omaha's police chief wrote:

> Omaha, because of her geographical position, appears to be visited by and harbor more criminals than any of the western cities which have a population greater than ours. Within twelve hours' time criminals who may be released or run out of Chicago, Denver, Kansas City, St. Joe, Des Moines, St. Paul, Minneapolis, and several other cities can come here, which they almost invariably do.[40]

The Omaha police chief might have been more perturbed had he realized that nymphs of the pavement were filtering into his city not only from cowtowns farther west but also from Michigan's ore mines. Nor did he know that ladies offering quick service possessed feet fleet enough to carry them from cattle centers, back through Omaha, and on to Chicago, Detroit, and eventually into Michigan towns such as Ishpeming and Marquette.[41]

That Ishpeming was not without sin's blemish is amply demonstrated by the antics of John Jones, marshal and police chief. When,

[40] *New York Evening Post*, August 8, 1834; City of St. Louis, *Mayor's Message with Accompanying Reports of City Officers . . . Second Stated Session, October 10, 1859* (St. Louis: Missouri Democrat Book & Job Office, 1859), p. 11; *Minneapolis Daily Tribune*, March 23, 1875; City of Omaha, *Omaha Municipal Reports, 1888* (Omaha: Dispatch Publishing Co., 1889), p. 246. See also *New Orleans Bee*, July 15, 1835; *La Crosse Independent Republican*, July 9, 1856; *Dubuque Daily North West*, July 26, 1857; *Winona Weekly Republican*, May 12, 1858; *Minneapolis Daily Tribune*, October 25, 1868, March 23, 1875, August 15, 1872; Harold Sinclair, *The Port of New Orleans* (New York: Doubleday, Doran & Co., 1942), p. 207; John H. Stevens, *Personal Recollections of Minnesota and Its People, and Early History of Minneapolis* (Minneapolis: Tribune Job Printing Co., 1890), p. 269.

[41] Interview with Toivo Bena, August 2, 1967, of near Marquette, who recalled hearing, as a young man, that prostitutes came into the area after working Kansas and Colorado cowtowns.

for example, he removed a young lady, come from Chicago, from an "establishment on the hill" in 1874, the local editor scoffed at Jones in print in Scandinavian dialect. Two years later, the council suspended Jones for intemperance, neglect of duty, and misbehavior in office, and, in the same session, reelected him marshal and chief. When, in 1877, the council passed an ordinance to suppress houses of ill fame, which seemed to be increasing in number, it directed the marshal to do the job, authorizing him to arrest and imprison managers of houses and their whores "upon the verbal complaint of any citizen or taxpayer."[42]

Inept as Ishpeming police might have been, they managed to snare at least some of the most persistent and disorderly prostitutes. Undoubtedly they favored friends from time to time. Officer Vivian, for example, when informed of the presence of a woman of ill repute, picked her up. However, instead of booking her, Vivian, with gallantry and generosity, hired a livery rig, and drove her to her house in Naugaunee. Mary Harrington, however, was another matter. By all accounts, she was poor, worthless, and a sot. She was described as a prostitute, as being beastly drunk, as having no visible calling or business to maintain herself, and as a wanton who did "go about from saloon to saloon in a drunken manner begging liquors and have slept in a barn ... in the company of several men." After a series of arrests, convictions, fines, and jail sentences, she, in 1884, was sent to the Detroit House of Corrections for six months.[43] No marshal ever raised a finger to help her and no policeman ever hired a buggy to take her anywhere.

Ishpeming and Marquette were centers of both mining and lumbering. Lumberjacks as well as miners thronged their streets before entering the woods, sought entertainment on weekends, and engaged in what mischief they might. Marquette's civic fathers passed the first city ordinance regulating vice in 1871 and another creating a police department a year later. The vice ordinance, amended in 1875, was a necessity, for Marquette, sprawled along the shore of Lake Superior, already was

[42] *Ishpeming Iron Home*, June 4, 1874; Ishpeming Records of the Common Council, 1874–1878, holographic volume in office of city clerk, February 11, 1876, May 4, September 5, 1877. Jones, born in Detroit, arrived in Ishpeming in 1872, served four years as marshal, and then established an omnibus and express line. See A. T. Andreas, prop., *History of the Upper Peninsula of Michigan . . .* (Chicago: Western Historical Co., 1883), 447–48.

[43] Records of the Ishpeming Common Council, October 2, 1878–April 6, 1887, November 8, 11, 1886. For the record of Mary Harrington, see Justice of the Peace Docket kept by Cornelius Kennedy, Ishpeming, April 1880–January 1903, holographic volume in police headquarters, pp. 41, 43, 143, 150.

flexing its muscles as the result of lumbering and mining. Lake vessels not only brought supplies but also put ashore surveyors, timber cruisers, miners, and ladies of easy virtue. Prostitutes settled on and adjacent to Lake Street. There were saloons for those who wished to quench their thirst, games of chance for those who desired to court Lady Luck, and numerous boarding and lodging houses for those who moved in and out of the woods. In truth, the Upper Peninsula might well be considered among the last frontiers.

The ordinance of 1875 was, in part, a vagrancy act, for it prescribed penalties for persons not having visible means to maintain themselves, for those who idled or rambled about, for those staying in drinking saloons or houses of bad repute or of ill fame, for those going about for the purpose of gaming or "watch stuffing" or using artifices to obtain money or any other valuable thing. For persons found guilty of keeping or being an inmate of a house of ill fame, the ordinance set a punishment of a fine of not less than ten nor more than one hundred dollars, or imprisonment in the county jail for a term of not more than ninety days, or both fine and imprisonment.[44] There's many a dry swallow, however, between well and lip, and, generally speaking, Marquette tolerated girls of the evening up to about the turn of the century. Until then, madams and their assistants were raided by police only when men came in from the woods and were fleeced of large sums of money in Lake Street establishments.

During the last decade of the century, the law was enforced more consistently. On June 13, 1892, for example, four girls—Kitty, Mabel, Beatrice, and Nettie—were convicted of keeping a house of ill fame. All were Americans. Kitty, age forty, was fined fifty dollars, just half of the maximum. Mabel, age twenty-two; Beatrice, age twenty-eight; and Nettie, age twenty-eight, each paid a fine of ten dollars, the minimum. Two years later, Nettie, was fined fifty dollars for the same offense. Other whores, ranging in age from fifteen to forty-five, gave their nationalities as Canadian, French, and Irish, but Americans were the most numerous. No particular conclusion is to be drawn from this statement, for marshals were apt to keep incomplete arrest books, and frequently entries concerning age and nationality were not made. It is, however, fair to state that not only were minimum fines consistently

[44] John L. Cochran, comp., *Charter of the City of Marquette as Amended February 27th, 1873 and the Ordinances* . . . (Marquette: Mining Journal Steam Presses, 1897), p. 62; also, George P. Brown, comp., *The Charter and Ordinances of the City of Marquette* (Marquette: Mining Journal Print, 1898), p. 128.

levied but also that some fines were below the amount prescribed by law. Of five girls convicted in May, 1900, the madam was fined fifteen dollars, and the remaining four paid seven dollars and a half each. In October, in one of the largest bags on record, two "landladies" and twenty-one "roomers" were each fined either ten or fifteen dollars. There was nothing unique about Marquette's vice ordinance, for it reflected adequately the state's statute. Indeed, it was only slightly different, for example, from the Texas statute in force in 1857.[45]

Prostitution probably was no better or worse in Michigan's iron-ore and timber country than it was elsewhere throughout the nation. In almost any town of consequence could be found, if one searched diligently, either a lone lady or a group. For the most part, the chippie rarely received newspaper notice unless she made a spectacle or nuisance of herself by engaging in fisticuffs with a rival or because she was far gone in drink. She came to public notice also if she were arrested and fined for soliciting, or if she ran such a disorderly emporium that the place was noted for its fights. The murder of a nymph of the pavements, of course, always made news. Raids and mob action also were newsworthy.

Extensive coverage was given the murder in New York, in 1836, of Helen Jewett by Richard P. Robinson. Two years later in Philadelphia, an affronted customer went after Susan McKean with a dirk. At a Chicago house of ill fame in 1853 three irate customers threatened Caroline Wilson, keeper of the brothel. Caroline drew a knife and, with the assistance of two loyal customers, threw the troublemaker out. In St. Cloud, Minnesota, a girl of tarnished character was shot by a patron. "Vice," said a magazine editor in 1862, "abounds on [New York's] Broadway." A shooting episode in a house in Des Moines, Iowa, in 1868, resulted in one death. Mrs. Catherine Edwards, it was charged, corrupted the youth of Blue Earth, Minnesota, in 1872.

A mob fired the bagnio of Mrs. Annie Hunter near Chippewa Falls, Wisconsin, in 1873. In the blaze a "girl known as Dora" and a "man

[45] Marquette, Marshal's Arrest Book, 1890–1900, holographic volume, police headquarters, Marquette, June 13, 1892, September 22, 1894; October 1, 1900; Marshal's Arrest Book, 1900–1922, May 3, 10, 1905. See *Penal Code of the State of Texas*, p. 74. The Marquette ordinance differed only slightly from that of Memphis, Tennessee, in 1857 or that of Atlanta, Georgia, in 1863. See L. J. Dupree, comp., *Digest of the Ordinances of the City Council of Memphis, from the Year 1826 to 1857* . . . (Memphis: Memphis Bulletin Co., 1857), p. 112; Jethro W. Manning, comp., *Code of the City of Atlanta* . . . (Atlanta: Intelligencer Steam-Power Presses, 1863), pp. 62–63.

named Cosgrove" burned to death.[46] Such examples could be multiplied many times over. In Kansas, an irritated male did make an assault upon one called Fanny—"throwed her on the floor, elevated her paraphanalia, spanked her, and finally busted her a left hander in the right eye, accompanying the same with a kick in the stomache." A fight between two doves of a roost was a magnificent sight: "Tufts of hair, calico, snuff and gravel flew like fir in a cat fight, and before we could distinguish how the battle waned a chunk of dislocated leg grazed our ear and a cheer from the small boys announced that a battle was lost and won."[47] Reporting, it seems, was more colorful, if not more accurate, in the post-Civil War West than it was east of the Mississippi during earlier decades, but the kind of news changed not one bit. Not even the whore's standard farewell to a departing customer altered: "Come back soon, honey."

How many greetings and how many farewells were uttered by how many joy Elsies to how many patrons is, obviously, impossible to determine. Now and then, however, one catches a glimpse of whores at work, of whores punished by legal or illegal means, of the number of whorehouses throughout the United States. Even statistics, when available, are not infallible. One can trust them no more than one can trust most streetwalkers.

Yet the brief glimpses and the incomplete, inaccurate statistics, when carefully pieced together, leave impressions and pictures of the trade. A New York reformer, for example, estimated that in 1817 there were no less than ten thousand abandoned females and said a considerable number of hacks were employed for no other purpose than that of transporting the miserable beings from one haunt of vice to another. The *New Orleans Picayune,* in 1848, wrote of the arrival in court of five nymphs of the pavement who were all "dressed richly and fashionably; some wore quilled muslin bonnets, others straw bonnets; some were attired in mulberry colored silk dresses, others in black silk, some

[46] *New York Evening Post*, April 11, July 11, August 1, 1836; *Philadelphia Public Ledger*, November 24, 1838; *Chicago Daily Tribune*, May 20, 1853; *Winona Daily Republican*, September 30, 1867; "Editor's Easy Chair," *Harper's Monthly Magazine* 24 (February 1862):409–10; *La Crosse Daily Republican*, September 28, 1868; *St. Paul Sunday Pioneer Press*, April 11, 1875.

[47] *Dodge City Times*, March 24, 1877, and *Ford County* (Kansas) *Globe*, January 21, 1879, quoted in Miller and Snell, *Great Gunfighters*, p. 12. For an illustration of brothel violence in New Orleans, see Herbert Asbury, *The French Quarter: An Informal History of the New Orleans Underworld* (New York: Garden City Publishing Co., 1938), pp. 372–73.

of them sported kid gloves, the finger casing of others were of open network silk; some had on prunella boots, others showed off morocco slippers; some wore their hair in romantic corkscrew curls, others had their locks drawn back *à la Chinoise;* all of them wore large dark veils, and superfluity of finger rings of the richest kinds, inlaid with precious stone of the most rare colors." [48]

Prostitution flourished near army camps during the Civil War. The provost marshal in Washington, D.C., in 1862, reported that 450 houses of ill fame were operating. A year later, the *Washington Star* put the number at no less than 7,500. Richmond, Virginia, became a mecca for prostitutes catering to Confederate troops. Their effect upon Johnny Rebs is dramatically apparent in venereal disease rates. One illustration must suffice: twelve regiments with men from five states and possessing a mean strength of 11,452 men reported 204 new cases of gonorrhea and 44 new cases of syphilis in July, 1861. [49]

In Nashville, Tennessee, in 1860, professional prostitutes totaled 207 out of the 13,762 free inhabitants of Nashville. The profile of the average Nashville prostitute in 1860, writes David Kaser, would show that she was "a white, Tennessee-born, twenty-three years old. Chances are about even that she was illiterate, and that she worked in a house with two or three colleagues." [50] The postwar years, a period which witnessed an increase of both minor and major crime of all types, brought new "statistics"—or at least attempts at statistics.

After March 31, 1872, when a St. Louis ordinance required registration of all prostitutes residing in private rooms, a tally showed 1,766 white bawds and 286 colored bawds. The top six, ranked as to nationality, were: United States, 1,378; United States (colored), 286; German, 139; Irish 122; English, 46; and Canadian, 40. Of the total number of arrests in St. Louis for 1872, the following groups produced the largest number: laborers, 5,371; prostitutes, 2,684; loafers, 515; servants, 493; rivermen, 401; gamblers, 374; saloonkeepers, 329. Throughout the city were 136 bawdy houses, 6 assignation houses, and 6

---

[48] Ward Stafford, *New Missionary Field: A Report to the Female Missionary Society for the Poor . . . March, 1817* (New-York: J. Seymour, 1817), p. 14; *New Orleans Picayune,* September 26, 1840, quoted in E. Merton Coulter, ed., *The Other Half of Old New Orleans* (Baton Rouge: Louisiana State University Press, 1939), pp. 29–32.

[49] Bell I. Wiley, *The Life of Billy Yank* (Indianapolis: Bobbs-Merrill Co., 1951–1952), p. 257, and his *The Life of Johnny Reb* (Indianapolis: Bobbs-Merrill Co., 1943), p. 55.

[50] Kaser, "Nashville's Women of Pleasure," p. 382.

keepers of single rooms, with a total of 703 bawds, of which 150 were colored.[51]

During 1874, Wichita's last big trail year, the number of city prostitutes ran between 45 and 50. Another author estimated the number of loose women in Denver in 1876 at approximately 1,000. Three years later, 17 common prostitutes were arrested in St. Paul, 3 keepers of disorderly houses, 74 keepers of houses of ill fame, and 29 persons for visiting houses of ill fame. So many streetwalkers crowded Keokuk, Iowa, in 1880, that street crossings were blocked by them.

The police judge of Omaha, Nebraska, reported cases for the year ending December 31, 1882. Among these were 2,212 drunks, 2,608 vagrants, 2,701 prostitutes, 1,113 disturbers of the peace, 276 inmates of houses of prostitution, and 329 drunk and disorderly persons. It is of some interest to note that citizens of Alexandria, Missouri, in 1909, tarred and feathered an experienced prostitute and her daughter who was learning the trade, and set them adrift in a leaky boat on the broad bosom of the Mississippi River.[52]

No one knows the number of houses, ranging from dreary cribs to fancy establishments, operating in the United States at any one time, although many persons are curious. The best estimate lies buried in the United States census of 1880. For that tenth census, Frederick Howard Wines, a clergyman, executive secretary of the Illinois Board of Public Charities, and the principal organizer of the National Conference of Charities and Corrections, was named a special adviser in the preparation of the report on the defective, dependent, and delinquent classes within the United States. Wines sent queries to 494 towns with populations of 5,000 or more. Among the questions asked was one concerning the number of houses of ill fame. One hundred and eighty-five towns submitted the information, 215 made no reply, and 94 said they lacked whorehouses.

A total of 4,067 houses were reported. Among the larger cities, New York admitted to 183, Philadelphia to 517, Chicago to 200, Boston to 100, Baltimore to 300, Cincinnati to 133, New Orleans to 305, and Pittsburgh to 100. St. Louis and San Francisco, with becoming modesty,

[51] St. Louis City Council, *Mayor's Message with Accompanying Documents* (St. Louis: St. Louis Times Co., 1872), pp. 94–96, 38.

[52] Miller and Snell, *Great Gunfighters*, p. 11; Parkhill, *Wildest of the West*, p. 13; *St. Paul Daily Globe*, June 7, 1879; *Keokuk Constitution*, January 12, 1880; *Omaha Municipal Reports, 1888* (Omaha: Dispatch Publishing Co., 1889), pp. 278–81; *Keokuk Constitution*, August 18, 1909.

made no returns. Among the Mississippi River towns were 3 in Minnesota. St. Paul said it had 7 houses, Minneapolis, 4, and Winona 3. In Illinois, Muscatine reported 5 and Rock Island, 2. Keokuk, Iowa, made a return of 4. Neither Dubuque nor Burlington, both Iowa river towns, furnished information. Fort Scott, Wyandotte, and Topeka, Kansas, made no response, Lawrence reported none, and Leavenworth said 6. Kansas City, Missouri; Nashville, Tennessee; and Santa Fé, New Mexico, did not answer. In Tennessee, Memphis put the figure at 29 and Knoxville at 30. Dallas and Fort Worth, Texas, reported 5 and 8 respectively, Louisville, Kentucky, set the figure at 126, and Atlanta, Georgia, at 6. In Colorado, Denver reported 7, and Leadville, as might be supposed, reported 100. In Nebraska, Omaha made a return of 17, and Lincoln 5. Virginia City, Nevada, reported 20 houses of ill fame, and Tucson, Arizona, 6.

Returns were so incomplete and so many communities failed to reply to the questionnaire that Wines became discouraged. He noted with that wry humor so characteristic of him that if the ninety-four towns which declared themselves without houses of ill fame "are as virtuous as they claim to be they are indeed fortunate; if not, the police are blind."[53] He, of course, was correct on each count—towns were not virtuous and the police were blind.

They failed to enforce statute and ordinance not only because the license system and the red-light district brought revenue into municipal coffers and segregated sin so that it did not annoy the passerby but also because a public, conceiving prostitution to be a picayune peccadillo, did not desire enforcement. Without enforcement, as Thomas Dekker wrote in his seventeenth-century play *The Honest Whore*,

> All here are but one swarm of bees, and strive,
> To bring with wearied thighs honey to the hive.

[53] Frederick H. Wines, *Report on the Defective, Dependent, and Delinquent Classes . . . as returned to the Tenth Census*, June 1, 1880 (Washington: G.P.O., 1888), table 136, pp. 566–74. In the eleventh census, Wines attempted to determine the number of females convicted and imprisoned for prostitution. Again, results were inadequate and incomplete. For the United States at large, the total was 353; for the North Atlantic division, 299; for the South Atlantic division, 4; for the North Central division, 41; for the South Central division, 9; for the Western division, none. See Wines, *Report on Crime, Pauperism, and Benevolence . . . Eleventh Census: 1890* (Washington: G.P.O., 1895), vol. 3, pt. 2, table 48, p. 202.

CHAPTER NINE

The Close and Stinking Jail

Close and Stinking Goal [sic] A Person would be in better Situation in the French Kings Gallies, or the Prisons of Turkey or Barbary, than in this Dismal Place—Which is a small House hir'd by the Provost Marshall containing 5 or 6 Rooms, about 12 feet square each and in one of these Rooms have 16 Debtors been crowded—And as the Heat of the Weather in C.[harles] T.[own] in Summer is almost intolerable, What must the Situation of Prisoners then be? They often have not Room to lye at length, but suceed each other to lye down—One was suffocated by the Heat of this Summer—and when a Coffin was sent for the Corps, there was no room to admit it, till some Wretches lay down, and made their wretched Carcasses, a Table to lay the Coffin on—Men and Women are crowded promiscuously —No Necessary Houses to retire too—The Necessities of Nature must be done by both Sexes in the presence of each other.[1]

This unflattering, but realistic, portrayal of their "close and stinking" jail set down by irate Carolinians in 1767 might well have been penned by indignant colonials throughout all of British America. Indeed, the depiction was apt and true long after the United States won its independence. Many a Mississippi River boatman, Arkansas traveler, hung-over cowpuncher, or lumberjack of the Pacific Northwest, blinking in sudden sunlight after stepping from confinement into freedom, left jails not unlike that in Charles Town. Prisons the nation over were crowded, many were unsegregated, more lacked proper sanitary facilities, and all stank all the time. Deaths of inmates were not uncommon. Yet the hoosegow was a necessity and, curiously enough, was ardently desired.

In 1632 Boston ordered a people pen to be constructed with all convenient speed, and in 1785 the Massachusetts General Court said that good and sufficient jails should be built in every town where a court was

[1] Charles Woodmason, *The Carolina Backcountry on the Eve of the Revolution*, ed. Richard J. Hooker (Chapel Hill: University of North Carolina Press, 1953), p. 236.

held. About 1642 the Virginia Grand Assembly ordered that "commissioners of the severall countyes doe take care that sufficient prisons be built for the use of the severall countyes respectively." The Dutch in New Amsterdam erected a jail-prison in 1642.[2]

William Penn, opposed as he was to capital punishment, approved of jails. The first Philadelphia jail, built late in 1682 or early in 1683, was a cage some seven feet long and five feet wide. A new jail was opened in 1776, but the structure was requisitioned by Congress and used for the confinement of military prisoners and British collaborators. When the Elizabeth, New Jersey, prison was burned by the enemy, the legislature graciously provided for the free use of the neighboring Essex County jail.[3]

As the new nation matured, consolidating itself in settled areas and pushing tentacles of vigor into new frontiers, the jails kept pace. Legislatures not only sought to improve conditions but also to make sure that each recently established community was provided with a courthouse and a jail. Georgia, for example, in 1796 was concerned with keeping its jails in repair. Tennessee authorized a score of counties to construct prisons and to erect stocks. Nashville was instructed in 1803 to build its jail on the bluff of the Cumberland River, so that it would be near water, and to erect a structure with at least three rooms —one for the jailer, one for felons, and one for debtors. In 1807, the Alabama jails were equipped with pillories, whipping posts, and stocks; further, they were to be well secured by timber, iron grates, bolts, and locks. By 1822 Mississippi also, in theory at least, insisted upon stone, brick, or timber jails with iron bars, and pillory, whipping post, and stocks.[4]

2 Nathaniel B. Shurtleff, ed., *Records of the Governor and Company of the Massachusetts Bay in New England, 1628–1686* (Boston: William White, 1853–1854), 1:100; *Laws of the Commonwealth of Massachusetts, 1780–1807* (Boston: F. T. Buckingham, 1807), 1:218; William W. Hening, ed., *The Statutes-at-Large: Being a Collection of All the Laws of Virginia, 1619–1792* (New York: R. & W. & G. Bartow, 1823), 1:264–65; Philip Klein, *Prison Methods in New York State* (New York: Columbia University Press, 1920), pp. 31, 33–34.

3 Thorsten Sellin, "Philadelphia Prisons of the Eighteenth Century," *Transactions of the American Philosophical Society*, vol. 43, pt. 1 (March 1953): pp. 326–30. See also J. Thomas Scharf and Thompson Westcott, *History of Philadelphia, 1609–1884* (Philadelphia: L. H. Everts & Co., 1884), 1:443–44; *Laws of the State of New-Jersey* (Trenton: Joseph Justice, 1821), p. 102.

4 Horatio Marbury and William H. Crawford, *Digest of the Laws of the State of Georgia, from Its Settlement as a British Province, in 1775, to the Session of the General Assembly in 1800, Inclusive . . .* (Savannah: Seymour, Woolhopter & Stebbins, 1802), pp. 171–72; Edward Scott, comp., *Laws of the State of Tennessee*

Two incidents illustrate the need for jails and the citizens' desire to have them. A fire in Detroit, Michigan, in 1805 destroyed the local jail, and the next year the federal government granted 10,000 acres of land to rebuild it. In 1810 a grand jury, in a strongly worded presentment, declared that, although five years had passed since the grant had been made, the territory was still without a jail, even though other, less worthy projects had been completed. The jury noted:

> It is strange to See a donation particularly appropriated to So necessary and usefull a purpose applied to So many disenterested objects . . . in this therefore We Consider it our duty to present that there has been a wanton violation and breach of the aforesaid act of Congress.[5]

Nineteen years later, in 1829, a grand jury in Key West, Florida, urged the propriety of a federal appropriation for the construction of a jail and gave plain reasons. Key West was an isolated spot, and the majority of those living there were mariners who were employed in the wrecking business.

> The habits the mode of life of Mariners when upon shore, are also well known—and though this Jury believe this population to be as good and orderly as in any other portion of the Union yet, here as in all other places, the strong arm of the Law is too often required to preserve order among them and punish the guilty.[6]

When Congress failed to act, another grand jury, convening in 1830, repeated the request. This also was ignored.

Finally, in 1831 the Legislative Council in desperation authorized the retention of $2,000 from the territorial tax on auction sales in Key West for the construction of a jail and a cistern. Two years later, a judge made it clear that West Florida was still without a jail:

> Except in the County of Jackson, I hold the Sessions of the Courts in private houses, which are rented, for that purpose by the Marshall. As we have no Jails at all, the Criminal law cannot be enforced, as it should be.[7]

. . . *1715–1820* (Knoxville: Heiskell & Brown, 1821), 1:502–4, 579–82, 790–92, 839–40, 969–70; 2:64, 214, 216–17; Harry Toulmin, comp., *Digest of Laws of Alabama* (Cahawba: Ginn & Curtis, 1823), p. 654; *Revised Code of the Laws of Mississippi* (Natchez: Francis Baker, 1824), p. 81.

[5] Clarence E. Carter, ed., *Territorial Papers of the United States* (Washington: G.P.O., 1936–62), 10:327–28 (Michigan Territory).

[6] Ibid., 24:215–16 (Florida Territory).

[7] Ibid., 24:417, 851–53 (Florida Territory).

As the 19th century civilized itself to the extent that imprisonment for debt was abolished and convicted criminals no longer were subjected to the indignities of whipping posts, stocks, and pillories, some of the harsher features of punishment were modified. Virtually all new states entering the Union standardized, at least to a degree, their criteria for jails, and the older states modified their previous requirements. Generally speaking, counties were to erect and maintain "good and sufficient" jails.[8]

Responsibility for the supervision of the jail and the safekeeping of prisoners was, of course, vested in the sheriff. This was traditional practice throughout the United States. Again and again, it was said that "The jail itself is the state's, but the keeping thereof is incident to the office of sheriff, and inseparable from it." The county jail, unfortunately, was the least of the sheriff's worries. Normally, he appointed a jailer who, in haphazard manner, supervised the jail and its assorted inmates. If the sheriff did double in brass as jailer, he devoted as little time as possible to the task. An elected official, he was busier mending his political fences than renovating the jailhouse. His guests, although distinguished enough in their peculiar professions, represented neither the local elite nor the county power structure.[9]

[8] See, for example, *Laws of the State of Missouri* (St. Louis: E. Charles, 1825), p. 258; *Revised Laws of Illinois* (Vandalia: Greiner & Sherman, 1833), pp. 336–37; *Revised Statutes of Wisconsin* (Southport: C. Latham Sholes, 1849), 735–36; Moses Sherburne and William Hollinshead, comps., *Public Statutes of the State of Minnesota, 1849–1858* (St. Paul: Pioneer Printing Company, 1859), p. 789; Cameron H. King, ed., *Revised Statutes of Arizona* (Prescott: Prescott Courier Print, 1887), p. 128; Will T. Little, L. G. Pitman, and R. J. Barker, comps., *Statutes of Oklahoma, 1890* (Guthrie: State Capital Printing Co., 1891), p. 408.

[9] Augustin S. Clayton, *The Office and Duty of a Justice of the Peace, and a Guide to Clerks, Constables, Coroners, Executors, Administrators, Guardians, Sheriffs, Tax-Collectors, and Receivers, and Other Civil Officers, According to the Laws of the State of Georgia* . . . (Milledgeville: S. Grantland, 1819), p. 218. See also Cyrus H. Karraker, *The Seventeenth-Century Sheriff: A Comparative Study of the Sheriff in England and the Chesapeake Colonies, 1607–1689* (Durham: University of North Carolina Press, 1930); John Bradford, *The General Instructor; Or, the Office, Duty, and Authority of Justices of the Peace, Sheriffs, Coroners and Constables in the State of Kentucky* (Lexington: John Bradford, 1800); Charles W. Hartshorn, *New England Sheriff: Being a Digest of the Laws of Massachusetts Relating to Sheriffs, Jailers, Coroners and Constables* (Worcester: Warren Lazell, 1844); John M. Krum, *The Missouri Justice: Being a Compendium of the Laws Relating to the Powers and Duties of Justices of the Peace, Executors, Administrators, Guardians, Constables, and Coroners* . . . *Adapted to the Revised Laws of 1845* (St. Louis: A. Fisher, 1845); William A. Jackson, *The Office of Sheriff in Iowa* (Iowa City & Cedar Rapids:

What buttered a sheriff's daily bread was not the per diem he received for feeding prisoners, but the fat fees he got from serving process.[10] Even today the lucrative fee system flourishes in some states. An Associated Press article published in the Minneapolis *Tribune* on March 4, 1968, reported the incomes of sheriffs in the state of Mississippi for the year 1966. The top income was $71,225, and the next highest was $48,755. The news story said: "Mississippi sheriffs' incomes vary because of the fee system, under which they keep the remainder of fees after paying expenses and salaries. There is no ceiling on the rakeoff."

Jail guest lists were set by law, and almost all states maintained identical admittance requirements. Jails were open for the detention of persons who were committed in order to assure their attendance as witnesses in criminal cases; for the detention of persons charged with crime and held for trial; for the confinement of persons committed for contempt, or upon civil process, or by other authority of law; and for the confinement of persons sentenced to imprisonment upon a convic-

---

Torch Press, 1924). For the Farther West, see, for example, Samuel Maxwell, *A Treatise on the Powers and Duties of Justices of the Peace, Sheriffs, and Constables in the State of Nebraska* (Lincoln: Journal Co., 1879); John Sayles, *A Treatise on the Civil Jurisdiction of Justices of the Peace in the State of Texas*, 2d ed. (Houston: E. H. Cushing, 1878); William S. Hawlow, *Duties of Sheriffs and Constables, Particularly under the Practice in California and the Pacific States and Territories*, 2d ed., rev. and ed. Fred L. Button (San Francisco: Bancroft-Whitney Co., 1895).

[10] *Alabama Acts, 1839–1841* (Tuscaloosa: Hale & Eaton, 1840), p. 61, provided that the sheriff of Marshall County receive 10 percent of all taxes collected by him. From colonial days throughout the 19th century, legislatures stipulated fee schedules. See, for example, Hening, *Statutes-at-Large, Virginia*, 1:305; William P. Van Ness and John Woodworth, eds., *Laws of the State of New York, 1784–1813* (Albany: H. C. Southwick & Co., 1813), 2:25–26; S. Garfielde and F. A. Snyder, *Compiled Laws of the State of California, 1850–1853* (Benicia: S. Garfielde, 1853), 724–25, 732–33; E. Estabrook, *Statutes of Nebraska* (Chicago: Culver, Page, & Hoyne, 1867), pp. 162–63. In addition to stated fees for transporting prisoners, serving summons, attending district court, serving execution or attachment, and other similar duties, sheriffs also were paid commissions on money collected without sale. In Montana, for example, the schedule was as follows: Commissions on all sums under $500, 2 percent; between $500 and $1,000, 2 percent on the first $500, and $1\frac{1}{2}$ percent on all such other sums; on all sums over $1,000, in addition to the percentage on the first $1,000, 1 percent. Commissions on money collected by sale: 2 percent on any sum under $1,000; between $1,000 and $5,000, 2 percent for the first $1,000, and 1 percent on all such additional amounts; on all sums over $5,000, the sheriff was to receive the fees above allowed for $5,000 and one-fourth of 1 percent on all such additional amounts. See *Revised Statutes of Montana, Twelfth Legislative Assembly* (Helena: Geo. E. Boos, 1881), pp. 530–31.

tion of crime. In addition, after the founding of the Republic, all states passed legislation providing for the hospitality of prisoners of the federal government.[11]

The sheriff's jailer, usually uncouth and frequently brutal, was the keeper of a mélange of human beings. Some were first offenders, and others were hardened criminals. Some were beardless youths, and others tottered on the edge of the grave. Others were confined only because they were being held as witnesses. There were those who had violated no section of the criminal code, but who were in jail because of some civil action. Federal prisoners mixed with those who had been tried, convicted, and sentenced and were awaiting transportation to a state penitentiary. According to law, each was entitled to a place to sleep, something to eat, and to medical care.

Theoretically, the care and feeding of inmates followed, as did so much of American legal procedure, the view of Sir William Blackstone, who wrote that a prisoner in a county jail should be used with the "utmost humanity, and neither be loaded with needless fetters, or subjected to other hardships than such as are absolutely requisite for the purpose of confinement only." Yet Blackstone recognized that jailers frequently were merciless men, and "by being conversant in scenes of misery, steeled against any tender sensation." Humanitarian sentiments were written into scores of statutes by the several states, but they were observed more in the breach than in the promise. It is difficult, indeed, to see how sheriffs and jailers could provide adequately for prisoners with the monies allotted by law.[12]

---

[11] King, *Revised Statutes of Arizona*, pp. 428–29; John R. Bartlett, ed., *Records of the Colony of Rhode Island and Providence Plantations in New England, 1630–1792* (Providence, Alfred Anthony, 1856–1865), 10:689–90: "An Act of Congress, March 4, 1789 recommended that the several states pass laws permitting jails to receive and keep federal prisoners with the United States paying fifty cents a month for each prisoner." The Rhode Island General Assembly, pursuant to the Congressional Act, passed a law in September, 1790, stipulating that the "keepers of the respective jails in the counties of Newport, Providence, Washington, and Kent" be ordered to receive and keep safe all prisoners committed under the authority of the United States. Other states enacted similar legislation. See, for example, *Revised Codes of North Dakota* (Bismarck: Tribune Co., 1895), pp. 1505–6.

[12] William Blackstone, *Commentaries on the Laws of England*, ed. with introduction and notes by George Sharwood (Philadelphia: J. B. Lippincott & Co., 1872, 1873), vol. 2, bk. 4, p. 298. Typical examples of state statutes may be found in Clayton, *Office and Duty*, Georgia, p. 219; Lucius Q. C. Lamar, comp., *Compilation of the Laws of the State of Georgia . . . 1810–1819* (Augusta: T. S. Hannon, 1821), pp. 163–64.

Tennessee sheriffs, for example, in 1796 were paid 25 cents a day per prisoner and for this sum were required to provide a daily ration of one pound of wholesome bread, one pound of good roasted or broiled fish, and a sufficient quantity of fresh water. During the 1820s, prisoners in Alabama county jails were fed on 50 cents a day. Some twenty years later, Louisiana sheriffs were given $37\frac{1}{2}$ cents a day and ordered to provide a daily allowance of one pound of beef or three-quarters of a pound of pork, one pound of wheaten bread, one pound of potatoes or one gill of rice, and one gill of whisky. Jailers were also obligated to furnish each prisoner, at the beginning of the winter season, a blanket capot, a shirt, a pair of woolen trousers, and a pair of coarse shoes. In summer, a shirt and a pair of trousers of coarse linen were to be provided. It is interesting to note that Nebraska, in 1867, allotted sheriffs not more than 25 cents a day for feeding prisoners, the same sum that Tennessee paid seventy-one years earlier.[13]

Other states were far less specific, legislating only in general terms and leaving actual details to the county commissioners or to the sheriffs to work out as best they might. Thus Iowa, for example, in 1851 required that jailers furnish prisoners daily with three wholesome and well-cooked meals in sufficient quantity, that they be supplied with sufficient clean water for personal use and for drinking, and that they be given a fresh towel and shirt once a week. The sheriff was also obliged to furnish necessary bedding, clothing, and medical aid. Several states required that Bibles be furnished, and all states, by the close of the 19th century, forbade the introduction of intoxicating liquors into county jails.[14]

[13] Scott, *Laws of Tennessee*, 1:554–55; Toulmin, *Digest of Laws of Alabama*, pp. 354–56; Meinrad Greiner, comp., *Louisiana Digest of Laws, 1804–1841* (New Orleans: Benjamin Levy, 1841), p. 418; Estabrook, *Statutes of Nebraska*, pp. 162–63. New Jersey sheriffs, in 1799, received 10 cents a day for victualing prisoners. See *Laws of the State of New-Jersey*, p. 489.

[14] *Code of Iowa, 1850–1851* (Iowa City: Palmer & Paul, 1851), pp. 428–30. For the supplying of Bibles, see, for example, *Revised Codes of North Dakota* (Bismarck: Tribune Co., 1895), p. 1499; Sherburne and Hollinshead, *Public Statutes of the State of Minnesota*, p. 789; Little, Pitman, and Barker, *Statutes of Oklahoma*, p. 1037. For laws pertaining to the introduction of intoxicating liquors into jails, see *Revised Code of Mississippi*, p. 254; *Revised Statutes of Wisconsin*, p. 736: "No sheriff, jailer or keeper of any prison shall, under any pretence, give, sell, or deliver to any person committed to prison for any cause whatever, any spirituous liquor, or any mixed liquor, part of which is spirituous, or any wine, cider or strong beer, unless a physician shall certify in writing that the health of such prisoner requires it, in which case he may be allowed the quantity prescribed and no more." Sheriffs, keepers, and

Although sheriffs were bonded and gave security, although jails, from earliest times, were inspected by official visitors, and although county trustees or commissioners were responsible, in part at least, for the proper functioning of the institution, jails seldom, if ever, met criteria prescribed by statutes. Prisoners, laws to the contrary, were mistreated or handled indifferently. One has only to scan reports of official inspectors to realize that conditions in jails were frightful in all parts of the nation.[15]

There is, perhaps, no better way to illustrate the point than to quote an inspector who visited the Mille Lacs jail in Princeton, Minnesota, in 1885. This wooden structure, built in 1876 at a cost of $450, was situated at the rear of the courthouse and was surrounded by a stockade of oak planks about ten feet high. The inspector wrote:

> The jail consists of a corridor 15 by 13 feet and two cells each $6\frac{1}{2}$ by 9 feet, the cell structure being composed of 2 by 6-inch oak scantling spiked together. The jail door is of the same, guarded by heavy iron bolts which give it the ponderous air of an old-style prison. The cell doors are of 2-inch pine stuff. Each cell is lighted and ventilated by a window 12 by 27 inches.[16]

But this was not all, for, according to the report, there was no way to heat the cells, and there were no sashes whatsoever in the windows. The

---

jailers convicted of violation for a first offense were subject to a fine of $25.00, and, upon a second conviction, were prohibited from holding office for a period of five years.

[15] For selected examples of bonds, securities, and oaths, see *Ohio State Constitution*, art. 6, sec. 1; Salmon P. Chase, ed., *Statutes of Ohio, 1788–1833* (Cincinnati: Corey & Fairbank, 1833–1835), 2:1351; *Missouri State Constitution*, art. 4, secs. 23, 24; *Wisconsin State Constitution*, art. 6, sec. 4. In November, 1801, the Maryland General Assembly authorized the appointment of eight discreet persons to visit and inspect the Baltimore County jail; in 1823 the Alabama Legislature placed the supervision of jails in the hands of the justices of county courts; in 1851 the Iowa Legislature authorized judges of district courts to appoint jail inspectors. After the Civil War, states such as Michigan and Minnesota, to offer only two examples, placed jail inspection in the hands of boards of correction and charities, but county commissioners still played a significant role. Penalties for the mistreatment of prisoners were generally provided for by law. See, for example, *Code of [the Territory of] Washington . . . Acts of a General Nature* (Olympia: C. B. Bagley, 1881), 175: "If any sheriff, jailer or other officer shall be guilty of willful inhumanity or oppression to any prisoner under his care or custody, he shall, on conviction thereof, be imprisoned in the county jail not more than one year nor less than one day, and be fined in a sum not exceeding one thousand dollars."

[16] Minnesota, *Executive Documents, 1886* (St. Paul: Pioneer Press Co., 1887), 1:643.

inspector commented caustically that this was the best ventilated jail in the state. The only furniture consisted of a broken bench, two chairs, two wooden pails, and a canvas cot covered with dirty blankets and quilts. The inspector continued:

> The sheriff was found in bed, but stated that the jail was unlocked. . . . It was utterly neglected, and without either stove or window sash, presented as depressing a spectacle as I have yet seen.[17]

Now and again, an enterprising sheriff not only posted rules for his jail, but also enforced them as best he could. Prisoners in the Otter Tail County jail in Minnesota were required to keep their cells and persons clean. They were not permitted to lie upon their beds during the daytime unless sick and were obliged to take weekly baths. Talking with prisoners in other cells was forbidden at any time, and inmates were not allowed to speak or motion to anyone through the jail windows. Defacing walls, loud talking, singing, profane language, and even whistling were not permitted. The use of intoxicating liquors was, of course, prohibited, and inmates using tobacco were warned to "spit only in the spittoons provided for that purpose." All prisoners remained locked in their cells except for brief exercise periods.[18]

Prisoners in the Polk County, Minnesota, jail, one of the worst in the state in 1892, formulated and posted their own awkwardly worded rules, which were enforced by a sort of kangaroo court:

1. Prisoners on the floor or in the cells shall be tried by this court.
2. Prisoners using water closet in the cage or the one outside, must not wet the floor or leave paper in the bowls or on the floor.
3. Every man must wash his clothes once a week and keep himself as clean as possible.
4. Each man takes his turn to sweep the floor and cells three times a day.
5. Officers of this jail infringing the rules of this jail is subjected to trial.
6. Any prisoner—an officer of this court not doing his duty is subject to trial by this court.
7. Any man whose turn it is to sweep, neglects to sweep three times a day or fails to clean wash bowls once a day shall be sentenced accordingly.
8. Any man spitting on stove is subject to trial by court.
9. All prisoners not complying with said rules, will be judged and sentenced by this court. Which should the prisoner have money will be obliged to donate so much tobacco. If without money, he will have a task set out for him to do around the jail. *Every new prisoner* coming to this

---

17 Ibid.

18 Ibid., 1:650–51. For model regulations, see Roy Casey, *The Modern Jail* (Keene, Texas: Continental Press, 1958), pp. 87–89.

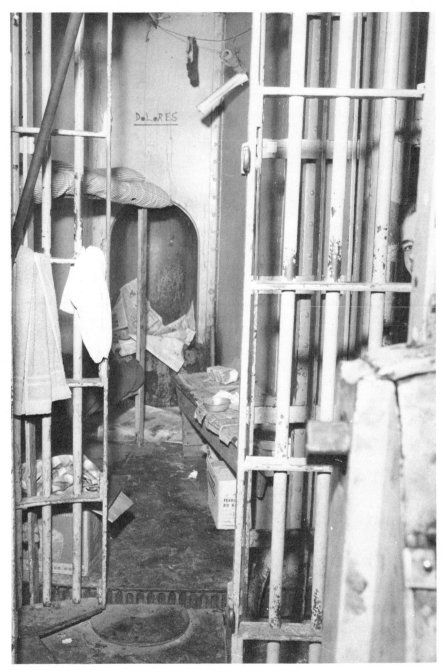

View of a cell in a county jail

204

JAIL REGISTER OF PRISONERS.

Geo. D. Barnard & Co., Blank Book Manufacturers

NAME	RESIDENCE	Time of Commitment M'th Day Year	CAUSE OF COMMITMENT	BY WHAT AUTHORITY COMMITTED	Sentence	When Liberated M'th Day Year
Jno A Swenson	Grantsburg	Apl 14 1907				Apl 12 1909
	Burnett	June 16 1908	Adultery			
Steve Wilson	Marshland	1 16 1897	held for Jury			18 1897
Joe Sawyer	Marshland					1 18 1897
Schmidt, August	Marshland	Mar 31 1897		Justice Ct.		May 30 1897
Schmidt, August	Wood Lake	May 24 1897	Rape	Justice Ct for Jury		Mar 2 1898
Seamon, Albert	Town of Reed	Mar 7, 1898	Rape	Justice Ct held for Jury		
Sigurdson, Gustafson	Town of Wood Row	Apr 16 1913	Insanity	County Judge		
Gundin, Fred	Town J W Marshland	Feb 8, 24 1913				
Smith, R C		July 18 1915	assault		100 & costs 6 days	Apr 21 1915
Dattie, Henry	Wood River	Mar 18 1917				
Behmen, Herman	Town Dann	May 6 1918				
Springer, Wm	Town of Union	Aug 6 1919		Justice Olson	released on bail	Aug 21 1918
Springer, Mabel		" " "	Adultery	"		
Springer, Wm		" " "	"	"		
Sundberg, Clara	Trade Lake	Oct 31 1921	"	Circuit Court		
Laura Dawew	" " "	May 25 1923	Insanity	County Court	1 year	
Ahlberg, Raymond	Village Grantsburg	Feb 4 1923	Larceny	County Judge		
Solander Albin	Town Trade Lake	Dec 26 1923	scott Bottles	Justice Court	fined	Dec 27 1923
S Hoagland John	Town Daniels	Dec 26 1923	scott Bottle	Justice Court	fined	Dec 27 1923

Courtesy of the Area Research Center, Wisconsin State University, River Falls

BURNETT COUNTY, WISCONSIN.

Printers, Lithographers and Stationers, St. Louis

Age	Height	Weight	Complexion	Color of Hair	Color of Eyes	By What Authority Liberated	PARTICULARS OF ESCAPE	Time of Escape M'th Day Year	REMARKS
40	5'10"	140	dark	Lit	Blue				
30	5'8-7in	165	light	Brown	Blue				
44	5 ♂		dark	Black	Blue	Discharged by Court			1 mo
44	5'5		dark	Black	Blue	Court Judge			Taken to hospital at Mankato Minn Taken to hospital at Mendota Minn
21	5'9	160	dark	dark	Blue				arrest (g) drap & paid fine.
	5'10	200	"	"	Blue				
40	5'9	158	Slight	Gray	Blue	returned	West som on you		returned finding judgment
27	5'10	140	dark	dark	Brown	Standfon chif	Standfon chif		Bandid manner
Aug. 13th 1921,									
27	5'10"	160	Med.	dark	Blue	Bound offers to Circuit Court.			Priton Courtip
63	5'1"	125	dark	"	Brown	"			Breathotoyed
21	5'10"	165	med	"	Blue	Sentenced to Green Bay for 1 year			
64	5'9	600	Taken to Black or Hospital at Ownn Minn Feb 4, 1923			Laken to State hospital at Ownn Minn May 26 1922			

Paid Fine
Paid Fine

Paid Fine

Courtesy of the Area Research Center, Wisconsin State University, River Falls

Lazy Susan jail, Pottawattamie County, Iowa

jail who states that he is without money—if not believed by the court—is subjected to a search, and should any money be found in his possession shall be tried by court and fined accordingly.[19]

Of greater interest than rules and regulations was the topic of escape. Sheriffs and jailers tried to keep their guests behind bars; prisoners worked to break out. The conflict is as old as time, for escaping from confinement seems to be an irresistible impulse. If convicts read the Bibles furnished them, they most certainly scoffed at Zophar's remark to Job: "But the eyes of the wicked shall fail, and they shall not escape." Equally absurd is the popular impression that prisoners whiled away the hours singing jailhouse ditties to the accompaniment of twanging banjos:

> One night when I was in prison I dreampt a happy dream,
> I dreampt I was in old Missouri down by some flowin' stream,
> With my darlin' girl beside me, she had come to go my bail,
> But I woke up broken-hearted in the Dallas county jail.[20]

It is almost a truism that escapes from state prisons, county jails, and town lockups were the rule rather than the exception. All sorts of statutes sought to prevent or curtail the practice. A Virginia statute of the 17th century required that

> if any person shall happen to escape from the hands or custody of any sheriffs of any severall countyes respectively for want of sufficient prison in each county, All such sheriffs shall find his remedie against the severall countyes which shall be delinquent in the building of prisons.[21]

A general law of Massachusetts in 1700 stipulated that jailers who voluntarily permitted prisoners to escape should suffer the penalties which the escapees would have had to suffer if they were apprehended.[22] A Michigan grand jury in 1836 complained of the large number of escapes and added, somewhat ruefully:

> But unless some more secure Prison be erected for this District, it seems to your Memorialists, hopeless to expect, that the prevalence of crime can be checked, by the mere force of the law.[23]

[19] Minnesota, *Executive Documents, 1892* (Minneapolis: Harrison and Smith, 1893), 3:748–49.

[20] For jail songs, see Vance Randolph, ed., *Ozark Folksongs* (Columbia, Mo.: State Historical Society of Missouri, 1946–1950), vol. 2, chap. 4.

[21] Hening, *Statutes-at-Large: Virginia*, 1:264–65.

[22] *Charter and General Laws of the Colony and Province of Massachusetts Bay, 1700 to 1814* (Boston: T. B. Wait, 1814), pp. 344–46.

[23] Carter, *Territorial Papers*, 12:1093–94 (Michigan Territory).

Through the years, most states adopted elaborate legislation designed not only to stem an increasing escape rate, but also to discourage individuals from helping friends to go over the wall. A Texas act is typical. It stipulated that any sheriff or peace officer who permitted a prisoner to escape was subject, upon conviction, to confinement in the penitentiary for not less than two or more than ten years and that any peace officer who negligently permitted a person convicted of a capital crime to escape was subject to a fine not exceeding $2,000. It also provided penalties for persons who smuggled instruments or arms into a jail and for persons who broke into a jail in order to help a prisoner escape. Finally, the act set a fine not exceeding $500 to be levied upon any person who aided a prisoner to escape from the custody of a peace officer and a fine not to exceed $1,000 for any person who used weapons in effecting such an escape.[24]

Such laws seemed to serve more as a challenge than as a deterrent, for jailbreaks occurred with monotonous regularity. Frequently, prisoners simply ambled away from courtroom or jail, perhaps, as in the case of one prisoner, to spend a quiet hour or so in a saloon, and then, thirst slaked, to return to his dry cell. A friendly soul opened the jail near Louisville, Kentucky, with a set of duplicate keys and invited six prisoners to walk freedom's road. A condemned man broke jail in Vicksburg, Mississippi, was apprehended by the sheriff, and then, armed with a long butcher knife, made "fearful lunges" at all who attempted to approach him. Finally, the sheriff shot him dead. In Erie County, New York, six prisoners broke open the jail and escaped. Peace officers in New Orleans arrested friends of inmates after they had placed a ladder against the jail wall. The rescuers were armed with three horse pistols and a large poniard. All these escapes and attempted escapes were made during the 1830s.[25]

Escapes were not, by any means, confined to the eastern or southern states. Citizens in all sections of the Union complained of poorly constructed prisons and of the inability of jailers to keep their prisoners confined. It was easy to saw through soft iron bars, to chip away rotting

---

[24] *Penal Code of State of Texas* (Galveston: News Office, 1857), pp. 58–63. See also *Ohio Acts, Sixteenth General Assembly, 1817* (Columbus: P. H. Olmsted, 1818), pp. 173–75; *Alabama Acts, 1839–1841*, p. 140; Garfielde and Snyder, *Compiled Laws of California, 1850–1853*, pp. 657–58; Estabrook, *Statutes of Nebraska*, pp. 613, 614.

[25] *Boston Courier*, September 30, 1831; *New Orleans Bee*, February 16, 1832, March 4, 1836, October 17, 1839; *Vicksburg Register*, March 26, 1834; *New York Evening Post*, July 9, 1834.

mortar, to pry apart loose stones, to simply walk away when permitted to go outside to a privy. To a jailer, of course, the height of indignity was for a prisoner to break jail, steal the marshal's gold watch, and ride away on the sheriff's horse. One determined individual broke jail four times in one month and was last seen poling down the Mississippi River in a leaky skiff. In Keokuk, Iowa, a determined inmate, emulating Jean Valjean, pried up a jail drain, made his way down it into a city sewer, crawled its length, and never was heard from again. Two of Sheriff Bat Masterson's prisoners escaped by cutting a hole through the pine ceiling of their cells.[26]

It is little wonder, in view of escape after escape, that grand juries should find that jails were unfit for the incarceration of criminals. They recommended that new and sturdier structures be built and that jails be better inspected. It was said repeatedly that "it is certain that either through remissness on the part of the jailor, or defects in the jail itself, prisoners succeed in making their escape with marvelous facility."[27] A Minnesota editor wrote, with heavy irony:

> We hope our citizens will demand the immediate building of a jail, for we have almost become hopeless as to their speedy movement in regard to schoolhouses; and we do say, if the children are doomed to suffer the want to Education, at least let our criminals be furnished with a commodious house of refuge.[28]

Curiously enough, although county commissioners desired escape-proof jails, they were blinded by architectural tradition and committed to age-old designing: that is, the customary jail, whether of stone, brick, wood, or adobe, was a square box whose interior was usually divided into cells partitioned by iron or steel bars. Reliance was placed upon barred windows, heavy doors, and ponderous locks.

[26] This paragraph is a composite based upon scores of accounts taken from newspapers of Minnesota, Wisconsin, Iowa, Illinois, and Missouri for the years from 1850 to 1870. The Masterson incident was reported in the *Dodge City Globe*, February 17, 1879, and it is cited in Nyle H. Miller and Joseph W. Snell, *Great Gunfighters of the Kansas Cowtowns, 1867–1886* (Lincoln: University of Nebraska Press, 1963), pp. 259–60.

[27] See, for example, grand jury reports on common jail, Hennepin County, Minnesota, District Court, court minutes, November 23, 1871, p. 446; May 27, 1873, p. 23; November 18, 1876, p. 462; May 16, 1877, p. 656; see also *Winona Weekly Republican*, June 29, 1859, March 12, 27, 1863. The quotation is from *Winona Times*, June 12, 1858.

[28] *Winona Weekly Republican*, September 8, 1857.

It made little difference whether such a jail stood by itself or was
fitted into a portion of a courthouse, for the essential design remained
unchanged. Cells were as cramped as coffins. An inspection team in
1865 reported that cells in the county jail in St. Louis, Missouri,
measured eight feet square and ten feet high and housed from three to
six prisoners.[29] Most prison planners felt that such cramped cubicles
were economical to build in jails. Only in eastern states did architects
begin to suggest radical changes in structures for the confinement of
prisoners. After the Civil War, the western states were hard put to
provide for adequate prisons, jails, and lock-ups. One example must
suffice.

The Utah territorial legislature in 1866 passed a resolution ordering
the directors of the penitentiary to employ a competent architect to pre-
pare plans and specifications for a new prison. A year later, the old
penitentiary was described as in very poor condition and as unfit for the
safekeeping of convicts. A memorial in 1869 again declared that the
prison was dilapidated and unsafe and was not suited to the purpose
for which it was used. It was pointed out that the "increase of population consequent upon the construction of the Union and Central Pacific
Railroad through the Territory, renders it necessary that accommoda-
tions of this class should be increased."

The memorialists requested permission to set aside the net proceeds
from the internal revenue of Utah Territory to be used for the erection
of a penitentiary, in the same manner as provided in "An Act setting
aside certain proceeds from Internal Revenue for the erection of Penitentiaries in the Territories of Nebraska, Washington, Colorado, Idaho,
Montana, Arizona and Dakota," which had been approved January
22, 1867.[30]

The point of all this is that, if penitentiaries were in such a deplorable
condition in the western country, county jails were as bad, if not worse.
Many newly created counties were poor; population increased, towns
boomed, and crime mounted after the Civil War, placing a heavy
burden upon law-enforcement agencies. Original prisons were no

[29] E. C. Wines and Theodore W. Dwight, *Report on the Prisons and Reformatories
of the United States and Canada* (Albany: Van Benthuysen & Sons' Steam Printing
House, 1867), p. 318.

[30] Territory of Utah, *Acts, Resolutions and Memorials . . . 1866* (Salt Lake City:
Henry McEwan, 1866); pp. 229–30; *Sixteenth Annual Session of the Utah Territorial
Legislature* (Salt Lake City: Geo. Q. Cannon, [1867]), pp. 36–37; *Eighteenth Annual
Session, Utah, 1869* (Salt Lake City: Geo. Q. Cannon, 1869), p. 33.

longer adequate. The Missouri River funneled thousands of men of every descripiton—some good, others bad—into the interior.[31]

Council Bluffs, Iowa, increased in population from 16,893 in 1870 to 39,846 in 1880, lending credence to the statement that

> Every new country, when first opened to emigration, is settled by a strange mixture of heterogeneous elements—by the enterprising and the virtuous seeking to improve their condition, and by the vicious of different grades who desire to escape from the trammels or the terrors of the law.[32]

The police chief of Omaha, Nebraska, made the same point in 1888, but in slightly different fashion. He noted that Omaha, because of its geographical position, appeared to harbor more criminals than other western cities with larger populations, adding:

> Within twelve hours' time criminals who may be released or run out of Chicago, Denver, Kansas City, St. Joe, Des Moines, St. Paul, Minneapolis and several other cities can come here, which they almost invariably do.[33]

Although architects customarily followed traditional design in planning new jails for a new age, there was a unique exception—the rotary jail, sometimes waggishly called the Human Squirrel Cage or the Lazy Susan Jail. At least six of these were built: the Montgomery County Jail, Crawfordsville, Indiana, in 1882; the Sedgwick County Jail, Wichita, Kansas, in 1884 or 1885; the DeKalb County Jail, Maysville, Missouri, in 1885; the Daviess County Jail, Gallatin, Missouri, in 1885; the Nodaway County Jail, Maryville, Missouri, in 1885; and the Pottawattamie County Jail, Council Bluffs, Iowa, in 1885. Of the six, only the last still stands.[34]

Although the mechanics of the rotary jail were complicated, the principle is understandable. In essence, the jail consisted of two cylinders,

[31] Betty B. Rosenbaum, "The Relationship between War and Crime in the United States," *Journal of Criminal Law and Criminology* 30 (1940): 722–40. For Missouri River traffic and freighting on the High Plains, see, for example, Henry P. Walker, *The Wagonmasters* (Norman: University of Oklahoma Press, 1966).

[32] Charles Summerfield [pseud.], *The Rangers and Regulators of The Tanaha; Or, Life among the Lawless* (New York: Robert M. DeWitt, 1856), p. viii.

[33] *Omaha Municipal Reports, 1888* (Omaha: Dispatch Publishing Co., 1889), p. 246.

[34] The discussion of the unique rotary jail is based upon Walter A. Lunden, "The Rotary Jail, or Human Squirrel Cage," *Journal of the Society of Architectural Historians* 18 (1959): 149–57. For a general, rather sketchy history of jail construction, see U.S. Bureau of Prisons, *Handbook of Correctional Institution Design and Construction* (n.p., [1949]).

one within the other, with the inner cylinder, containing cells, capable of revolving. In order to make the jail secure, only one passageway was cut from the outside to the inner, circular cage. The inner cylinder was rotated by a hand-cranking device attached to a huge gear ring. When the jail's inventors, W. H. Brown and B. F. Haugh, filed for a United States patent in July, 1881, they called attention to the fact that the jail's design prevented prisoners from communicating with one another.

> The cell structure is rotated until the door opening of the cell desired is brought opposite the general door opening in the outside grating, and while one cell occupies this position the rest must of necessity be securely closed. This arrangement makes the whole prison as convenient to the keeper as though it consisted of but a single prisoner.[35]

The grotesque, madman's jail in Council Bluffs, which cost some $28,000, began to malfunction within two years after it received its first prisoners. The inner drum failed to "scour," and inmates sustained fractured arms, legs, feet, and hands when these members were caught between the bars during the revolving of the cylinder. Nevertheless, the jail was held up as escape proof.

The crowning blow came in December, 1888, when eleven prisoners released themselves from the inner drum, climbed the grating of the outer shell, and coolly walked out the front door. In 1938, after successive grand jury investigations, the rotary cylinder was welded to the stationary outer shell. The squirrel cage became just another jail, no better or worse than thousands of others throughout the land, some of which, even in the 20th century, bore remarkable likeness to primitive lock-ups built when the nation was young.

[35] Lunden, "The Rotary Jail," p. 153.

CHAPTER TEN

The Law—Western Style

On the fifteenth day of October, 1866, two freedmen of color were jolting along in a wagon on a road near Brooksville, Texas. Charley was driving, and Seal, formerly the property of William H. Swinney, sat beside him in a vehicle, which was jumbled with bedding and blankets. The pair, Charley and Seal, no doubt lounged indolently upon the wagon's seat, perhaps—although this is conjecture—thanking their lucky stars that slavery had ceased to exist in the Lone Star state as the result of proclamations of President Johnson, General Gordon Granger, and Provisional Governor Andrew J. Hamilton. Charley and Seal had, therefore, become free during the summer and autumn of 1865. The two freedmen, clucking their horse along a dirt road, had among the bedclothing a collar and bell which only recently had decorated the neck of an ox belonging to William B. Henry, a white man. Henry valued the collar and bell at $2.50.

Mr. Henry, knowing no black men lived in Brooksville and having seen Charley and Seal drive through the community, suspected them of the theft and took off in relative hot pursuit. He caught up with the wagon, searched it, and found both collar and bell. Henry, taking the stolen property, inquired where Charley and Seal had acquired it. Each maintained it had been purchased that very morning from a Negro man, riding a white horse, who offered the collar and bell to them for six bits in specie. After the sale was consummated, the vendor disappeared, still riding his white horse. Seal, who, it was charged, made the purchase, was arrested, indicted, brought to trial, and convicted of theft. Charley testified in Seal's behalf.

The legal proceedings pertaining to the conviction of Seal and to the right of Charley to take the stand as a witness were justified, for the eighth section of the Texas constitution of 1866 stated specifically that criminal prosecutions against Africans and their descendants should be conducted in the same manner as prosecutions for like offenses against white men. Penalties for each race were the same. Furthermore, the constitution stipulated that Negroes could testify in court under the same rules of evidence which applied to white men. The only witness for the state was Henry, owner of the purloined bell and collar. He told the judge and jury that the collar of his ox had been severed by a knife with a dull blade and that he found such a knife in Seal's possession.

When the judge charged the jury, he defined theft and said:

> If from the evidence you believe that the defendant Seal, did unlawfully, feloniously, and fraudulently take, steal, and carry away the bell and bell-collar, or either of them was of some value, and that the bell and bell-collar, or either of them, was the property of William B. Henry, and said taking was done in this county, then it is your duty to find the defendant guilty, and assess his punishment to confinement in the penitentiary for two years, but if these facts are not proved by the evidence, then it is your duty to find the defendant not guilty.

Seal's counsel entered in the court record a charge to the effect that a jury must be satisfied of his client's guilt beyond a reasonable doubt, that the possession of stolen property raised only a presumption of guilt, "which may be explained away, if the explanation be satisfactory." The jury found Seal guilty and fixed the sentence at two years in the penitentiary, then the exact penalty for petty larceny. An appeal was carried by Seal's attorney to the Texas Supreme Court. It was based upon the argument that, among other errors, the lower court had misdirected the jury and that the evidence presented was not reasonably sufficient to satisfy jurymen of the truth of the charges against Seal.

The Supreme Court, however, possessed a tidy sense of the law if not of justice. It, in its decision affirming Seal's conviction, held that it was not a judge's duty to instruct a jury, even "though instructions though correct as abstract principles of law, were not authorized by the testimony produced upon the trial." The Supreme Court admitted there was conflict between the testimony given by Henry and that presented in behalf of Seal. "The jury," said the court, "had the witnesses before them, and were the best judges of their credibility. . . . They [the jury] have chosen to disregard the statements of the defendant's witness and give credit to the evidence offered by the state." Finally, as a sort of grand close, the court added:

> And as the judge who tried the case . . . and who of course had every opportunity of seeing the manner of the witnesses at the time of giving their testimony, and of knowing all the other circumstances under which

their evidence was taken, did not see proper to set aside the verdict, we see no reason why this court should disturb it.[1]

Even today one may properly wonder whether or not Seal actually made away with that collar and bell and, what is more significant, whether he received the unprejudiced and full protection of the law. Andrew Jackson, it might appear, was not entirely accurate when he opined that "the great can protect themselves, but the poor and humble require the arm and shield of the law."[2] He, of course, was correct enough when he indicated that underprivileged citizens desperately needed the cloak of the law, but in error if he believed that they invariably received it.

A few years before black Seal was shipped off to languish in the penitentiary, another Texan, this time not a man of color, was in 1857 indicted and found guilty of murder in the district court of Freestone County. He, said a jury, killed a gentleman by the name of William N. Self with a bowie knife. Cockrum (no first name appears in the Supreme Court record), enjoyed a reputation according to one witness of being a horse thief and of having been run out of Hill County by indignant citizens. And Cockrum looked with no particular relish upon spending the remainder of his life in solitary confinement in the penitentiary, the sentence which the jury agreed to be equitable and just. He felt the law had wronged him not only because, as his attorney argued, that the Texas penal code violated both the federal and state constitutions which extended to citizens the right to bear arms but also that he was denied his right to elect whether he should be tried under an original section of the penal code or under an amendment to it. This was vital, for the unamended code prescribed as the only penalty for murder, such as occurred in Cockrum's case, solitary confinement for life. The amended code obliterated this penalty and increased the "possibilities of diminished punishment, and reduced the amount of severity of the punishment for any but the highest grade of murder."[3] In short, Cockrum, as indicated, did not look with joy upon spending the remainder of his life by himself in a cell. This, I would venture to say, was no unnatural reaction.

Cockrum's dexterous handling of the bowie knife with which he carved the life from Mr. Self was, to some degree, legal filigree. The

[1] *Seal, A Freedman* v. *The State of Texas*, 28 Tex., 492, 1866.
[2] Quoted in Herbert J. Doherty, "Andrew Jackson's Cronies in Florida Territorial Politics," *Florida Historical Quarterly*, 34 (July 1955):10.
[3] *Cockrum* v. *The State of Texas*, 24 Tex., 395, 1858.

counsel argued, as had been done in western states for years, that "a bowie knife or dagger, as defined in the code, is an ordinary weapon, one of the cheapest character, accessible even to the poorest citizen." Warming to his argument, Cockrum's attorney told the court that a common butcher knife, costing not more than half a dollar, came within the description of a bowie knife or dagger, and was frequently worn upon the person. "To prohibit such a weapon," he emphasized, "is substantially to take away the right of bearing arms, from him who has not money enough to buy a gun or pistol." The Supreme Court rejected this flatly:

> The article of the code which provides that a homicide which would otherwise be a case of manslaughter, if committed with a bowie-knife or dagger, shall be deemed murder, and punished as such, is not in violation of the constitutional right of every citizen to bear arms in the lawful defense of himself or the state; but is in restraint of an abuse growing out of such right.

Bowie knives, although frequently favorite weapons and used with marvelous success by gentlemen of quality such as Cassius Marcellus Clay of Kentucky, were easy to come by and relatively inexpensive, although not as costly as a fine gun or a matched set of dueling pistols. Clay, known affectionately as the Lion of Whitehall, once wrote out meticulous, blood-curdling instructions for bowie-knife mayhem. Obtain a headlock with your left arm on your enemy, he said, and then drive viciously back of the clavicle to sever the jugular vein. Never, he warned, strike at the chest walls. If the headlock fails and the clavicle is missed, Clay recommended sinking the knife to the hilt on a line with the navel.[4]

After disposing of the bowie-knife argument, the court centered on the nub of the principle involved in Cockrum's appeal, and it wasted no words: "The amendment to the code establishing degrees in murder, and affixing its punishment accordingly, limits the discretion of the jury, and is more often prejudicial than beneficial to a defendant; the court cannot, therefore, say that the punishment has been ameliorated

---

[4] William H. Townsend, *The Lion of Whitehall Cassius Marcellus Clay* ("Sellanraa," Dunwoody, Georgia: Norman S. Berg, 1967), p. 24; Townsend, *Hundred Proof Salt River Sketches and Memoirs of the Bluegrass* (Lexington: University of Kentucky Press, 1964), pp. 122–23. For an inadequate, but helpful, account of the bowie knife, see Raymond W. Thorp, *Bowie Knife* (Albuquerque: University of New Mexico Press, 1948); for a study of the statutes regulating weapons and their use, see "The Wearing of Weapons in the Western Country," p. 1 in this volume.

by the amendments." This meant that Cockrum had not received the full protection of the law in the district court. The Supreme Court, therefore, decided that judgment must be reversed and the cause remanded.

The misfortunes which befell both black Seal, who may or may not have made off with collar and bell, and of the bowie-wielding Cockrum, who was deprived of his right to go to trial under the new code, most certainly demonstrate that the law in Texas and other areas of the Southwest was no fixed concept of justice, even though justice might have been achieved in the end. It might be said, of course, that the human animal instinctively knows right from wrong and, furthermore, possesses access to ordinances and statutes which spell out the nature and punishment of crime. If a citizen is in doubt as to what the law says, he always has recourse to professional advice from an attorney. All this is not necessarily true.

Oliver W. Holmes, Jr., once pointed out that the common man, whoever he is, and especially the bad man, usually viewed the law, "mainly, and in the first place, [as] a prophecy that if he does certain things he will be subjected to disagreeable consequences by way of imprisonment or compulsory payment of money."[5] Few ranchmen, cowboys, sheepherders, merchants, thieves, arsonists, murderers, rapists, and just plain hell-raisers ever realized that the law is an inexact science and that members of the bar "deal in probabilities, not in certainties."[6] Frontiersmen were unaware that, as settlement edged in irregular thrusts westward, statutes and ordinances were, in too many instances, unavailable to citizen, counselor, and judge. In short, the notion that the American knew his rights and could expect justice is untenable. At times, not even lawyers could comprehend the wording of statutes, even if they had access to them.

Both law books and law libraries were scarce on the frontier. Salmon P. Chase complained in 1833 that it was absolutely impossible to obtain a complete set of the territorial laws of Ohio; before 1830 the state statutes of Louisiana not only were out of print, but, when issued,

---

[5] Quoted in M. P. Golding, ed., *The Nature of Law Readings in Legal Philosophy* (New York: Random House, 1966), p. 179. For a definition of crime, see Leonard Savitz, *Dilemmas in Criminology* (New York: McGraw-Hill Book Co., 1967), pp. 13–14; "Crime is prohibited, punishable *behavior;* the criminal is the judicially proven, culpable *perpetrator* of the crime."

[6] The layman will find an excellent summary of the law's inexactitude in G. Gordon Post, *An Introduction to the Law* (Englewood Cliffs, N.J.: Prentice-Hall, 1965), pp. 8–10.

appeared with errors on almost every page, which, a legal compiler complained, made the laws of little or no use to the public. Judge Edward Scott, of Tennessee, wrote in 1821 of the difficulty of even procuring the laws, adding: "In a free government, it is of the utmost consequence to the great body of the people, to be rightly informed of those laws and regulations, by which their duties are defined and their rights secured."[7] Time and again, lawyers, legislators, and politicians from Michigan to Florida complained of the lack of legal references.[8] A Nebraska editor, looking at a volume of statutes published in 1869, found "some bills which never passed, and what is worse, we find that some acts which did pass both houses and were duly signed by the Governor *are not among the published laws.*"[9]

Texas sought in its penal code of 1857 to set down principles according to the "plain import of the language in which it is written." No person was to be punished for an offense which was not made penal by easily understood words, under the pretense that an accused had merely offended against the spirit of the laws. Yet early copies of law books of Texas became so scarce that Judge A. H. White wrote in 1888 that but few copies were in existence.[10] One other example nails down the point: "There is probably no civilized community in the world, governed by written statutes," exclaimed an irate compiler in New Mexico in 1880, "where it is so impossible to obtain possession of the statutes themselves as in this Territory." He continued with rich rancor:

> So long as eight years ago, the Territorial legislature memorialized Congress on the subject, stating that they had been unable to obtain a copy of the statutes, even for their own use, during the session. . . . In 1880, neither the governor, the legislature, the chief justice, the United States attorney, nor any Territorial official, except the secretary, was in possession of the laws they were expected to be guided by and to administer; and it was believed

[7] Salmon P. Chase, ed., *Statutes of Ohio, 1788–1833* (3 vols.: Cincinnati: Corey & Fairbank, 1833), 1:5; Meinrad Greiner, comp., *Louisiana Digest, 1804–1841* (New Orleans: Benjamin Levy, 1841), pp. vii–viii; Edward Scott, comp., *Laws of the State of Tennessee . . . 1715–1820*, 2 vols. (Knoxville: Heiskell & Brown, 1821), 1:[1].

[8] See, for example, Clarence Edwin Carter, ed., *The Territorial Papers of the United States*, 24 vols. (Washington: G.P.O., 1934–1962), 10:712, 713, 737; 11:57; 24:360, 361, 362; 25:468; 26:420.

[9] *Nebraska Herald* (Plattsmouth), August 12, 1869.

[10] *Penal Code of the State of Texas* (Galveston: New Office, 1857), p. 2; John and Henry Sayles, comps., *Early Laws of Texas, General Laws from 1836 to 1879 . . . Also Laws of 1731 to 1835 as Found in the Laws and Decrees . . .*, 3 vols. (St. Louis: Gilbert Book Co., 1888), 1:viii.

that not a single probate judge, board of county commissioners or justice of the peace in the whole of New Mexico was the owner of a complete set.[11]

If statutes, codes, and legal digests were unavailable, this was bad enough, but another difficulty presented itself. Not only were the laws loosely drawn, worded in illogical fashion, and inadequately printed, but also they could not be read, let alone understood, by some natives and by members of foreign-born or foreign-language groups. A large number of Americans, during the nineteenth century, could not read at all and others could spell out simple sentences only with the greatest difficulty. Other residents might be able to follow a text in Spanish, French, German, and the Scandinavian tongues, but be utterly incompetent to read even a local ordinance printed in English.

Perhaps a solution to this dilemma was to print the laws in at least two languages. This was done by legislatures and town trustees in some areas where it was necessary. It is quite true that, for example, statutes were printed in both English and Spanish in Louisiana and Texas and in Norwegian and Swedish in, again for example, Minnesota. Yet, in some instances, a bilingual publication resulted only after pressure by citizens was exerted. One early example must suffice. In 1809, the French-speaking citizens of the Territory of Michigan petitioned Congress, saying:

> That your petitioners derive great inconvenience from not being able to refer in their mother tongue to the general laws by which they are governed at present as well as the local ones. Sincerely attached to the government of the United States and viewing with appreciation and approbation the care which has been taken for the welfare of their local government, it is knowledge and not good intentions which your petitioners need to make them capable of satisfying their ambition to show themselves worthy citizens of this young and splendid republic of which they have the happiness

11 L. Bradford Price, comp., *General Laws of New Mexico* (Albany, N.Y.: W. C, Little & Co., 1880), pp. iii–v; also, Moses Sherburne and William Hollinshead, comps., *Public Statutes of the State of Minnesota, 1849–1858* (St. Paul: Pioneer Printing Co., 1859), p. 3; Will T. Little, comp., *Statutes of Oklahoma, 1890* (Guthrie: Capital Printing Co., 1891), p. v: "Most intimate with life of parent state, each member [of the legislature] championed some of its statutory provisions. These circumstances, augmented by contention born of urban ambition and varying natural conditions, retarded legislation, alienating men otherwise of one mind. . . . Overworked clerks were relieved by some inexperienced assistants whose labors culminated in grave and irreparable injury to enrolled bills. Unreasonable speed was demanded. Technical accuracy vanished. Legal sense was often lost. Construction was thrown in medley. Punctuation ran riot."

and of which they are proud to be a part. As soon as the Congress of
the United States is informed that outside of the garrisons and their
neighborhoods nineteen-twentieths of the inhabitants of this country
speak only the French language and that most of them are completely
ignorant of the English language, your petitioners flatter themselves that
the generosity and policy of the Congress of the United States will willingly
bear the expense of authorizing an edition of their new territorial code in
the French language as well as several of the more important laws of the
Union.[12]

Printed statutes, whether in English or in bilingual editions, generally
were issued in limited number and were distributed and circulated in a
slipshod fashion. Virginia, in 1666, stipulated that law books "be kept
at James City, and paid for out of the two shillings per hogshead; and
that the like books be sent for by some of the commissioners of the
severall county courts for the use of the respective counties, and paid
for out of the county levy." The laws of the United States, to the end
of the second session of the fourth congress, were issued gratis only to
selected officials of the Northwest Territory, but "application for those
Laws must be accompanied with a Receipt to the Governour, acknowl-
edging them the Property of the Territory, and obligatory of delivering
them over undefaced to Successors in office." Ohio, in 1809, would
issue no laws unless an individual applied for a copy. In 1825, Kentucky
distributed books to public officers and allowed forty days for delivery.
During the 1860s Kansas printed only eighteen hundred copies of the
session laws and three hundred copies of the legislative journals.
Texas, in 1870, provided for a public printer, the establishment of an
official journal, the distribution of the journal, and the printing of the
laws.[13] Other states followed much the same practice.

Even the nature and duties of courts, from those presided over by
justices of the peace to the supreme court itself, were a baffling maze of
hocus-pocus to many citizens.[14] So many officers of the lower courts—

[12] Carter, *Territorial Papers*, X:266–68.

[13] William W. Hening, ed., *The Statutes-at-Large: Being a Collection of All the
Laws of Virginia, 1619–1732*, 13 vols. (New York: R. & W. & G. Bartow, 1823),
2:246; Carter, *Territorial Papers*, 3:493; Chase, *Statutes of Ohio*, 1:637–38; *Kentucky Acts of the General Assembly, December Session, 1836* (Frankfort: A. G.
Hodges, 1837), p. 349; *Kansas General Laws . . . in Force at the Close of the Session of
the Legislature Ending March 6th, 1862* (Topeka: J. H. Bennet, 1862), pp. 675–78;
Sayles, *Early Laws of Texas*, 3:31–32.

[14] For early acts establishing courts, see Sayles, *Early Laws of Texas*, 1:213–16,
An act to establish and organize the supreme court and to define the powers and

justices of the peace, sheriffs, coroners, clerks—were so ignorant of their duties that they depended upon special simply worded manuals issued for their instruction. These useful, privately printed volumes, relied upon since colonial days, followed the advancing frontier. Generally the manuals offered sample forms of warrants, writs, and attachments, summarized the laws, and translated Latin legal phrases into English. Many a Texas magistrate relied upon John Sayles' treatise on the civil jurisdiction of justices of the peace, a second edition of which was printed in Houston in 1878. Sayles, it is said, was the ablest and most prolific author of legal volumes that the Lone Star state ever produced.[15]

With law an inexact science, with statutes incorrectly printed, and with books published in strange tongues and in small editions, it is little wonder that numerous Americans held only a dim concept of what was legal or illegal and frequently either ran afoul of the law deliberately or innocently netted themselves in its obscure web; or, possessing contempt for the law, or the lack of it, dispensed precarious justice at the whim and hand of Judge Lynch.

Certainly the ancient bromide which promised that the righteous man could tread the path of justice without fear of evil's serpent comes close to being preposterous, if not ridiculous. A good man, for example, might not know the legal difference between a mule and a horse; a member of an incorporated protective agency, which conferred police power upon him, might be brought to trial for impersonating a peace officer; a gentleman could easily be confused about sleeping with his wife, or, indeed with another woman who believed he was her husband. A sixteen-year-old boy, convicted of the "unnatural and shocking"

---

jurisdiction thereof, December 15, 1836; ibid., 1:217–18, An act organizing justices' courts, and defining the powers and jurisdiction of the same, and also creating and defining the powers of commissioners of roads and revenue, December 18, 1836; ibid., 1:218–19, An act organizing the inferior courts, and defining the powers and jurisdiction of the same, December 20, 1836; ibid., 1:225–30, An act establishing the jurisdiction and power of the district courts, December 22, 1836; ibid., 2:50–53, An act to organize the district courts and to define their powers and jurisdiction, May 11, 1846; ibid., 2:70–71, An act to organize justices' courts and to define the powers and jurisdiction of the same, May 11, 1846; ibid., 2:344–45, An act regulating justices' courts in the city of San Antonio, February 13, 1854; ibid., 3:369–76, An act to organize the county courts, and define their powers and jurisdiction, June 16, 1876.

15 *A Treatise on the Civil Jurisdiction of Justices of the Peace in the State of Texas,* 2d ed. (Houston: E. H. Cushing, 1878).

crime of parricide, might be first convicted, and, upon appeal, have the judgment reversed.[16]

Reversals, of course, are heady successes, but the law, upon occasion, could fill its hand and stand pat. Take, for example, N. Salazar, a man no better or worse than the lower social class to which he belonged. On November 11, 1883, Salazar and José Martin were relaxing with liquor and cards in a New Mexico saloon. What caused an ensuing quarrel is uncertain, but it appears that, during the dispute, Martin, forgetting for a moment parlor etiquette, called Salazar a son-of-a-bitch. This overused epithet, although not a particularly original figure of speech, then and now possesses a certain bite if not charm. Salazar drew a pistol, but friends dissuaded him from using it. He then left the saloon, presumably to raise twenty-one dollars which he owed the proprietor. Instead of this, Salazar hotfooted it to the house of Manuel Salazar, where he took another pistol. With it in hand, he ran as fast as possible back to the drinking establishment, looked Martin straight in the eye, and said loudly and clearly: "You are the one who called me a son-of-a-bitch." Then he shot Martin dead. In short, the killing, was a willful and premeditated murder. No self-defense was involved.

Salazar was arrested, indicted, brought to trial on a charge of murder in the first degree, and found guilty of second-degree murder. A motion for a new trial was denied, and Salazar was sentenced to imprisonment for life. He appealed to the Supreme Court of the Territory of New Mexico, his attorneys arguing that the lower court erred on several counts, including a failure to instruct the jury properly. The superior court, however, held, first, that a lower court is not bound to instruct a jury as to any degree of crime not supported by evidence; second, that it is within the province of a lower court to decide, upon the evidence, whether the time which elapsed between the provocation and the stroke was sufficient for passion to subside; and, third, that while the evidence was sufficient to convict of murder in the first degree, the instruction, though erroneous, was more favorable to the defendant than the evidence would warrant. In short, the superior court affirmed Salazar's sentence.[17] The moral of this and similar cases is simple: it is

[16] *State* v. *C. J. Ost and Others*, 129 Minn., 1915; *Fouts* v. *The State of Ohio*, 113 Ohio State Reports, 1926; *Cooper* v. *State of Texas*, 22 Texas, Court of Appeals, 419, 1886; *W. A. Stagner* v. *State of Texas*, 9 Texas, Court of Appeals, 440, 1881. For a discussion of rape by fraud and impersonation, see Robert Traver, *The Jealous Mistress* (Boston: Little Brown & Co., 1967), chap 11.

[17] *Territory of New Mexico, Appellee*, v. N. Salazar, *Appellant*, 3 N.M. 21, 1885.

better to be called a son-of-a-bitch than to go to the penitentiary for life. This sage statement may appear obvious, but many a man in many a western community remembered it too late.

Yet even remembering, in some instances, may be of slight avail. No doubt exists but that the three Booth boys—Zack, Nick, and John —knew generally that it was highly improper to steal. On a February night in 1893, in Payson, then a rough-and-tumble town in the Territory of New Mexico, a thousand pounds of flour was stored in James Callahan's house. Sometime between then and March 2, probably on the latter date, Callahan missed his store of bread-making ingredients. A cart dusted with flour was found at Piper's livery stable after it had been tracked from Callahan's house to the gate of old man Booth, the father of Zack, Nick, and John. The flour itself was stacked in the old gentleman's house. Zack might have been an accomplished and successful thief had he not possessed a flannel mouth. Indeed, Zack talked, according to a witness, of taking the flour, although he spoke in a joshing manner. The three brothers were arrested and hustled off to the local pokey, and the law went to work. They were jointly indicted and convicted of burglary in the first degree. A motion for a new trial was overruled, and eventually the case made its weary way to the supreme court, where a reversal was requested on the single ground that the evidence was insufficient to support the jury's verdict. There is no question but that the evidence was all circumstantial. Yet the facts —such as they were—strongly tended to connect Zack Booth with the theft. But nothing indicated that either Nick or John plundered Callahan's stock of flour. Indeed, the two supposedly were snoring in their beds when the theft occurred; yet, it will be recalled, they were tried and found guilty. Thus it was that the high court affirmed Zack's sentence and reversed and remanded for new trial the sentence of Nick and John.[18] Here also a bit of advice comes in handy: if you steal, keep your big mouth shut, or, better yet, keep your mouth closed and stay in bed.

Yet, if cleverly done, a man may murder and make a monkey of the law. In Galveston County, Texas, on an early evening in May in 1872, Green Butler and a friend were standing on the gallery of the Butler residence, having just stepped out from the supper table. At that moment two men rode into the yard and asked if they could get a bite to eat. Butler replied, "Certainly, light and come in." The hungry travelers

---

[18] *Territory of Arizona, Plaintiff and Respondent*, v. *Zack Booth et al., Defendants and Appellants*, 4 Ariz., 148, January 10, 1894.

dismounted, tied their mounts to a hitching post, and walked toward the house. Butler started out to greet them. He never took more than a few steps, for one of the wayfarers drew a pistol and shot him. Then both mounted their horses and galloped—if one wishes to add a fictitious flourish—into the lengthening shadows of a western sun.

Mrs. Butler, rushing to the side of her prostrate husband, asked with scant tact: "Are you dead? Who killed you?"

Butler replied, "Yes, Annie, Andrew Walker killed me; little Isham was with him." He said this twice and then died, so that Annie finally got a definite answer to her first question, "Are you dead?"

About this time, poor Isham, whom Butler in a deathbed statement had positively identified as one of his killers, rode up, together with several neighbors. This was Isham's second appearance that fateful evening, for he had, indeed, ridden into the yard just as one of the two strangers shot Butler. Frightened by the pistol shot, Isham's horse bolted and ran away with him. Clearly, Butler was mistaken about Isham, but correct enough when he named Andy Walker. Walker was riding a dun-colored horse, and his companion a sorrel one. Isham's mount was of another color. Walker's friend was soon identified as Jeff Black. Both Walker and Black were arrested, brought to trial, and convicted of murder in the first degree. Walker drew the death penalty, and Black was sentenced to life imprisonment. They, as might be expected, appealed, saying the lower court had erred in its instructions to the jury and that the jury had misbehaved. Both men had rested their case in the lower court on an alibi, maintaining they were nowhere near Butler's place when the killing took place.

The question of alibi may be considered first. The trial court instructed the jury that "an *alibi* is a species of defense often set up in criminal cases, and one which seems to figure in this case." The supreme court, in turn, commented that "this language was well calculated to convey to the jury the impression that the court regarded that particular defense as a pretense, without foundation in fact." Thus, in this instance, the lower court was in error. The trial court also was at fault when it permitted jurors to read newspapers containing "imperfect or incorrect" accounts of the trial. Even Butler's dying declaration, in which he correctly identified one man and incorrectly named another, was mishandled by the trial judge, for, said the supreme court, "Dying declarations are admitted in evidence as an exception to the general rule regulating the admissibility of hearsay evidence, and it is the province of the jury alone to say what credence shall be given it." For these and other reasons, the judgment of the lower court was reversed, and the cause remanded.[19] It is interesting to note that in this affair no mention of motive is made in the arguments of either party.

Relatively few individuals, throughout the West, committed crimes which eventually were decided in supreme courts, for superior courts of appeal generally, although not always, heard cases which possessed some legal uniqueness. Far more actions were decided in district courts, and, as is obvious, most incidents involving misdemeanors— gambling, vagrancy, prostitution, petty crimes—came to the benches of justices of the peace or police judges.[20] These were the bars of the people, brought there by the night watch or by a town marshal to face their fate. There, indeed, the law touched the common man—plain and fancy drunks, raunchy bullies, peddlers who vended without licenses, those charged with assault or with assault and battery, and the rank and file of misfits, unfortunates, and maladjusted ones. In endless ragged procession, they paid their fines, went to insanitary jails, or worked out sentences on the streets. Both in the nation and throughout the South- west, remnants of humanity—some poor, others rich, some ignorant, others intelligent, some depraved and others normal—teetered pre- cariously upon the uncertain, and, at times, unreliable, swaying scales of justice. For those found guilty, the barbed-wire fence of the law shut them in and marked them and branded them as unworthy. Even those found innocent learned too frequently to their horror that they, although without sin, were marked with the sign of Cain.

Few tears may be cried for the horse thief who, caught in the act, was strung up by court order or by vigilantes. He is unworthy of sorrow, except that the loss of a human life is always a tragedy. But the little people, guilty of no unrighteousness except that occasioned by poverty and ignorance, merit grief to the cup's full measure. In 1887, when northern Michigan was about as much of a frontier as were south- western states, Catherine Wren, poor and hungry, took from a vegetable stand three bunches of pie plant and seven bunches of radishes. The total value of her larceny amounted to sixty cents. She was fined a total of seven dollars, one dollar of which was her fine and six dollars of which covered the costs. The costs went into the pocket of Cornelius Kennedy, justice of the peace, who represented the law's majesty

[19] *A. J. Walker and Jeff Black* v. *The State of Texas*, 37 Tex. 366, 1872–73.

[20] For gambling, see "Lady Luck and Her Knights of the Royal Flush"; for prostitution, "Come back Soon, Honey," pp. 43 and 115, respectively, of this volume.

and who never during a long life knew the growling of an empty belly.[21]

The essential and fundamental characteristics of the law beyond the wide Missouri, throughout the Great Plains, across the Rocky Mountains, and on to California and the Pacific Northwest were, of course, no different than was the philosophy of the law and of legal procedure in colonial days and during the early years of the Republic, although, to be neat, variations existed. There is no time here for a discussion of civil law and civil actions as the emphasis is upon criminal codes. It is well, therefore, to establish specifically, as did Anglo-Saxon law, five necessary and theoretical elements involved in any crime.

Professor Leonard Savitz explained these well in a slight volume with which any historian who treats of law either in established judicial districts or on any one of the advancing frontiers should be acquainted. Savitz points out that first a crime must involve a conscious, voluntary, external harm; second, that the act must have been legally prohibited at the time it was committed; third, the offender must have possessed criminal intent (*mens rea*) when he participated in the crime; fourth, that there must be a causal relationship between the voluntary misconduct and the legally forbidden result; fifth, that there must be some legally prescribed punishment for a person convicted of the crime.[22] Some of these axioms were violated, sometimes too frequently and too flagrantly, in the backcountry which was only gradually assuming social and legal maturity. It must be remembered also that every new statute or ordinance automatically creates new lawbreakers. To be crisp: laws, old or new, result in human conflict.[23]

It was no slight task, however, to adopt, as so many states did, the common law of England, and to determine what this common law really meant. The superior judges of Orleans in 1804, of Missouri in 1812, of Arkansas in 1819, and of Florida during the early 1820s—all frontier communities—held jurisdiction over both criminal and civil cases. In Louisiana and in Florida it was not clear whether Spanish law or English law was to be relied upon. The Indiana legislature, in a memorial to Congress in 1814, asked the same question about the Ordinance of 1787:

[21] Cornelius Kennedy, Justice of the Peace Docket, Ishpeming, Michigan, April, 1880–January, 1903, p. 236, MS vol., Ishpeming, Michigan Police Station.

[22] Savitz, *Dilemmas in Criminology*, pp. 10–13. The paragraph leans heavily upon these pages, where discussion is more extended than I have indicated.

[23] Post, *An Introduction to the Law*, pp. 5–6.

... what common law the ordinance refers to, whether the common law of England, of France, or of the Territory over which the ordinance is the constitution. If it should be determined that, by the expression of the ordinance, a common law jurisdiction should be located on the common law of England, it is essential to define to what extent of that common law the judges shall take cognizance; whether the customs, or unwritten law shall be taken with the statute law, and that to form the common law to govern the judges; or whether the unwritten and statute law is to be taken in contradistinction to the laws, customs, and rules of chancery; or whether it includes that law which is common to all.[24]

Once the English common law was accepted, jurists, fortunately or unfortunately, conceived of law "as the imperative of the state, applied mechanically by tribunals in the administration of justice."[25] Such an attitude, of course, clarifies the decisions of not only western "hanging judges," but also the, at times, irregular and irresponsible actions of vigilante groups. Neither Judge Isaac Charles Parker, presiding in the Indian Territory at Fort Smith, nor a sheriff who combined the talents of prosecutor, jury, judge, and executor probably ever gave serious thought to the law as a woman "sitting by the wayside, beneath whose overshadowing hood every man shall see the countenance of his deserts or needs." This was Oliver Wendell Holmes' figure of speech. He said further that "the timid and overborne gain heart from her protecting smile." Holmes, in a brilliant essay, added: "The wretch who has defied her [the law's] most sacred commands, and has thought to creep through ways where she was not, finds that his path ends with her, and beholds beneath her hood the inexorable face of death."[26]

The great gunfighters, the rogues like the bandit Sam Bass, the ugly ones like Joaquín Miller, the vigilantes of Montana—all these and

[24] William Wirt Blume and Elizabeth Gaspar Brown, "Territorial Courts and Law: Unifying Factors in the Development of American Legal Institutions," *Michigan Law Review* 61 (November 1962): 52.

[25] Roscoe Pound, *The Formative Era of American Law* (Gloucester, Mass.: Peter Smith, 1960), p. 110.

[26] For Judge Parker, see Glenn Shirley, *Law West of Fort Smith: A History of Frontier Justice in Indian Territory, 1834–1896* (Lincoln: University of Nebraska Press, 1968); also, Oliver Wendell Holmes, *Collected Legal Papers* (New York: Peter Smith, 1952), pp. 27–28. Numerous instances of frontier "justice" may be found in Wayne Gard, *Frontier Justice* (Norman: University of Oklahoma Press, 1949). Although not identified with nineteenth-century frontier law and justice, the following sheds general insight: Jerome H. Scholnick, *Justice without Trial: Law Enforcement in Democratic Society* (New York: John Wiley & Sons, 1967).

more recognized that death face from experience, yet few of them comprehended not only the nature of law but also the significance which evidence played throughout the legal process.[27] One historian of the region of the Great Plains writes that the West was Godless, quoting the popular bromide that there was "no Sunday west of Junction City and no God west of Salina." A long-time western resident contradicts this by saying that his grandfather's friends were, by and large, "moral and law-abiding—maybe even religious. They shot other men when they had to, and most of them drank whiskey and gambled; but those things were part of the times."[28] Yet each of these affirmations hangs upon hearsay, and the truth lies somewhere between. The same is true of the law, for the scale seldom comes to rest, as does a wheel of fortune, upon a specific, absolute number, even though a win or lose is decided.

Take, for example, the case of Charley Keys, who was tried on a charge of stealing a horse. Charley appeared before the United States Court of Appeals, Indian Territory, just before Oklahoma entered the Union, and was convicted. He was, unfortunately, not an altogether upright person of integrity, for he had, upon several occasions, served time in various jails. Upon conviction, he carried his case to the superior court. The court, somewhat puzzled, rummaged through its law library and eventually found help in an Arkansas statute, or, to be truthful, in several statutes. One said, in effect, that owners of cattle, hogs, or sheep running at large must be branded if over twelve months old. Another set a penalty of imprisonment in the penitentiary at hard labor for any person convicted of marking, stealing, killing, or wounding any kind of cattle, pigs, hogs, sheep, or goats. A third stated plainly

[27] Nyle H. Miller and Joseph W. Snell, *Great Gunfighters of the Kansas Cowtowns, 1867–1886* (Lincoln: University of Nebraska Press, 1963); Charles L. Martin, *A Sketch of Sam Bass The Bandit*, introduction by Ramon F. Adams (Norman: University of Oklahoma Press, 1956); Yellow Bird [John Rollin Ridge], *The Life and Adventures of Joaquin Miller, the Celebrated California Bandit*, introduction by Joseph Henry Jackson (Norman: University of Oklahoma Press, 1955); Thos. J. Dimsdale, *The Vigilantes of Montana; or, Popular Justice in the Rocky Mountains*, introduction by E. Degolyer (Norman: University of Oklahoma Press, 1953). Also, D. J. Cook, *Hands Up; or, Twenty Years of Detective Life in the Mountains and on the Plains*, introduction by E. Degolyer (Norman: University of Oklahoma Press, 1958); Edward Bonney, *The Banditti of the Prairies; or, The Murderer's Doom!! A Tale of the Mississippi Valley*, introduction by Philip D. Jordan (Norman: University of Oklahoma Press, 1963).

[28] Everett Dick, *Vanguards of the Frontier* (New York: D. Appleton-Century Co., 1941), p. 514; John Leakey, *The West That Was* (Lincoln: University of Nebraska Press, 1967), pp. 28–29.

that any person convicted of stealing any horse, mare, gelding, filly, foal, mule, ass, or jenny must be sentenced to the penitentiary for not less than five nor more than fifteen years.

All this is plain enough. Charley, however, argued that the horse he was alleged to have stolen was four years old, was unmarked and unbranded, and was running at large on the open range. Thus the case centered on the first statute, namely, that concerning the age of an animal—cattle, hogs, or sheep—and whether or not it was branded. Charley contended, with a good deal of ingenuity, that the term *cattle* excluded horses and that, therefore, he was not guilty of larceny in taking the animal from the range. The superior judge must have scratched his judicial brow, for he himself was uncertain when he wrote:

> There are some authorities to the effect that the term "cattle" in a penal statute includes horses. So far as we have been able to ascertain, these authorities are confined to the earlier cases and where the statutes construed use that term alone and without any words of qualification. In its primary sense the word "cattle," according to Webster, includes "animals, horses, asses, and all the varieties of domesticated horned beasts of the bovine genus." According to Webster it was used in this general sense in the Scriptures. . . . If the Legislature had intended that the word "cattle" should include all species of domesticated animals, the words "hogs or sheep" would not have been used. The mere fact that the words "hogs or sheep" appear is conclusive that the word "cattle" was not used in its primary sense, but in the common acceptation of the term, and was not intended to cover any other kind of animals. . . . We are driven to the conclusion that the word "cattle" . . . was used in the sense in which it is commonly used, and not to include horses.

If a horse is not classified as cattle, then, in layman's language, Charley was no horse thief. Yet another issue faced the superior court. When Charley went to trial in the lower court, much was made of his several periods of rest and relaxation in numerous jails. So much, indeed, was made of this that it constituted one of the reasons for appeal, for Charley's attorney thought it improper, if not a downright violation of rights, for Charley to be subjected to this type of questioning. The prosecution hammered him hard in cross-examination which went like this:

Question: "Have you ever been in jail, Charley?"

Charley's attorney: "We object to that question."

The Court: "I will overrule that objection. He may answer the question."

Charley's attorney: "The defendant excepts to the court's ruling."

The Court: "Yes, sir."

Question: "How many times have you been in jail, Charley?"

Charley's attorney: "The defendant objects to the question, for the reason it is incompetent, immaterial, irrelevant, and not proper cross-examination."

The Court: "The objection will be overruled."

Charley's attorney: "The defendant excepts."

Charley: "I have been in jail three times."

Question: "Is that all, Charley?"

Charley: "Yes, sir."

Question: "You have been in jail at Ft. Smith, Ark., haven't you?"

Charley's attorney: "The defendant objects to this question, for the reason it is incompetent, immaterial, irrelevant, and not proper cross-examination."

The Court: "The objection is overruled."

Charley's attorney: "The defendant excepts."

The Court: "Yes, sir."

Question, "You have been in jail at Muskogee?"

Charley: "Yes, sir, but that was the same transaction. They moved me from Muskogee up here."

Question: "You have been in jail at Vinita?"

Charley: "Yes, sir, but that is the same thing. They moved me from Muskogee to Vinita, and then up here."

Question: "You have been in jail at Coffeeville, Kan., haven't you?"

Charley: "No, I was at Independence."

Question: "Where else, Charley?"

Charley: "That's all."

Question: "How long have you been in jail, Charley, all your life, all told?"

Charley's attorney: "Defendant objects to the question for the reason it is incompetent, immaterial, irrelevant, and not proper cross-examination."

The Court: "The objection is overruled."

Charley's attorney: "The defendant excepts."

Charley, it is plain to see, was being shanghaied, first by being tried under a statute which did not pertain to his alleged theft and second by being forced, with the aid of the court, into revealing what had no bearing on the case at issue. The higher court, to Charley's great delight, found the trial court to be in error and ordered that the case be reversed and remanded to the district court of Nowata County with directions to grant the defendant a new trial.[29] In short, as a lawyer friend of mine put it, the supreme court judge finally figured out the difference between a horse and his ass.

The case of Charley Keys exemplifies true justice at work, a far more meaningful expression of the law than that set down by some western authors who concentrate upon brawls, shoot-outs, and impromptu hangings. Retribution and punishment are not necessarily synonymous with justice, not even if a culprit is believed in the popular mind to be guilty. All things considered, it is better for society, although perhaps not so dramatic, to indict and bring to trial a keeper of a San Antonio whorehouse, situated on Alamo Square, than it is, as was customary in many communities throughout the nineteenth century, for disgruntled citizens to burn down the joint.[30]

Such taking of the law into one's own hands, as is generally known, was not atypical, but both attitudes and actions of those who did do so deserve more attention than some historians have given them. Luke Short, a faro dealer in Tombstone's Oriental Saloon and Gambling House, was table master at a game in which Charlie Storms, known as a bad man, lost heavily. Charlie thereupon threw a handful of chips into Short's face, and said loudly: "When I come in the morning, I'm coming a shooting." On the following morning, true to his promise, Charlie, six-shooter in hand, crossed a street to where Short stood. Luke shot Charlie through the heart.[31]

No one can argue reasonably that Charlie, even though drunk or semi-intoxicated, did not threaten Luke or that Charlie, gun in hand, crossed the street and approached Luke. But Luke, had he wished, might have attempted to avoid the final encounter by ducking into a building, by attempting to dissuade Charlie, by not being on the street in the first place. In other words, was Charlie's provocation so great and so immediate and was his intent to shoot Luke so obvious that Luke's only recourse was to kill in self-defense? No one knows. Luke

[29] *Charley Keys* v. *United States*, 2 Okla., Crim. App., 647, 1909.

[30] *James Couch* v. *State of Texas*, 24 Tex., 558, 1859. For raids, see, for example, *La Crosse Independent Republican*, July 8, 1857; *Dubuque Daily Express and Herald*, November 3, 1857; *Oquawka Spectator*, January 12, 1865. See also "Come Back Soon, Honey," p. 115 in this volume.

[31] Lorenzo D. Walters, *Tombstone's Yesterday* (Glorieta, N. Mex.: Rio Grande Press, 1968), p. [282]. The accuracy of the details in this account may be questioned, for the publisher's introduction says source material may be taken "with a box of salt handy." Nevertheless, the episode is typical of numerous other similar affrays.

was not arrested, and he left town soon after, only to slay another man within a relatively short time. One wonders what might have happened had Luke been brought to trial in time-honored manner.

The ugly suspicion raised as to the propriety of such events which pocked, like smallpox scars, one frontier after another, reflects no contemporary, twentieth-century hindsight. "The people, too, are not content with the slow but sure workings of the law," said the editor of the *Frontier Echo* on February 11, 1876, "but must violate the law by [the use of] lynch law." [32] Whether or not he realized it, this Lone Star editor was speaking of a cult of violence—not only physical, sweat-dripping, illegal force but also lawless passion permeating American literature. [33] Each is equally evil if both its roots and its results remain unclear. Perhaps this all means that historians of the lawless, woolly, gun-slingin' Wild West should turn to and study seriously—in addition to their stock-in-trade frontier sources—codes, digests, statutes, ordinances, and the written and printed findings and decisions of courts of both low and high degree. [34]

[32] Quoted in W. C. Holden, " Law and Lawlessness on the Texas Frontier, 1875–1890," *Southwestern Historical Quarterly* 44 (October 1940):189.

[33] See, for example, Otto N. Larsen, ed., *Violence and the Mass Media* (New York: Harper & Row, 1968), pp. 74–78; David Brion Davis, *Homicide in American Fiction, 1798–1860: A Study in Social Values* (Ithaca: Cornell University Press, 1968).

[34] Ervin H. Pollack, *Fundamentals of Legal Research*, 2d ed. (Brooklyn: Foundation Press, 1962) is the best volume of its type.

Index